L. F.

D0845321

# INTRODUCTION TO
# INFORMATION THEORY

**CLAUDE E. SHANNON**
**The Father of Information Theory**
(Photo by Frank Ross, Cape May Courthouse, New Jersey)

# INTRODUCTION TO
# INFORMATION THEORY

**Masud Mansuripur**
College of Engineering
Boston University

PRENTICE-HALL, INC.
Englewood Cliffs, New Jersey 07632

ALBRIGHT COLLEGE LIBRARY

**Library of Congress Cataloging-in-Publication Data**

Masud Mansuripur (date)
Introduction to information theory.

Bibliography: p.
Includes index.
1. Information theory. I. Title.
Q360.M3215   1987      001.53'9      86-17033
ISBN 0-13-484668-0

Cover Design: Diane Saxe
Manufacturing Buyer: Rhett Conklin

Copyright © 1987 by Prentice-Hall, Inc.
A division of Simon & Schuster
Englewood Cliffs, New Jersey 07632

All rights reserved. No part of this book may be reproduced,
in any form or by any means,
without permission in writing from the publisher.

Printed in the United States of America

10  9  8  7  6  5  4  3  2  1

ISBN   0-13-484668-0      025

Prentice-Hall International (UK) Limited, London
Prentice-Hall of Australia Pty. Limited, Sydney
Prentice-Hall Canada Inc., Toronto
Prentice-Hall Hispanoamericana, S.A., Mexico
Prentice-Hall of India Private Limited, New Delhi
Prentice-Hall of Japan, Inc., Tokyo
Prentice-Hall of Southeast Asia Pte. Ltd., Singapore
Editora Prentice-Hall do Brasil, Ltda., Rio de Janeiro

ALBRIGHT COLLEGE LIBRARY

001.539
M 424 i

205351

32. 00

To Anne and Kaveh

# CONTENTS

# PREFACE

This book has been developed out of a course in information theory that I have taught at Boston University during the past several years. The course is intended for beginning graduate students, as well as advanced undergraduates who desire a conceptual understanding of the foundations of information theory. It is thus designed to cover the major ideas involved in this important branch of modern science and to give the student an overview of the subject without getting nailed down in more advanced and sometimes less intuitive issues. The required background is probability theory at an undergraduate level. Although some basic concepts of probability are reviewed in the beginning, it is essential that the reader be familiar with the techniques of probability theory in general. A certain degree of mathematical maturity and capacity for abstract thinking on the part of the reader is also assumed.

Several excellent textbooks on information theory are available at this time, and it may seem inappropriate to write yet another one on the subject. I found it difficult, however, to find a text that addressed all the major concerns of the theory at the proper level for my intended audience. Some of the books were written for the Ph.D. level students and researchers and thus required a much higher knowledge base than introductory probability theory, while others, although appropriate for the less advanced student, were not comprehensive enough in their coverage. The present book is thus the outcome of my effort to bridge this gap; although it contains some of the more recent developments in information theory, which, to my knowledge, have not yet appeared in any textbook, it remains an introductory exposition of the basic concepts at the core. In organizing the book, I have been guided by the original paper of C. E. Shannon, "A Mathematical Theory of Communication" and by the monumental work of R. Gallager, *Information Theory and Reliable Communication.* I also benefited from the books *Information Theory and Coding,* by N. Abramson, *Information Theory,* by R. Ash, *The Theory of Information and Coding,* by R. McEliece, *Coding and Information Theory,* by R. Hamming, and *Rate Distortion Theory,* by T. Berger. The chapter on universal source coding is based on the original papers of B. Fitingof and the section on numerical computation of channel capacity is based on the papers of R. Blahut and S. Arimoto.

Although intuitive development of concepts has been my goal in this book, I have tried not to achieve this goal at the expense of mathematical rigor. All the results are derived from the basic principles, and every step in the derivation is carefully described. The problems are an important part of the book in that they either give a different perspective on a subject that has already been developed in the text or try to extend and generalize the concepts.

Chapter 1 is a review of the mathematical tools that are required for the understanding of the book. It is not necessary, however, to cover this material in the beginning; the reader can refer to it as the need arises. Chapter 2 concerns entropy and its properties; typical or likely sequences are introduced here, and a first hint of the usefulness of the concept in data-compression applications is given. Chapter 3 expands on the idea of source coding for data compression and introduces various properties of variable-length source codes. In Chapter 4 we look at source coding from a different point of view and introduce the idea of universal coding. This is a departure from the classical information theory in that a previous knowledge of the probabilistic structure of the source is no longer required for the construction of an optimum universal code. Chapters 5 and 6 are concerned with the discrete memoryless channel; after defining conditional entropy and mutual information and familiarizing the reader with some elementary discrete memoryless channels in Chapter 5, we prove the noisy channel theorem and its converse in Chapter 6. Chapter 7 is an elementary treatment of the rate-distortion theory. Here the concept of source coding with a fidelity criterion is introduced and the rate-distortion function is defined; the fundamental theorem of rate-distortion theory for the discrete memoryless source with single-letter fidelity criterion and its converse are then established.

I found it hard to completely ignore the problems associated with the more practical aspects of information theory, which, more often than not, are treated independently under the name of Coding Theory. I thus included some material on error-correcting codes, addressing the elementary aspects of linear codes for error correction in Chapter 8. Both block codes and convolutional codes are discussed here. It is hoped that through this chapter the reader will see the relation between theory and practice. I deliberately avoided any mention of cyclic codes in order to stay away from algebraic field theory; that would have been beyond the scope of this book. Finally, in Chapter 9, some advanced topics relating to stationary and ergodic sources and continuous channels are discussed. This can be viewed as an extension of some of the ideas developed in the previous chapters and is aimed at students who like to have a glimpse at what could be the subject of a second course in information theory.

I have used the book for a one-semester, four-credit course in information theory at Boston University. Chapters 1 through 6 are usually covered in the beginning and then, depending on the level of understanding and the interest of students, I have selected topics from the remaining three chapters. Chapter 8 on linear codes has always been a favorite of engineering students. If I were to teach the course in a school with the quarter system, I would probably teach the first six chapters in the first quarter and use some additional material with the last three chapters for the second quarter.

I would like to thank Professor Lev Levitin who inspired me and spent many of his precious hours discussing the more subtle points of information theory with me. He also honored me by agreeing to write an introductory chapter for this book. I would also like to thank Dean Louis Padulo of the College of Engineering who encouraged me in writing this book and provided me with the time needed for completing it. Thanks are due to Mr. Tim Bozik, the editor, for his support of the project. Finally, I would like to thank my wife, Annegret, without whose patience and encouragement this book would not have become a reality.

### Acknowledgments

Problems 1.1, 2.1, 2.2, 2.6, 3.1, 3.4, 3.9, 3.10, 3.11, 3.12, 5.4, 5.5, 5.6, 6.4, 6.9, 7.4, 8.8, 8.9, 8.10, and 9.5 are from R. G. Gallagher, INFORMATION THEORY AND RELIABLE COMMUNICATION. New York: Wiley, 1968. Copyright © 1968 by John Wiley & Sons, Inc. Reprinted with permission.

Problems 2.4, 2.5, 2.9, 6.8, 8.2, 8.5, and 8.6 are from R. Ash, INFORMATION THE-ORY. New York: Interscience, 1965. Copyright © 1965 by John Wiley & Sons, Inc. Reprinted with permission.

Problems 2.11, 2.13, 3.15 (adapted), and 8.16 are from R. J. McEliece, THE THEORY OF INFORMATION AND CODING: A MATHEMATICAL FRAMEWORK FOR COMMUNICATION. New York: Cambridge, 1977. Copyright © 1977 by Cambridge University Press. Reprinted with permission.

# INFORMATION THEORY AND THE MODERN SCIENTIFIC OUTLOOK

*Lev B. Levitin*

One of the greatest revolutions in the scientific world outlook in our century is the turn from Laplacian determinism to a probabilistic picture of nature. The development of statistical mechanics and (even in a more categorical way) of quantum theory has brought us to the appreciation of the fact that the world we live in is essentially probabilistic. A natural extension of this point of view is an understanding that our knowledge is of a probabilistic nature, too. Any information we obtain affects the probabilities of possible alternatives, rather than indicates uniquely one particular outcome (as "genuine" deterministic knowledge was supposed to do).

Therefore, it seems to be not just a sheer coincidence that information theory emerged after statistical and quantum mechanics had been developed, and that it shares with statistical physics the fundamental concept of entropy.

Mathematically, information theory is a branch of the theory of probabilities and stochastical processes. It has won its first victories by answering the most basic questions concerning information transmission over communication channels. In the past, communication engineers believed that the rate of information transmission over a noisy channel had to decline to zero, if we require the error probability to approach zero. Shannon was the first to show that the information-transmission rate can be kept constant for an arbitrarily small probability of error. Besides its technological importance, this result has a remarkable philosophical meaning. Information theory not only gives a quantitative measure of information common for both deterministic and probabilistic cases, but it also shows the qualitative equivalence of these two kinds of knowledge in the following sense: even if the input and the output of a communication channel are only statistically dependent, it is possible to transmit an amount of data that is arbitrarily close to the amount of information in the output about the input, with a vanishing error probability (i.e., in almost deterministic way).

The development of information theory is an excellent illustration of the statement that "nothing is more practical than a good theory." Indeed, at the time when the basic results of information theory related to communication channels had first been formulated, communication technology was not at all able to implement them in practice. It took a long time, about a quarter of a century, until the development of practical methods of data encoding and decoding together with new computer technology made it possible to process information in real time in accordance with the recommendations following from information theory, and thus to make the theoretical limits attainable. The results regarded once by some too "practical" people as "academic exercises" have become a matter of today's engineering practice. We are witnessing now the ongoing information revolution, the vigorous development of new means of information transmission, storage, and retrieval that may lead to profound changes in the nature of our society in ways that could hardly be envisioned by the most daring utopians. And information theory plays a crucial role in this development by providing not only a theoretical basis, but also a deep philosophical insight into new and challenging problems we have to encounter — today and tomorrow.

However, the importance and generality of information theory concepts and approaches go far beyond the area of communication engineering. The ideas of information theory were applied in a variety of diverse fields from physics to linguistics, from biology to computer science, and from psychology to chemistry and proved to be productive and innovative — of course, in the hands of those who knew how to handle them properly. Thus information theory has become not just another special branch, but an indispensable part of the modern scientific outlook. It should be borne in mind, however, that "seldom do more than a few of nature's secrets give way at one time," as the founder of information theory, Claude E. Shannon, observed, warning against immature attempts to use information theory just because it had become "something of a scientific bandwagon."

> A thorough understanding of the mathematical foundation and its communication application is surely a prerequisite to other applications. I personally believe that many of the concepts of information theory will prove useful in these other fields — and, indeed, some results are already quite promising — but the establishing of such applications is not a trivial matter of translating words to a new domain, but rather the slow tedious process of hypothesis and experimental verification [1].

Historically, the basic concepts of information theory, such as entropy, mutual information, equivocation, and redundancy were first introduced by Shannon in connection with cryptographic systems [2], rather than the usual communication channels. The modern development of cryptography added an important aspect of complexity to be taken into consideration. Information-theoretical analysis plays a significant role in the theory of computational and structural complexity and in the design of effective decision algorithms (e.g., [3]). (An elementary example of such a decision algorithm is that related to the famous counterfeit coin problem [4].)

Another important area of the application of information theory to computer science is fault-tolerant computing. Although the first attempts in this direction were unsuccessful, more thorough investigations [5, 6, 7] have shown that it is possible to achieve arbitrarily small probability of error in data storage and computation at the expense of limited redundancy, exactly as in the case of communications.

Essential interconnections between information theory and statistics have been found [8] and new methods of statistical analysis based on information theory have been suggested [9].

A number of interesting attempts have been made to apply information theory in political economy and economics. For instance, the theory of optimal investment appears to be exactly parallel to the theory of optimal source coding [10].

Application of information theory to linguistics seem to be highly relevant (e.g., [11–15]). Indeed, a natural language gives us a remarkable example of a system used for generating long sequences of symbols (i.e., texts) that can be considered as realizations of a random process. But, in contrast with other random processes that exist in nature, this random process was developed, modified, and selected during a long period of evolution and "natural selection," being specially intended for meaningful communication between human beings. Information-theoretical studies of texts have revealed a number of significant linguistic features. For instance, they provide objective criteria for the characterization of different styles and different schools in poetry and prose, and even for identification of individual authors [16]. An illustration of the importance of the information-theoretical characteristics of a language is given by the fact (noted first by Shannon) that large crossword puzzles are only possible if the redundancy of a language does not exceed 50 percent (on the vocabulary level). If the entropy of a language were two times less than its actual value, poetry in its usual form (with rhymes and meters) would be impossible.

Application of information theory t experimental psychology made it possible to discover some remarkable facts related to sensory organs and neural systems [17]. It was found, for example, that the reaction time of a subject is a linear function of the amount of information contained in the stimulus [4, 18, 19]. Moreover, our sensory organs can be characterized by a certain information capacity, as engineering communication lines are.

Perhaps the most important and meaningful are interconnections between information theory and statistical physics. Long before information theory was founded, L. Boltzman and later L. Szilard [20] attributed an information meaning to the thermodynamical notion of entropy. On the other hand, D. Gabor [21] pointed out that "the communication theory should be considered as a branch of physics." In the classical work of L. Brillouin [22], a profound relationship between physical entropy and information was first formulated in a general form. Later the "entropy defect principle" was established in the quasiclassical [23, 24] and the quantum [25, 26] form. According to this principle, any information is represented by a certain ensemble of states of a physical system and associated with its deviation from the thermodynamic equilibrium. Thus the basic concepts of information theory can be defined on the basis of statistical physics, and a way is open to develop a consistent physical information theory. The subject of this theory is investigation of the physical nature of information transmission, storage, retrieval, and processing (so called physics of communication and physics of computation) (e.g., [27–29]). On the other hand, the information-theoretical approach has been applied to statistical physics [30–34]. Information theory shed a new light on the classical problems of Maxwell's demon, Gibbs' paradox [22, 34], and on the foundations of statistical physics in general. There is a hope that further development in this direction will eventually bridge the gap between physical and cybernetical descriptions of a complex system and will lead to formulation of a physical theory of high-organized systems, both artificial and natural (biological). The progress on this way is slow and difficult [35], but the goal is worth all the efforts.

Here we have to touch on another philosophical problem. Since the time of Newton (or even Democritus), scientists believed that the most fundamental laws, the most hidden secrets of nature, are those of elementary particles and elementary forces acting between them. Indeed, if everything that happens in the universe is no more than a combination of these elementary acts, then isn't the knowledge of laws that govern the interactions between elementary particles sufficient to describe any phenomenon in the world, to predict theoretically outcomes of any experiment? Today we have achieved incredible progress in discovering and describing the nature of elementary particles and interactions, and have learned that this knowledge is incredibly insufficient for the ambitious purpose of "explaining everything," of building an accomplished scientific picture of the world.

It seems that we know, indeed, how to derive the behavior of a system, even as large as stars and galaxies, from the "first principles," if we deal with a low-organized, chaotic system. But we find our knowledge almost irrelevant when we have to face a system at a higher level of organization (whatever it means, I should add, since we still lack even a good definition of "level of organization"). For instance, we have a wonderful theory of electromagnetic interactions that predicts the experimental results with an accuracy of 15 decimal digits, and we know that the processes in a human body are mostly electromagnetic, but this perfect theory tells us very little, if anything, about how our bodies function.

There has occurred another revolutionary shift in the minds of scientists: to become aware that the greatest secrets of nature, the hardest to discover — and the most important for us — are the laws of organization, the understanding of how a certain complex "combination" of particles and processes can emerge and persist as an organized system among the chaos of myriads of elementary interactions; how it can be formed and sustained by those interactions; how a "more organized" system can be built from "less organized" parts; why, when, and how such a system becomes able to display the properties of "high organization" such as self-regulation, self-organization, learning, adaptivity, expedient behavior, self-reproduction, and, eventually, intelligence. These are the crucial problems of life and death. Until we solve them, we remain, with all our knowledge and technology, helpless children in the cradle of nature.

Three geniuses of our time, J. von Neumann, N. Wiener, and C. E. Shannon, were the most influential in recognizing the problem with all its generality and consequence and bringing it to our attention [36–39]. And all of them stressed the importance of the concepts of entropy, information, and control for developing a general theory of high-organized systems, a new science for which Wiener coined the name cybernetics, but which is still waiting to be created. Today, information theory provides the only existing narrow bridge between the two different worlds of chaotic and organized systems. And I strongly believe that information theory will win its new triumphs by helping us on our way to the ultimate knowledge intellectual beings desire—the knowledge of ourselves.

## References

1. C. E. Shannon, "The Bandwagon," *Trans. IRE, IT-2*, No. 1, 1956.

2. C. E. Shannon, "Communication Theory of Secrecy Systems," *BSTJ*, 28, No. 4, 1949.

3. C. R. P. Hartmann, and others, "Application of Information Theory to the Construction of Efficient Decision Trees," *IEEE Trans.*, IT-28, No. 4, 1982.

4. A. M. Yaglom and I. M. Yaglom, *Probability and Information.* Hingham, Mass.: D. Reidel Publishing Co., 1983.

5. S. Winograd and J. D. Cowan, *Reliable Computation in the Presence of Noise.* Cambridge, Mass.: MIT Press, 1963.

6. M. C. Taylor, "Reliable Information Storage in Memories Designed from Unreliable Components" and "Reliable Computation in Computing Systems Designed from Unreliable Components," *BSTJ*, 47, No. 10, 1968.

7. A. V. Kuznetsov, "Information Storage in a Memory Assembled from Unreliable Components," *Problems in Information Transmission*, 9, No. 3, 1973.

8. S. Kulback, *Information Theory and Statistics.* New York: Wiley, 1959.

9. S. Watanable, "Information-Theoretical Analysis of Multivariate Correlation," *IBM J. Res. Develop.*, 4, No. 1, 1960.

10. T. M. Cover, "Information Theory and Investment," *1985 IEEE Intern. Symp. Information Theory*, Brighton, England, June 1985. Also "An Algorithm for Maximizing Expected Log Investment," *IEEE Trans.*, IT-30, No. 2, 1984.

11. C. E. Shannon, "Prediction and Entropy of Printed English," *BSTJ*, 30, No. 1, 1951.

12. B. Mandelbrot, "An Informational Theory of the Statistical Structure of Language." In *Communication Theory,* W. Jackson, ed. New York: Academic Press, 1953.

13. I. M. Yaglom, R. L. Dobrushin, and A. M. Yaglom, "Information Theory and Linguistics," *Voprosy yazykoznaniya (Problems of Linguistics),* No. 1, 1960 (in Russian).

14. T. M. Cover and R. C. King, "A Convergent Gambling Estimate of the Entropy of English," *IEEE Trans.,* IT-24, No. 4, 1978.

15. L. Levitin and Z. Reingold, "Evaluation of the Entropy of a Language by an Improved Prediction Method," *Proc 11th IEEE Convention in Israel,* Tel-Aviv, 1979.

16. A. M. Kondratov, "Information Theory and Prosody (Entropy of the Rhythm of Russian Speech)," *Problemy Kibernetiki (Problems of Cybernetics),* 9, 1963 (in Russian).

17. H. Quastler ed., *Information Theory in Psychology.* New York: Free Press, 1955.

18. J. A. Leonard, "Choice Reaction Time Experiments and Information Theory." In *Information Theory,* C. Cherry ed., London, Eng.: Butterworth, 1961.

19. A. T. Welford, "The Measurement of Sensory-Motor Performance: Survey and Reappraisal of Twelve Years Progress," *Ergonomics,* 3, No. 3, 1960.

20. L. Szilard, "Uber die Entropieverminderung in einem Thermodynamischen System bei Eingriff Intelligenter Wesen," *Z. Physik,* 53, No. 5, 1929.

21. D. Gabor, "Communication Theory and Physics," *Phil. Mag.,* 41, No. 7, 1950.

22. L. Brillouin, *Science and Information Theory.* New York: Academic Press, 1956.

23. D. S. Lebedev and L. B. Levitin, "Information Transmission by Electromagnetic Field," *Information and Control,* 9, No. 1, 1966.

24. L. B. Levitin, "A Thermodynamic Characterization of Ideal Physical Information Channels," *Journal of Information and Optimization Sciences,* 2, No. 3, 1981.

25. L. B. Levitin, "On the Quantum Measure of the Amount of Information," *Proc. IV National Conf. Information Theory,* Tashkent, 1969 (in Russian).

26. L. B. Levitin, "The Amount of Information and the Quantum-Mechanical Irreversibility of Measurements," *Proc. II Intern. Symp. Information Theory,* Yerevan, 1971 (in Russian).

27. V. V. Mityugov, "Physical Grounds of Information Theory," *Sovietskoe Radio.,* Moscow, 1976 (in Russian).

28. R. Landauer, "Fundamental Physical Limitation of the Computational Process." In *Noise in Physical Systems,* P. H. E. Meijer, R. D. Mountain, R. J. Soulen, eds., NBS Spec. Pub. 614, Washington, D.C.: 1981.

29. L. B. Levitin, "Physical Limitations of Rate, Depth and Minimum Energy in Information Processing," *Intern. J. Theoretical Physics,* 2.1, No. 2/3, 1982.

30. E. T. Jaynes, "Information Theory and Statistical Mechanics," *Phys. Rev.,* Part I, 106, 620–630, 1957; Part II, 108, 171–190, 1959.

31. A. Katz, *Principles of Statistical Mechanics. The Information Theory Approach.* San Francisco: W. H. Freeman, 1967.

32. R. S. Ingarden, "Information Theory and Thermodynamics," Part I, Torun, Poland, 1974; Part II, Torun, Poland, 1975.

33. R. S. Ingarden, "Quantum Information Theory," Torun, Poland, 1975.

34. L. B. Levitin, "Quantum Amount of Information and Maximum Work," *Proc. 13th IUPAP Conf. Statistical Physics*, D. Cabib, D. G. Kuper, I. Riess, eds., Bristol, Eng.: A. Hilger, 1978.

35. H. P. Yockey, R. L. Platzman, and H. Quastler, eds., *Information Theory in Biology*, Elmsford, N.Y.: Pergamon Press, 1958.

36. N. Wiener, *Cybernetics, or Control and Communication in the Animal and Machine*, 2nd ed. Cambridge, Mass.: MIT Press, 1961.

37. J. von Neumann, "The General and Logical Theory of Automata," *The Hixon Symposium*, 1948, L. Jeffres, ed., Wiley, 1951.

38. C. E. Shannon, "Computers and Automata," *Proc. IRE*, 41, No. 10, 1953.

39. C. E. Shannon, "Von Neumann's Contributions to Automata Theory," *Bull. Amer. Math. Soc.*, 64, No. 2, 1958.

# 1

# MATHEMATICAL PRELIMINARIES

**Introduction** The purpose of this chapter is to familiarize the reader with some of the mathematical tools that are needed for the study of information theory. Although the tools are simple and their mastering requires no knowledge of advanced mathematics, the reader must have a certain level of mathematical maturity and sophistication in order to use them effectively. Knowledge of probability theory at an introductory level and familiarity with combinatorial techniques are the only prerequisites for the study of this book; although Section 1.1 is devoted to a review of probability, it is no substitute for formal education in this area. Section 1.2 describes the Chebyshev inequality and the weak law of large numbers. In Section 1.3 we define convexity and prove an important relationship, known as the Jensen inequality, for convex functions. A simple derivation of Stirling's approximation to the factorial function is given in Section 1.4.

## 1.1 REVIEW OF PROBABILITY

In a probability experiment the outcome can be any member of a given set $E$. The set $E$ is known as the sample space of the experiment. Certain subsets of $E$ are defined as events. If the outcome of a trial belongs to the event $E_i$, then $E_i$ is said to have occurred. To each $E_i$, a probability $p_i$ is assigned. The assignment is not arbitrary, and the collection of $p_i$'s must satisfy the axioms of probability theory. For the most part, in this book we assume either that the set $E$ is countable or that it is divided into a countable number of elementary events. In either case, we have a discrete probability space.

**Example 1**

In a coin-flipping experiment, $E = \{H, T\}$. If the coin is fair $P\{H\} = P\{T\} = 0.5$.

**Example 2**

If the experiment is to throw a die, then $E = \{1, 2, 3, 4, 5, 6\}$. If the die is fair, $P\{1\} = P\{2\} = \cdots = P\{6\} = \frac{1}{6}$, $P\{2, 5\} = \frac{1}{3}$, $P\{1, 3, 5\} = \frac{1}{2}$.

**Example 3**

Let the experiment be the weather forecast for a certain day; then $E = \{$sunny, cloudy, rainy, snowy$\}$. A possible probability assignment is $P\{$sunny$\} = \frac{1}{2}$, $P\{$cloudy$\} = \frac{1}{4}$, $P\{$rainy$\} = \frac{1}{8}$, $P\{$snowy$\} = \frac{1}{8}$.

**Example 4**

Take a typical English text and pick a letter at random; then $E = \{a, b, c, \ldots, x, y, z\}$. The probability distribution will be $P\{a\} = 0.0642, \ldots, P\{e\} = 0.103, \ldots, P\{z\} = 0.0005$.

If the outcome of an experiment is always the same, it is said to be a degenerate (or certain) experiment.

**Example 5**

In the English language, the letter that follows q in a word is always u. The experiment is to open a book at random and to pick the letter following the first q encountered. The sample space is $E = \{a, b, c, \ldots, x, y, z\}$, but $P\{u\} = 1$ and $P\{a\} = \cdots = P\{z\} = 0$.

A discrete random variable $\mathbf{x}$ is defined by assigning a real number $x_i$ to each elementary event $E_i$ in a discrete sample space. The probability of $x_i$ is then denoted by $p(x_i)$. The average (or expected value) and the variance of $\mathbf{x}$ are defined as follows:

$$E(\mathbf{x}) = \bar{x} = \sum_i x_i p(x_i)$$

$$\text{Var}(\mathbf{x}) = E((\mathbf{x} - \bar{x})^2) = \sum_i (x_i - \bar{x})^2 p(x_i)$$

$$= \sum_i (x_i^2 + \bar{x}^2 - 2x_i\bar{x}) p(x_i)$$

$$= E(\mathbf{x}^2) + \bar{x}^2 - 2\bar{x} \cdot \bar{x} = E(\mathbf{x}^2) - \bar{x}^2$$

where $E(\mathbf{x}^2)$ is the expected value of $\mathbf{x}^2$. In general, the expected value of a function of $\mathbf{x}$, such as $f(\mathbf{x})$, is given by

$$E(f(\mathbf{x})) = \sum_i f(x_i) \cdot p(x_i)$$

A pair of random variables $(\mathbf{x}, \mathbf{y})$ associated with an experiment forms a joint random variable. If $\mathbf{x}, \mathbf{y}$ are discrete, the joint probability distribution is defined as $\{p_{ij}\}$, where $p_{ij} = P\{\mathbf{x} = x_i, \mathbf{y} = y_j\}$.

**Example 6**

The experiment is to throw a coin and a die. The possible outcomes are

$$(H, 1), (H, 2), \ldots, (H, 6), (T, 1), (T, 2), \ldots, (T, 6)$$

If the coin and the die are fair and independent, $p_{ij} = \frac{1}{12}$ for all $i, j$. The diagram of Figure 1.1 is often helpful in visualizing the situation. Using the diagram, it is easy to verify that

  (i)   The sum of the probabilities $p_{ij}$ is equal to 1.
  (ii)  $P\{\text{Coin} = \text{Head}\} = P\{(H, 1)\} + P\{(H, 2)\} + \cdots + P\{(H, 6)\} = \frac{1}{2}$.
  (iii) $P\{\text{Die} = 5\} = P\{(H, 5)\} + P\{(T, 5)\} = \frac{1}{6}$.

Now assume that the coin and the die are somehow interacting and as a result their outcomes are not independent. The joint density may have the distribution shown in Figure 1.2. The following statements can be directly verified from the diagram.

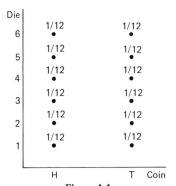

**Figure 1.1**

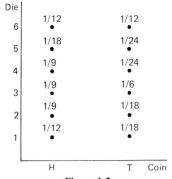

**Figure 1.2**

(i)   $P\{(H, 5)\} = \frac{1}{18}$
(ii)  $P\{Coin = H\} = \frac{5}{9}$
(iii) $P\{Coin = T\} = \frac{4}{9}$
(iv)  $P\{Die = 5\} = \frac{7}{72}$
(v)   $P\{Die = 5 \text{ given } Coin = H\} =$

$$\frac{1/18}{(1/12) + (1/18) + (1/9) + (1/9) + (1/9) + (1/12)} = 1/10$$

The conditional density of **y** given **x** is defined as

$$p(y_j \,|\, x_i) = \frac{p(x_i, y_j)}{p(x_i)}$$

where the marginal density $p(x_i)$ is assumed to be nonzero. The marginal densities are defined as follows:

$$p(x_i) = \sum_j p(x_i, y_j)$$

$$p(y_j) = \sum_i p(x_i, y_j)$$

The random variables **x** and **y** are said to be independent if $p(x_i, y_j) = p(x_i)p(y_j)$ for all $i, j$.

The correlation $C$ between **x** and **y** is defined as the expected value of $(\mathbf{x} - \bar{x})(\mathbf{y} - \bar{y})$:

$$C(\mathbf{x}, \mathbf{y}) = E((\mathbf{x} - \bar{x})(\mathbf{y} - \bar{y})) = \sum_i \sum_j (x_i - \bar{x})(y_j - \bar{y})p(x_i, y_j)$$

$$= E(\mathbf{xy}) - \bar{x}\bar{y}$$

In the special case where **x** and **y** are independent,

$$E(\mathbf{xy}) = \sum_i \sum_j x_i y_j p(x_i)p(y_j) = \sum_i x_i p(x_i) \sum_j y_j p(y_j) = \bar{x}\bar{y}$$

Independence thus results in a lack of correlation. The opposite, however, is not true (see Problem 1.3).

## 1.2 CHEBYSHEV INEQUALITY AND THE WEAK LAW OF LARGE NUMBERS

Given a random variable **x** with average $\bar{x}$ and variance $\sigma_x^2$, the Chebyshev inequality for an arbitrary positive number $\delta$ is

$$P\{|\mathbf{x} - \bar{x}| \geq \delta\} \leq \frac{\sigma_x^2}{\delta^2}$$

A simple proof of this result is given here (for another proof, see Problem 1.4). Define the function $f(x)$ as follows:

$$f(x) = \begin{cases} 1, & \text{if } |x - \bar{x}| \geq \delta \\ 0, & \text{if } |x - \bar{x}| < \delta \end{cases}$$

Then

$$P\{|\mathbf{x} - \bar{x}| \geq \delta\} = \sum f(x_i)p(x_i)$$

Upon inspection of Figure 1.3, it is obvious that

$$f(x) \leq \left[\frac{x - \bar{x}}{\delta}\right]^2$$

Therefore,

$$P\{|\mathbf{x} - \bar{x}| \geq \delta\} \leq \sum_i \left[\frac{x_i - \bar{x}}{\delta}\right]^2 p(x_i) = \frac{\sigma_x^2}{\delta^2}$$

The Chebyshev inequality can now be used to derive the weak law of large numbers. Consider a binary experiment where the outcomes are 0 and 1 with probabilities $p_0$ and $1 - p_0$, respectively. This experiment is repeated $N$ times independently, and the average output is defined as $\mathbf{y}_N$; that is, $\mathbf{y}_N$ is equal to the total number of 1's in the $N$ trials divided by $N$. Obviously, $\mathbf{y}_N$ is a random variable with sample space $\{0, 1/N, 2/N, \ldots, 1\}$. Defining $\mathbf{x}^{(n)}$ as the r. v. associated with the outcome of the $n$th trial, we have

$$\mathbf{y}_N = \frac{1}{N} \sum_{n=1}^{N} \mathbf{x}^{(n)}$$

The average and variance of $\mathbf{y}_N$ are obtained as follows:

$$\bar{y}_N = \frac{1}{N} \sum_{n=1}^{N} E(\mathbf{x}^{(n)}) = \frac{1}{N} \sum_{n=1}^{N} \bar{x} = \bar{x}$$

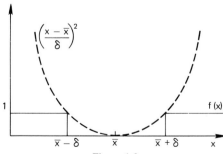

**Figure 1.3**

$$\sigma_y^2 = E((\mathbf{y}_N - \bar{y}_N)^2) = \frac{1}{N^2} E\left(\left[\sum_{n=1}^{N} (\mathbf{x}^{(n)} - \bar{x})\right]^2\right)$$

$$= \frac{1}{N^2} \sum_{n=1}^{N} E((\mathbf{x}^{(n)} - \bar{x})^2) = \frac{\sigma_x^2}{N}$$

For an arbitrary positive number $\varepsilon$, the Chebyshev inequality

$$P\{|\mathbf{y}_N - \bar{y}_N| \geq \varepsilon\} \leq \frac{\sigma_y^2}{\varepsilon^2}$$

leads to the following statement of the weak law of large numbers:

$$P\left\{\left|\left[\frac{1}{N} \sum_{n=1}^{N} \mathbf{x}^{(n)}\right] - \bar{x}\right| \geq \varepsilon\right\} \leq \frac{\sigma_x^2}{N\varepsilon^2}$$

Notice that the right side approaches zero with increasing $N$. The weak law of large numbers thus asserts that the sample average of $\mathbf{x}$ approaches the statistical average $\bar{x}$ with high probability as $N \to \infty$.

## 1.3 CONVEX SETS AND FUNCTIONS: JENSEN'S INEQUALITY

In the Euclidean space, a set $S$ is convex if, for every pair of points $P_1, P_2$ in $S$, the straight line connecting $P_1$ to $P_2$ is completely contained in $S$. Figure 1.4a shows two convex sets in the two-dimensional Euclidean space. The sets of Figure 1.4b are not convex.

If $P_1 = (x_1, \ldots, x_n)$ and $P_2 = (y_1, \ldots, y_n)$ are points in the Euclidean $n$-space, then the straight line connecting them is represented by the set of points

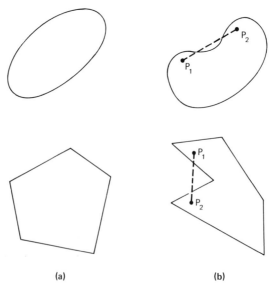

(a)                                    (b)

**Figure 1.4**

$P$, where $P = \lambda P_1 + (1 - \lambda)P_2 = [\lambda x_1 + (1 - \lambda)y_1, \ldots, \lambda x_n + (1 - \lambda)y_n]$, and $\lambda$ is a real number in the interval $[0, 1]$. An important example of a convex set is the set of all $n$-dimensional probability distributions $\{p_1, \ldots, p_n\}$ (see Problem 1.6).

The real function $f(P)$, defined on a convex set $S$, is convex cap ($\cap$) if for every pair of points $P_1, P_2$ in the set and for every $\lambda$ in $[0, 1]$ the following inequality is satisfied:

$$f[\lambda P_1 + (1 - \lambda)P_2] \geq \lambda f(P_1) + (1 - \lambda)f(P_2)$$

This property is shown graphically in Figure 1.5 for a function defined on a one-dimensional space. If the direction of inequality is reversed (for all $P_1, P_2, \lambda$), then the function is convex cup ($\cup$).

**Theorem.**    If $\lambda_1, \ldots, \lambda_N$ are nonnegative numbers whose sum is unity, then, for every set of points $P_1, \ldots, P_N$ in the domain of the convex $\cap$ function $f(P)$, the following inequality is valid:

$$f\left(\sum_{n=1}^{N} \lambda_n P_n\right) \geq \sum_{n=1}^{N} \lambda_n f(P_n)$$

*Proof.*    We use induction on $N$. For $N = 2$, the inequality is valid by definition of convexity. Assuming the validity of the theorem for $N - 1$, we prove it for $N$.

$$f\left(\sum_{n=1}^{N} \lambda_n P_n\right) = f\left(\lambda_N P_N + (1 - \lambda_N) \sum_{n=1}^{N-1} \frac{\lambda_n}{1 - \lambda_N} P_n\right)$$

$$\geq \lambda_N f(P_N) + (1 - \lambda_N)f\left(\sum_{n=1}^{N-1} \frac{\lambda_n}{1 - \lambda_N} P_n\right)$$

$$\geq \lambda_N f(P_N) + (1 - \lambda_N) \sum_{n=1}^{N-1} \frac{\lambda_n}{1 - \lambda_N} f(P_n)$$

$$= \sum_{n=1}^{N} \lambda_n f(P_n)$$

The proof is thus complete.

A direct consequence of the preceding theorem is Jensen's inequality for discrete random variables. Let r. v. $\mathbf{x}$ assume the values $x_1, \ldots, x_n$ with probabilities $p_1, \ldots, p_n$. Let $f(x)$ be a convex $\cap$ function whose domain includes $x_1, \ldots, x_n$. Now $E(\mathbf{x}) = \sum_i p_i x_i$ and $E(f(\mathbf{x})) = \sum_i p_i f(x_i)$. Therefore,

$$f(E(\mathbf{x})) \geq E(f(\mathbf{x}))$$

This is known as Jensen's inequality.

## 1.4 STIRLING'S FORMULA

In this section we derive Stirling's formula, which provides upper and lower bounds to $N!$. Consider the function $\ln(x)$ whose integral from 1 to $N$ is given

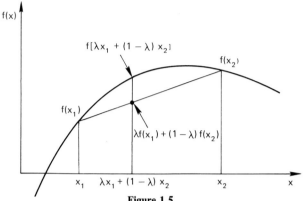

**Figure 1.5**

by

$$\int_1^N \ln(x)\,dx = [x\,\ln(x) - x]_1^N = N\,\ln(N) - N + 1$$

This integral is underapproximated by the trapezoid method of Figure 1.6a and overapproximated by the midpoint method of Figure 1.6b. Consequently,

$$\int_1^N \ln(x)\,dx \geq \ln 2 + \ln 3 + \cdots + \ln(N-1) + \tfrac{1}{2}\ln(N) = \ln(N!) - \tfrac{1}{2}\ln(N)$$

$$\int_1^N \ln(x)\,dx \leq (\tfrac{1}{8}) + \ln 2 + \ln 3 + \cdots + \ln(N-1) + \tfrac{1}{2}\ln(N)$$

$$= \ln(N!) + (\tfrac{1}{8}) - \tfrac{1}{2}\ln(N)$$

Therefore,

$$N\,\ln(N) + \tfrac{1}{2}\ln(N) - N + (\tfrac{7}{8}) \leq \ln(N!) \leq N\,\ln(N) + \tfrac{1}{2}\ln(N) - N + 1$$

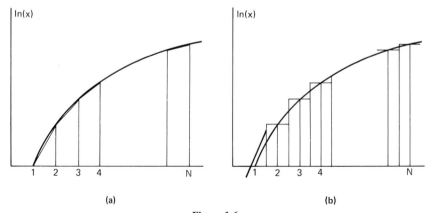

(a)                                          (b)

**Figure 1.6**

which yields Stirling's formula as

$$N^N e^{-N} \sqrt{N}\, e^{\,7/8} \leq N! \leq N^N e^{-N} \sqrt{N}\, e$$

## PROBLEMS

**1.1.** Three events $E_1, E_2$, and $E_3$, defined on the same space, have probabilities $P(E_1) = P(E_2) = P(E_3) = \frac{1}{4}$. Let $E_0$ be the event that one or more of the events $E_1, E_2, E_3$ occurs.

(a) Find $P(E_0)$ when:

(1) $E_1, E_2, E_3$ are disjoint.

(2) $E_1, E_2, E_3$ are statistically independent.

(3) $E_1, E_2, E_3$ are three names for the same event.

(b) Find the maximum values that $P(E_0)$ can assume when:

(1) Nothing is known about the independence or disjointness of $E_1, E_2, E_3$.

(2) It is known that $E_1, E_2, E_3$ are pairwise independent; that is, the probability of realizing both $E_i$ and $E_j$ is $P(E_i)P(E_j)$, but nothing is known about the probability of realizing all three events together.

**Hint:** Use Venn diagrams.

**1.2.** A box contains two dice, one fair and the other loaded, so that for the first one $P(1) = P(2) = \cdots P(6) = \frac{1}{6}$ and for the second one $P(6) = \frac{2}{3}$, $P(1) = \cdots = P(5) = \frac{1}{15}$. We choose one die from the box at random and roll it. If the outcome is the number 6, what is the probability that the loaded die has been selected? What if the die is rolled twice and the outcome of both trials is the number 6?

**1.3.** Let $\mathbf{x}$ and $\mathbf{y}$ be discrete random variables,

(a) Prove that $E(\mathbf{x} + \mathbf{y}) = E(\mathbf{x}) + E(\mathbf{y})$

(b) If $\mathbf{x}$ and $\mathbf{y}$ are independent, prove that $E(\mathbf{xy}) = E(\mathbf{x}) \cdot E(\mathbf{y})$; that is, $\mathbf{x}$ and $\mathbf{y}$ are uncorrelated.

(c) Is it possible for $\mathbf{x}$ and $\mathbf{y}$ to be dependent but uncorrelated? Give an example.

(d) If $\mathbf{x}$ and $\mathbf{y}$ are independent, prove that $\text{Var}(\mathbf{x} + \mathbf{y}) = \text{Var}(\mathbf{x}) + \text{Var}(\mathbf{y})$. Is this relationship valid when $\mathbf{x}$ and $\mathbf{y}$ are dependent but uncorrelated?

**1.4.** (a) For any random variable $\mathbf{y}$ that assumes only nonnegative values, prove the following inequality:

$$P\{\mathbf{y} \geq \delta\} \leq \frac{\bar{y}}{\delta}$$

where $\delta$ is an arbitrary positive number.

(b) Let $\mathbf{x}$ be a random variable with average $\bar{x}$ and variance $\sigma_x^2$. Define a nonnegative random variable $\mathbf{y} = (\mathbf{x} - \bar{x})^2$ and show that

$$P\{|\mathbf{x} - \bar{x}| \geq \delta\} \leq \frac{\sigma_x^2}{\delta^2}$$

This is the Chebyshev inequality derived in Section 1.2.

**1.5.** A sequence of independent identically distributed random variables $\mathbf{y}_1, \ldots, \mathbf{y}_N$ with average $\bar{y}$ and standard deviation $\sigma_y$ is given. Define the random variable $\mathbf{x}$ as follows:

$$\mathbf{x} = \frac{1}{N} \sum_{n=1}^{N} \mathbf{y}_n$$

Show that the Chebyshev inequality for $\mathbf{x}$ is

$$P\{|\mathbf{x} - \bar{y}| \geq \delta\} \leq \frac{\sigma_y^2}{N\delta^2}$$

and investigate the limit when $N \to \infty$.

**1.6.** Prove that the set of all $n$-dimensional probability distributions $\{p_1, \ldots, p_n\}$ is convex. For $n = 3$, show the set graphically.

**1.7.** The function $f(x)$ is defined on the open interval $(a, b)$ and is convex $\cap$. Prove that $f(x)$ is continuous. Would this conclusion be valid if the domain of the function were a closed interval?

**1.8.** The function $f(x)$ is defined and has second derivative on the interval $(a, b)$. Prove that the necessary and sufficient condition for $f(x)$ to be convex $\cap$ is

$$\frac{d^2 f(x)}{dx^2} \leq 0$$

for all points in $(a, b)$.

# 2

# ENTROPY, DISCRETE MEMORYLESS SOURCE, AND BLOCK ENCODING

**Introduction** The concept of entropy is the central concept in information theory. The entropy of a random variable is defined in terms of its probability distribution and can be shown to be a good measure of randomness or uncertainty. This chapter begins by introducing the entropy for a discrete random variable in Section 2.1 and describes some of its properties in Section 2.2. Other important properties of entropy are discussed in the problems at the end of the chapter.

The importance of entropy in practical applications has much to do with its relationship with long sequences of a random variable. It turns out that repeated trials of a probabilistic experiment give rise to outcomes that can, under quite general circumstances, be divided into two categories. The first category consists of sequences that have a very small probability of occurrence; in fact, the probability of occurrence of this category as a whole approaches zero with the increasing length of the sequences. The second category consists of the remaining sequences; these sequences, which are known as likely or typical sequences, all have more or less the same probability and, as their length increases, they become closer and closer to being equally likely. The number of typical sequences and their individual probabilities are functions of the entropy, and it is this relationship that gives entropy a major role in the theory of data compression and error control coding. Sections 2.3 and 2.4 explore this relationship.

The concept of entropy as developed in the original work of C. E. Shannon [1] has been used in several branches of science, but its most significant applications to date have been in the areas of data communication and signal processing. We will therefore restrict our discussion in this book to situations that arise in source coding (data compression) and channel coding (error correction). This chapter and the next focus on the problem of source coding for discrete memoryless sources, where the goal is to accurately represent (encode) the output of the information source with as few code words as possible.

This chapter deals with situations where a fixed-length block of data is mapped onto a fixed-length block of code letters. Section 2.5 considers the case where the code letters are of equal duration in time, while Section 2.6 considers situations such as telegraphy, where different code letters have different durations. In both cases, typical sequences produced by the information source are encoded (represented) by sequences of code letters, and the minimum required rate of generation of code letters is shown to be equal to the source entropy. In Chapter 3, fixed-length blocks of data are mapped onto variable-length blocks of code letters, and encoding schemes are described for the minimization of the average code-word length. It is shown that the minimum achievable code-word length, on the average, is equal to the source entropy.

## 2.1 ENTROPY OF A DISCRETE RANDOM VARIABLE

Let $\mathbf{x}$ be a random variable (r. v.) with sample space $X = \{x_1, \ldots, x_N\}$ and probability measure $P(x_n) = p_n$. The entropy of $\mathbf{x}$ is defined as

$$H(\mathbf{x}) = -\sum_{n=1}^{N} p_n \log(p_n) \tag{2.1}$$

The base of the logarithm is arbitrary and amounts to a constant multiplicative factor. [Remember that $\log_a^p = (\log_a^b)(\log_b^p)$.] If this base is 2, the entropy is said to be in *bits* (for binary digits); if the base is $e$, the entropy is said to be in *nats* (for natural units). A plot of the function $-p \ln(p)$ is shown in Figure 2.1. Note that at $p = 0$ we have set the function equal to zero, in agreement with the fact that $x \ln(x) \to 0$ as $x \to 0$. Also notice that the function $-p \ln(p)$ is a convex $\cap$ function of $p$.

**Example 1**

Let $X = \{0, 1\}$, $P(0) = p$, and $P(1) = 1 - p$. Then

$$H(\mathbf{x}) = -p \log(p) - (1 - p) \log(1 - p)$$

A plot of $H(\mathbf{x})$ (in bits) versus $p$ is shown in Figure 2.2. This function is convex $\cap$ and

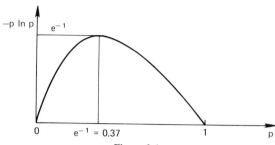

**Figure 2.1**

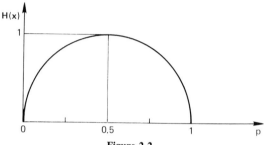

**Figure 2.2**

has symmetry about $p = 0.5$. Note that at $p = 0$ and $p = 1$ the function is tangent to the vertical axis.

## 2.2 *H*(x) AS A MEASURE OF UNCERTAINTY

The entropy as defined by Eq. (2.1) has several properties. These properties make $H(\mathbf{x})$ a good measure of the uncertainty about the outcome of a probabilistic experiment. In this section, we describe some of these properties.

(i)  If $p_1 = 1$ and $p_n = 0$ for $n \neq 1$, then $H(\mathbf{x}) = 0$; that is, the uncertainty about an experiment with deterministic outcome is zero.

(ii)  If $p_1 = p_2 = \cdots = p_N = 1/N$, then $H(\mathbf{x}) = \log N$. Note that, if the number of equiprobable outcomes of an experiment increases (i.e., if $N$ increases), then the entropy of the experiment increases.

(iii)  $H(\mathbf{x}) \leq \log N$ with equality iff[†] $p_n = 1/N$ for all $n$. The proof of this statement is based on the important inequality $\ln(x) \leq x - 1$, whose validity becomes obvious upon inspection of Figure 2.3. In this figure the functions $\ln(x)$ and $x - 1$ are plotted on the same set of axes. Note that the two functions are equal only at $x = 1$.

---

[†]iff means if and only if.

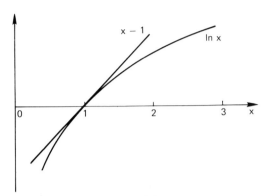

**Figure 2.3**

We now proceed with the proof:

$$H(\mathbf{x}) - \ln(N) = -\sum_{n=1}^{N} p_n \ln(p_n) - \sum_{n=1}^{N} p_n \ln(N) = \sum_{n=1}^{N} p_n \ln\left(\frac{1}{Np_n}\right)$$

$$\leq \sum_{n=1}^{N} p_n \left(\frac{1}{Np_n} - 1\right) = \sum_{n=1}^{N} \left(\frac{1}{N}\right) - \sum_{n=1}^{N} p_n$$

$$= 1 - 1 = 0$$

Therefore, $H(\mathbf{x}) \leq \ln(N)$ with equality iff $Np_n = 1$ for all $n$; that is, $p_n = 1/N$ for all $n$. This implies that the uncertainty of an experiment is highest when the outcomes are equiprobable.

(iv) Let the r.v. $\mathbf{x}$ have sample space $X = \{x_1, \ldots, x_N\}$ and the r.v. $\mathbf{y}$ have sample space $Y = \{y_1, \ldots, y_M\}$. Then the joint r.v. $\mathbf{z} = (\mathbf{x}, \mathbf{y})$ has sample space $Z = \{(x_1, y_1), \ldots, (x_1, y_M), (x_2, y_1), \ldots, (x_2, y_M), \ldots, (x_N, y_1), \ldots, (x_N, y_M)\}$ with $NM$ elements. Let $\mathbf{x}$ and $\mathbf{y}$ be independent and have equiprobable outcomes. Then $H(\mathbf{x}) = \log(N)$, $H(\mathbf{y}) = \log(M)$, and $H(\mathbf{z}) = \log(MN) = \log(M) + \log(N) = H(\mathbf{x}) + H(\mathbf{y})$; that is, the uncertainty of the joint experiment $(\mathbf{x}, \mathbf{y})$ is the sum of the uncertainties of the independent experiments $\mathbf{x}$ and $\mathbf{y}$. This property remains valid even if $\mathbf{x}$ and $\mathbf{y}$ have nonuniform distributions. In this case,

$$H(\mathbf{z}) = -\sum_{n=1}^{N} \sum_{m=1}^{M} P(x_n, y_m) \log P(x_n, y_m)$$

$$= -\sum_{n=1}^{N} \sum_{m=1}^{M} P(x_n)P(y_m) [\log P(x_n) + \log P(y_m)]$$

$$= -\sum_{n=1}^{N} P(x_n) \log P(x_n) \sum_{m=1}^{M} P(y_m)$$

$$- \sum_{m=1}^{M} P(y_m) \log P(y_m) \sum_{n=1}^{N} P(x_n)$$

$$= H(\mathbf{x}) + H(\mathbf{y})$$

(v) If an experiment is decomposed into two subexperiments, the original uncertainty will be the uncertainty associated with the first experiment plus the average uncertainty associated with the second experiment. This is the *grouping property* of the entropy. To explain this property, consider the r.v. $\mathbf{x}$ with sample space $X = \{x_1, \ldots, x_n, x_{n+1}, \ldots, x_N\}$ and probability measure $P(x_i) = p_i$. Let us decompose $X$ into two subspaces, $Y = \{x_1, \ldots, x_n\}$ and $Z = \{x_{n+1}, \ldots, x_N\}$. The probabilities associated with $Y$ and $Z$ are given by $P(Y) = \sum_{i=1}^{n} p_i$ and $P(Z) = \sum_{i=n+1}^{N} p_i$. Furthermore, let us define random variables $\mathbf{y}$ and $\mathbf{z}$ by $P(y_i) = P(x_i)/P(Y)$, $i = 1, 2, \ldots n$ and $P(z_i) = P(x_{n+i})/P(Z)$, $i = 1, 2, \ldots N - n$. $H(\mathbf{x})$ can now be written as

$$H(\mathbf{x}) = -\sum_{i=1}^{N} p_i \log p_i = -\sum_{i=1}^{n} p_i \log p_i - \sum_{i=n+1}^{N} p_i \log p_i$$

$$= -P(Y) \sum_{i=1}^{n} P(y_i)(\log P(y_i) + \log P(Y))$$

$$- P(Z) \sum_{i=1}^{N-n} P(z_i)(\log P(z_i) + \log P(Z))$$

$$= -[P(Y) \log P(Y) + P(Z) \log P(Z)] + [P(Y)H(\mathbf{y}) + P(Z)H(\mathbf{z})].$$

In the final expression, the first bracket represents the uncertainty associated with the first experiment and the second bracket is the average uncertainty associated with the second experiment.

*Note:* The preceding properties of the function $H(\mathbf{x})$ defined by Eq. (2.1) are reasonable properties for a measure of uncertainty. It is possible to prove, however, that this function is the only one that satisfies a small set of reasonable requirements. In reference [4], it is shown that the entropy *must* be defined by Eq. (2.1) if properties (ii), (iv), and (v), plus a continuity property, are required.

## 2.3 ENTROPY AND SEQUENCES OF A RANDOM VARIABLE

The following example is designed to bring out the significance of $H(\mathbf{x})$ as related to long sequences of the random variable $\mathbf{x}$.

**Example 2**

Consider the r.v. $\mathbf{x}$ with sample space $X = \{x_1, x_2\}$, $P(x_1) = \frac{1}{3}$, and $P(x_2) = \frac{2}{3}$. The entropy of $\mathbf{x}$ is given by

$$H(\mathbf{x}) = -(\tfrac{1}{3}) \log(\tfrac{1}{3}) - (\tfrac{2}{3}) \log(\tfrac{2}{3}) = 0.918 \text{ bits}$$

Let us repeat this experiment $N$ times to obtain a sequence of $N$ independent, identically distributed (i.i.d) random variables. In general, there are $2^N$ possible sequences. If the number of occurrences of $x_1$ in a certain sequence is $n$, the probability of that sequence is given by

$$p_1^n(1 - p_1)^{N-n}$$

Since there are $\binom{N}{n} = N!/n!(N - n)!$ such sequences, their total probability is equal to

$$\binom{N}{n}p_1^n(1 - p_1)^{N-n}$$

Table 2.1 shows probabilities of various sequences for $N = 15$. Notice that the most probable sequences are those for which $n$ is close to $Np_1 = 5$. In fact, the probability of $2 \le n \le 8$ is 0.95. In other words,

The probability of occurrence of a sequence for which $n$ is significantly different from $Np_1$ is very small.

Also notice that the individual probabilities of these sequences are between $2^{-15 \times 0.718}$ and $2^{-15 \times 1.18}$, which are fairly close to $2^{-NH(x)} = 2^{-15 \times 0.918}$. In other words,

All the likely sequences are more or less equiprobable with probability about $2^{-NH(x)}$.

Finally, notice that the total number of sequences with $2 \le n \le 8$ is $22,803 = 2^{15 \times 0.965}$, which is not far from $2^{NH(x)}$. In other words,

The total number of likely sequences is about $2^{NH(x)}$.

**TABLE 2.1**

| $n$ | No. of Sequences $\binom{N}{n}$ | Probability of Each Sequence $p_1^n(1 - p_1)^{N-n}$ | Total Probability $\binom{N}{n}p_1^n(1 - p_1)^{N-n}$ |
|---|---|---|---|
| 0 | 1 | $2^{-15 \times 0.585}$ | 0.002284 |
| 1 | 15 | $2^{-15 \times 0.652}$ | 0.017127 |
| 2 | 105 | $2^{-15 \times 0.718}$ | 0.059946 |
| 3 | 455 | $2^{-15 \times 0.785}$ | 0.129883 |
| 4 | 1365 | $2^{-15 \times 0.852}$ | 0.194825 |
| 5 | 3003 | $2^{-15 \times 0.918}$ | 0.214307 |
| 6 | 5005 | $2^{-15 \times 0.985}$ | 0.178589 |
| 7 | 6435 | $2^{-15 \times 1.052}$ | 0.114807 |
| 8 | 6435 | $2^{-15 \times 1.118}$ | 0.057404 |
| 9 | 5005 | $2^{-15 \times 1.185}$ | 0.022324 |
| 10 | 3003 | $2^{-15 \times 1.252}$ | 0.006697 |
| 11 | 1365 | $2^{-15 \times 1.318}$ | 0.001522 |
| 12 | 455 | $2^{-15 \times 1.385}$ | 0.000254 |
| 13 | 105 | $2^{-15 \times 1.452}$ | 0.000029 |
| 14 | 15 | $2^{-15 \times 1.518}$ | 0.000002 |
| 15 | 1 | $2^{-15 \times 1.585}$ | 0.000000 |

The last conclusion is consistent with the previous two conclusions: if a subset of nearly equiprobable elements has a total probability close to 1, then the number of elements in the subset must be approximately the inverse of the probability of each element.

The three conclusions of Example 2 are quite general. In the next section we will show that the degree of approximation can be arbitrarily improved by letting $N$ assume larger and larger values. Later we will see that the sequences that behave in this manner are far more general than the memoryless binary sequences considered in this section.

The practical significance of these results in data compression should be quite clear. To represent a binary sequence of $N$ digits in our example, we only need $NH(\mathbf{x}) = 0.918N$ bits, which constitutes an 8.2 percent reduction in the volume of data. Any degree of accuracy can then be achieved by choosing sufficiently large values of $N$.

## 2.4 DISCRETE MEMORYLESS SOURCE AND LIKELY SEQUENCES

We now put the conclusions of the previous section on a firm basis. We will need the weak law of large numbers, which asserts that, if the experiment corresponding to the r. v. $\mathbf{x}$ is repeated $N$ independent times with $\mathbf{x}^{(j)}$ the outcome of the $j$th trial, then

$$P\left\{\left|\frac{1}{N}\sum_{j=1}^{N}\mathbf{x}^{(j)} - \bar{x}\right| \geq \delta\right\} \leq \frac{\sigma_x^2}{N\delta^2}$$

Here $\bar{x}$ and $\sigma_x$ are the average and standard deviation of $\mathbf{x}$, respectively, and $\delta$ is an arbitrary positive number. For a proof of the weak law, the reader is referred to Section 1.2 and Problem 1.5.

Suppose a source generates a letter belonging to the alphabet $\{a_1, \ldots, a_K\}$ every $T$ seconds. The probability of $a_k$ is $p(a_k)$, and each letter in the sequence is generated independently. Starting at time $t = 0$, the source will have produced $N = t/T$ symbols at time $t$. The number of possible sequences generated in this period is thus $K^N$, and each sequence $S_i$ has probability of occurrence $P(S_i)$. $P(S_i)$ is the product of $N$ terms $p(a^{(j)})$, where $a^{(j)}$ is the $j$th letter of the sequence.

We now define a random variable $\mathbf{z}$ corresponding to the set of sequences $S_i$. The value $z_i$ assigned to $S_i$ is given by

$$z_i = -\log P(S_i) = -\sum_{j=1}^{N} \log p(a^{(j)})$$

$\mathbf{z}$ is thus the sum of $N$ i. i. d. random variables $\mathbf{x}$ with outcomes $x_k = -\log p(a_k)$. The weak law of large numbers asserts that, if $\delta$ and $\varepsilon$ are arbitrary positive numbers, there exists $N_0$ such that for $N \geq N_0$

$$P\left\{\left|-\frac{1}{N}\sum_{j=1}^{N}\log p(a^{(j)}) - H(\mathbf{x})\right| \geq \delta\right\} \leq \varepsilon$$

Notice that

$$\overline{x} = -\sum_{k=1}^{K} p(a_k) \log p(a_k) = H(\mathbf{x})$$

has been used in the preceding equation. We conclude that, with probability greater than $1 - \varepsilon$,

$$-\delta \leq -\left(\frac{1}{N}\right) \log P(S_i) - H(\mathbf{x}) \leq \delta, \qquad \text{for large } N$$

Using 2 as the base of the logarithm, this yields

$$2^{-N[H(\mathbf{x})+\delta]} \leq P(S_i) \leq 2^{-N[H(\mathbf{x})-\delta]} \tag{2.2}$$

The number of sequences for which Eq. (2.2) is valid can now be bounded. Denoting by $\nu$ the number of such sequences, we will have

(a) $P(S_i) \geq 2^{-N[H(\mathbf{x})+\delta]}$ and $\nu[P(S_i)]_{\min} \leq 1$
(b) $P(S_i) \leq 2^{-N[H(\mathbf{x})-\delta]}$ and $\nu[P(S_i)]_{\max} > 1 - \varepsilon$

Therefore,

$$(1 - \varepsilon)2^{N[H(\mathbf{x})-\delta]} \leq \nu \leq 2^{N[H(\mathbf{x})+\delta]} \tag{2.3}$$

Equations (2.2) and (2.3) imply that the probability of each likely sequence is about $2^{-NH(\mathbf{x})}$ and the number of these sequences is about $2^{NH(\mathbf{x})}$. Furthermore, since $H(\mathbf{x}) \leq \log K$ (see Section 2.2, property (iii) of the entropy function), we conclude that

$$\nu \cong 2^{NH(\mathbf{x})} \leq 2^{N\log(K)} = K^N \tag{2.4}$$

where $K^N$ is the maximum possible number of sequences $S_i$. Equality holds iff $p(a_k) = 1/K$ for all $k$.

## 2.5 BLOCK ENCODER WITH FIXED-LENGTH ALPHABET

To encode the output of the source described in the preceding section, consider a binary encoder that can create binary sequences at a rate of $\beta$ bits per second. After $t = NT$ seconds, the total number of sequences generated by the encoder is $2^{N\beta T}$. ($\beta T$ can be interpreted as the number of bits generated by the encoder per source symbol.) We wish to encode the source into binary sequences, that is, to assign a unique binary sequence to each source sequence. We also wish to use a machine with finite (and otherwise unlimited) memory so that, aside from an initial delay, data can be encoded as they are generated by the source. Under these circumstances, if a unique binary word is assigned to each of the likely sequences and the remaining (unlikely) sequences are ignored, an error will be committed with probability less than $\varepsilon$ provided that enough binary sequences are available to cover all the likely source sequences. Thus, if $2^{N\beta T} \geq 2^{N[H(\mathbf{x})+\delta]}$, or equivalently $\beta T > H(\mathbf{x})$, the probability of error will be less than $\varepsilon$.

As long as the binary sequences are generated with a rate (per source symbol) greater than the entropy of the source $H(\mathbf{x})$, the probability of error can be made as small as desired.

Conversely, if $\beta T < H(\mathbf{x})$, say $\beta T = H(\mathbf{x}) - 2\gamma$, set $\delta = \gamma$ and choose an arbitrarily small positive number $\varepsilon$. There exists a time $t_0$ after which, with probability greater than $1 - \varepsilon$, the source sequence $S_i$ will be a likely sequence. The probability of $S_i$ is bounded by

$$P(S_i) \leq 2^{-N[H(\mathbf{x})-\gamma]}$$

The number of available binary sequences, however, is

$$2^{N\beta T} = 2^{N[H(\mathbf{x})-2\gamma]}$$

Therefore, the probability of having a code for a likely sequence is at most

$$2^{N[H(\mathbf{x})-2\gamma]} \cdot 2^{-N[H(\mathbf{x})-\gamma]} = 2^{-N\gamma}$$

We could also have assigned some codes to the unlikely sequences; but since these sequences have probability less than $\varepsilon$, the probability of having a code for a source sequence will, in general, be less than $\varepsilon + 2^{-N\gamma}$. For very long sequences, this probability will be extremely small.

If the binary sequences are generated with a rate (per source symbol) less than the entropy of the source $H(\mathbf{x})$, the probability of error will be as close to 1 as desired, irrespective of the manner in which sequences are encoded.

*Note:* If $\beta T$ is larger than $H(\mathbf{x})$ but very close to it, the output of the binary encoder, in the long run, will have $2^{\beta t}$ sequences with equal probabilities $\sim 2^{-NH(\mathbf{x})} \cong 2^{-\beta t}$. This means that the encoder is working close to its maximum entropy with $P(0) \cong P(1) \cong 0.5$.

**Exercise**

The results of this section are not restricted to binary encoders. It is quite straightforward to generalize the results to an encoder with $D$ different symbols in its alphabet. Carry out this generalization.

## 2.6 BLOCK ENCODER WITH VARIABLE-LENGTH ALPHABET

Consider an encoder with alphabet $\{x_1, \ldots, x_D\}$, where the duration of $x_i$ is $T_i$. It is assumed that the encoder can generate every possible sequence of $x_i$'s. To determine the number of different sequences the device can generate in $t$ seconds, we define the function $N(t)$ as

$$N(t) = \begin{cases} 0, & \text{if } t < 0 \\ 1, & \text{if } 0 \leq t < T_{min} = \min\{T_i\} \\ \text{no. of possible sequences in } [0, t], & \text{if } t \geq T_{min} \end{cases}$$

It is not difficult to verify that, for $t \geq T_{min}$,

$$N(t) = N(t - T_1) + N(t - T_2) + \cdots + N(t - T_D) \qquad (2.5)$$

Thus $N(t)$ is the solution of a linear difference equation. Before proceeding further, let us consider a simple example.

**Example 3**

Let $D = 2$, $T_1 = 1$, and $T_2 = 2$. It can readily be verified that Figure 2.4 is the correct representation of $N(t)$ for the first few units of time. The difference equation $N(t) = N(t - 1) + N(t - 2)$ has continuous solutions of the form $\lambda^t$, where $\lambda$ is found by substitution in the equation:

$$\lambda^t = \lambda^{t-1} + \lambda^{t-2}$$

From the characteristic equation $\lambda^2 - \lambda - 1 = 0$, the values of $\lambda$ are found to be $(1 \pm \sqrt{5})/2$. The general solution is therefore given by

$$N(t) = A\left(\frac{1 + \sqrt{5}}{2}\right)^t + B\left(\frac{1 - \sqrt{5}}{2}\right)^t$$

The initial conditions $N(1) = 1$ and $N(2) = 2$ are satisfied with $A = (\sqrt{5} + 1)/2\sqrt{5}$ and $B = (\sqrt{5} - 1)/2\sqrt{5}$. Therefore,

$$N(t) = \frac{1}{\sqrt{5}}\left\{\left(\frac{\sqrt{5} + 1}{2}\right)^{t+1} + \left(\frac{\sqrt{5} - 1}{2}\right)^{t+1} e^{j\pi t}\right\}; \qquad (j = \sqrt{-1})$$

At noninteger values of $t$, the preceding function is quite different from the function represented in Figure 2.4. It assumes correct values, however, at integer times $t = n$. Since our main interest is in the integer values of $t$, we ignore these differences and take the preceding function to represent $N(t)$.

We can now write

$$N(t) = \frac{1}{\sqrt{5}}\left(\frac{\sqrt{5} + 1}{2}\right)^{t+1}\left\{1 + \left(\frac{\sqrt{5} - 1}{\sqrt{5} + 1}\right)^{t+1} e^{j\pi t}\right\}$$

which can equivalently be written as

$$\log N(t) = t \log\left(\frac{\sqrt{5} + 1}{2}\right) + \log\left(\frac{\sqrt{5} + 1}{2\sqrt{5}}\right) + \log\left\{1 + \left(\frac{\sqrt{5} - 1}{\sqrt{5} + 1}\right)^{t+1} e^{j\pi t}\right\}$$

For large $t$, the last term of this equation is very close to zero and may be ignored, yielding

$$\beta = \left(\frac{1}{t}\right)\log N(t) \cong \log\left[\frac{\sqrt{5} + 1}{2}\right] = 0.694 \text{ bits/unit time}$$

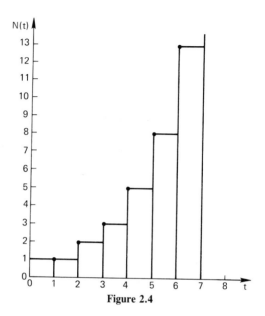

**Figure 2.4**

$\beta$ is sometimes referred to as the capacity of the encoder. If the entropy of the source is less than $\beta$, long blocks of data can be encoded with high accuracy. If the entropy is larger than $\beta$, however, the probability of error approaches 1 with increasing length of the sequences.

Returning now to Eq. (2.5), the general equation for $N(t)$, the characteristic equation can be written as

$$\lambda^{-T_1} + \lambda^{-T_2} + \cdots + \lambda^{-T_D} = 1 \tag{2.6}$$

This equation can have both real and complex solutions, but the solution with the largest absolute value, $\lambda_{max}$, is always real and positive (see Problem 2.8). Furthermore, $\lambda_{max}$ can be determined graphically, as shown in Figure 2.5.

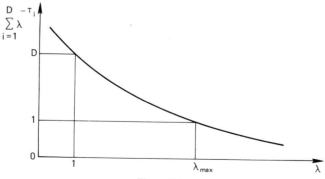

**Figure 2.5**

From Example 3 it must be clear that $\lambda_{max}$ determines the capacity of the encoder and that this capacity is given by $\beta = \log(\lambda_{max})$. To achieve reliable encoding, the entropy of the source must be less than the capacity of the encoder.

## PROBLEMS

**2.1.** Let $E = \{e_1, \ldots, e_N\}$ be a set of disjoint events, and let $p_1, \ldots, p_N$ and $q_1, \ldots, q_N$ be two different probability assignments on $E$, with $\Sigma p_n = \Sigma q_n = 1$. Prove that:

(a) $\displaystyle\sum_{n=1}^{N} p_n \log(p_n/q_n) \geq 0$

(b) $\displaystyle\sum_{n=1}^{N} (p_n)^2/q_n \geq 1$

**2.2.** A random variable $\mathbf{x}$ assumes nonnegative integer values $0, 1, 2, \ldots$. Find the probability assignment $p_n$ that maximizes $H(\mathbf{x})$ subject to the constraint that the mean value of $\mathbf{x}$ is a fixed value $A$; that is,

$$\sum_{n=0}^{\infty} np_n = A$$

Evaluate the resulting $H(\mathbf{x})$. (*Hint:* Use Lagrange multipliers. See, for example, F. B. Hildebrand, *Advanced Calculus for Applications*, 2nd ed., Prentice-Hall, Inc., Englewood Cliffs, N.J., 1976, Chap. 7.)

**2.3.** Prove that any transfer of probability from one member of a discrete sample space to another that makes their probabilities more nearly equal will increase the entropy.

**2.4.** Let $A = [a_{ij}]$ be an $N \times N$ doubly stochastic matrix; that is,

$$a_{ij} \geq 0 \quad \text{for all } i, j, \qquad \sum_{i=1}^{N} a_{ij} = 1 \quad \text{for all } j, \qquad \text{and} \qquad \sum_{j=1}^{N} a_{ij} = 1 \quad \text{for all } i.$$

Given a set of probabilities $p_1, \ldots, p_N$, we define a new set of probabilities $q_1, \ldots, q_N$ by

$$q_i = \sum_{j=1}^{N} a_{ij} p_j$$

Show that $H(q_1, \ldots, q_N) \geq H(p_1, \ldots, p_N)$ with equality iff $q_1, \ldots, q_N$ is a rearrangement of $p_1, \ldots, p_N$.

**2.5.** Let $x_1, \ldots, x_n$ be arbitrary positive numbers, and let $a_1, \ldots, a_n$ be positive numbers whose sum is unity. Prove that

$$x_1^{a_1} \cdots x_n^{a_n} \leq \sum_{i=1}^{n} a_i x_i$$

with equality if and only if all $x_i$ are equal. Note that the inequality still holds if some of the $a_i$ are allowed to be zero. However, the condition for equality becomes: All $x_i$ corresponding to positive $a_i$ are equal.

**2.6.** A source produces a sequence of statistically independent binary digits with the probabilities $P(1) = 0.005$ and $P(0) = 0.995$. These digits are taken 100 at a time and a binary code word is provided for every sequence of 100 digits containing three or fewer 1's.

   **(a)** If the code words are all of the same length, find the minimum length required to provide the specified set of code words.

   **(b)** Find the probability of getting a source sequence for which no code word has been provided.

   **(c)** Use the Chebyshev inequality to bound the probability of getting a sequence for which no code word has been provided and compare with part (b).

**2.7.** Let $\mathbf{x}$ be a discrete random variable with probabilities $p_1 \leq p_2 \leq \cdots \leq p_N$. Show that

   **(a)** $H(\mathbf{x}) \geq \displaystyle\sum_{n=1}^{N} p_n(1 - p_n) \geq 1 - p_N$    (in nats)

   **(b)** $H(\mathbf{x}) \geq H(p_N)$, where $H(p_N) = -p_N \log(p_N) - (1 - p_N) \log(1 - p_N)$

   **(c)** $H(\mathbf{x}) \geq -\log(p_N)$

   **(d)** $H(\mathbf{x}) \geq 2(1 - p_N)$    (in bits)

   **(e)** Compare the lower bounds obtained for $H(\mathbf{x})$ in terms of $p_N$ in parts (a) and (d). Which bound is stronger and why?

   *Hint:* Use part (b) when $p_N \geq 0.5$ and part (c) when $p_N \leq 0.5$ to prove part (d).

**2.8.** The construction of Figure 2.5 guarantees that a real, positive solution can always be found for Eq. (2.6). Denoting this solution by $\lambda_0$, show that if $\lambda$ is a complex solution of the equation its magnitude must be less than $\lambda_0$. (*Hint:* Represent complex numbers $\lambda^{-T_i}$ as vectors in the complex plane and use the fact that a straight line connecting two points in this plane is the shortest path between them.)

**2.9.** For the following binary code, let $N(k)$ be the number of messages that can be formed using exactly $k$ code characters. For example, $N(1) = 1$ (i.e., $x_1$), $N(2) = 3$ $(x_1x_1, x_2, x_3)$, and $N(3) = 5$ $(x_1x_1x_1, x_1x_2, x_1x_3, x_2x_1, x_3x_1)$. Find a general expression for $N(k)$ $(k = 1, 2, \ldots)$.

$$
\begin{array}{cc}
x_1 & 0 \\
x_2 & 10 \\
x_3 & 11
\end{array}
$$

**2.10.** **(a)** Show that the function $\log x$ in the region $0 < x < \infty$ is convex $\cap$.

   **(b)** Using Jensen's inequality, prove that

$$
H(\mathbf{x}) = -\sum_{n=1}^{N} p_n \log p_n \leq \log N
$$

**2.11.** Let $f(y)$ be an arbitrary function defined for $y \geq 1$. Let $\mathbf{x}$ be a discrete random variable with range $\{x_1, \ldots, x_N\}$ and probability distribution $\{p_1, \ldots, p_N\}$. Define the $f$-entropy of $\mathbf{x}$ by

$$
H_f(\mathbf{x}) = \sum_{n=1}^{N} p_n f\left(\frac{1}{p_n}\right)
$$

If $f(y)$ is convex $\cap$, show that the following inequality is always satisfied:

$$
H_f(\mathbf{x}) \leq f(N)
$$

**ALBRIGHT COLLEGE LIBRARY**    205351

**2.12.** Let

$$A = \sum_{n=2}^{\infty} \frac{1}{n \log^2 n}$$

and define the random variable **x** by

$$P\{\mathbf{x} = n\} = \frac{1}{An \log^2 n}, \qquad \text{for } n = 2, 3, \ldots, \infty$$

**(a)** Show that $A$ exists; that is, the sum defining $A$ converges.

**(b)** Find the entropy of the random variable **x**.

**2.13.** Let $P = (p_1, p_2, \ldots)$ be a countable probability distribution; that is, $p_n \geq 0$ for $n = 1, 2, \ldots$ and $\sum_{n=1}^{\infty} p_n = 1$.

**(a)** Show that if $\sum_{n=1}^{\infty} p_n \log n$ converges then $H(P)$ is finite.

**(b)** Assuming that $p_1 \geq p_2 \geq \cdots \geq p_n \geq \ldots$, show that the existence of $H(P)$ implies the existence of $\sum_{n=1}^{\infty} p_n \log n$.

# 3

# VARIABLE-LENGTH SOURCE CODING

**Introduction**   In Chapter 2 we studied the problem of source coding using fixed-length code words for fixed-length blocks of data. The likely (typical) sequences were encoded into equal-length code words and, as long as the encoder was capable of producing letters above a certain rate, the encoding process was apt to go smoothly. There are two problems with this scheme. First, the atypical or unlikely sequences cannot be reproduced from the code, and, second, the encoding/decoding procedures are not practical. The first problem is not a serious one because the probability of occurrence of an atypical sequence is extremely small and, in practice, small failure rates are almost always acceptable. The second problem arises from the fact that a code table must be stored in the memory of the encoder and decoder, relating each block of data to a corresponding code word. Moreover, this table must be searched for each block until a match is found. The required amount of memory and the search times thus grow exponentially with the block length and soon become impractically large.

Variable-length source coding, which is the subject of this chapter, is, in a sense, the answer to the preceding problems. Here again one chooses a fixed-length block of data but assigns a variable-length code to it. In practice, the length of the block of data is short, and more often than not this block is composed of only one or two letters from the source alphabet. The code-word lengths are related to the probability of their occurrence and, in general, shorter code words are assigned to more probable blocks of data. The average code-word length will be shown to be bounded from below by the source entropy. Moreover, we will show that this lower bound can be approached in the limit of long sequences.

In Section 3.1 we address the problem of unique decodability. Prefix-free codes will be defined in this section and their properties explored in Sections 3.2 and 3.3. The Shannon–Fano coding scheme is described in Section 3.4, and upper and lower bounds on the average code-word length are established in this section. Finally, in the remainder of the chapter, an optimum encoding scheme known as Huffman coding is described.

## 3.1 UNIQUE DECODABILITY AND PREFIX CONDITION

Consider an information source with alphabet $\{a_1, \ldots, a_K\}$. The source produces a sequence of independent, identically distributed letters with probability distribution $P(a_i) = p_i$ ($1 \leq i \leq K$). Next, consider an encoder with alphabet $\{x_1, \ldots, x_D\}$, where all $x_i$ have the same duration. Depending on the duration of source letters, there may be a waiting line at the input to the encoder. We assume that the system has infinite memory and thereby ignore the waiting line problem. The encoder encodes a sequence of source letters by assigning a predetermined sequence of $x_i$'s to each incoming letter. Suppose the code word assigned to $a_i$ is $x_{i1} \ldots x_{in_i}$, where $n_i$ is the length of the code word. The average length of this code $\bar{n}$ is given by

$$\bar{n} = \sum_{i=1}^{K} p_i n_i$$

From the law of large numbers, we know that for long source sequences the average code-word length will be close to $\bar{n}$ with high probability. Our goal in this chapter is to provide insight into methods of encoding that minimize $\bar{n}$.

Obviously, not all codes that can be imagined are useful. The most general requirement is that all finite sequences of code words must be uniquely decodable. In other words,

For each source sequence of finite length, the sequence of code letters corresponding to that source sequence must be different from the sequence of code letters corresponding to any other source sequence.[†]

---

[†]R. G. Gallagher, *Information Theory and Reliable Communications*. New York: John Wiley & Sons, 1968, p. 45. Copyright © 1968 by John Wiley & Sons. Reprinted with permission.

We restrict attention here to the class of all uniquely decodable codes. There is a subset of this class with which we will be mainly concerned. This is the class of prefix-free codes.

A prefix-free code is a code in which no code word is the prefix of any other code word.[†]

A string of code words from a prefix-free code is uniquely decoded by starting from the first letter and decoding one word at a time. Table 3.1 is a collection of several binary ($D = 2$) codes for a given source. Code I is not uniquely decodable because, among other things, the code words for $a_1$ and $a_2$ are the same. Code II is not uniquely decodable because $a_1a_1$ is not distinguishable from $a_3$. Code III is uniquely decodable because it is a prefix-free code. Code IV, although not prefix free, is uniquely decodable. In this code, 0 signals the beginning of a new word and the number of 1's that follow identifies the word uniquely.

## 3.2 KRAFT INEQUALITY

Let $n_1, \ldots, n_K$ represent the lengths of code words in a prefix-free code, and let $D$ be the size of the encoder's alphabet. Then

$$\sum_{i=1}^{K} D^{-n_i} \leq 1 \tag{3.1}$$

Conversely, if integers $n_1, \ldots, n_K$ satisfy Eq. (3.1), a prefix-free code can be found whose word lengths are given by $n_1, \ldots, n_K$.

For a proof of this theorem, consider the tree depicted in Figure 3.1. Starting at the root, the tree branches in $D$ directions to create $D$ nodes. Each

**TABLE 3.1**

| Source Letter | $P(a_i)$ | Code I | Code II | Code III | Code IV |
|---|---|---|---|---|---|
| $a_1$ | 0.5 | 0 | 0 | 0 | 0 |
| $a_2$ | 0.25 | 0 | 1 | 10 | 01 |
| $a_3$ | 0.125 | 1 | 00 | 110 | 011 |
| $a_4$ | 0.125 | 10 | 11 | 111 | 0111 |

*Source*: R. G. Gallagher, *Information Theory and Reliable Communications*. New York: John Wiley & Sons, 1968, p. 45. Copyright © 1968 by John Wiley & Sons. Reprinted with permission.

[†]R. G. Gallagher, *Information Theory and Reliable Communications*. New York: John Wiley & Sons, 1968, p. 45. Copyright © 1968 by John Wiley & Sons. Reprinted with permission.

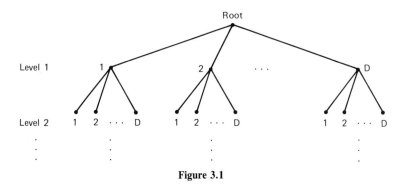

**Figure 3.1**

node, in turn, creates $D$ new branches and the process continues. The nodes at level $i$ can be associated with code words of length $i$. Assuming that the word lengths are arranged in increasing order (i.e., $n_1 \leq n_2 \cdots \leq n_K$), we assign a node at level $n_1$ to the first code word. The code being prefix free, no other code word should stem from the node associated with $n_1$. Therefore, the first word disables a fraction $D^{-n_1}$ of branches. When the second code word is assigned to a node at level $n_2$, the total fraction of disabled branches becomes $D^{-n_1} + D^{-n_2}$. This process can continue as long as a fraction of branches remains. It is therefore necessary that Eq. (3.1) be satisfied in order to have a node associated with each and every code word.

Conversely, if integers $n_1 \leq n_2 \leq \cdots \leq n_K$ satisfy the Kraft inequality, one can assign nodes to code words beginning with $n_1$. The Kraft inequality then assures that at each stage of assignment the necessary nodes are available.

## 3.3 SIGNIFICANCE OF THE PREFIX CONDITION

In Section 3.2 we proved that a prefix-free code satisfies the Kraft inequality. We now take this one step further and prove that any uniquely decodable code satisfies this inequality. This will help us establish the important result that for any uniquely decodable code there exists a prefix-free code with the same word lengths.

Let the word lengths of a uniquely decodable code be $n_1 \leq n_2 \leq \cdots \leq n_K$, and let the code have $D$ symbols in its alphabet. With $N$ an arbitrary integer, we can write

$$\left( \sum_{i=1}^{K} D^{-n_i} \right)^N = \sum_{i_1=1}^{K} \cdots \sum_{i_N=1}^{K} D^{-(n_{i_1} + \cdots + n_{i_N})}$$

Now, $n_{i_1} + \cdots + n_{i_N}$ is the length of a sequence of $N$ code words and can be anywhere between $Nn_1$ and $Nn_K$. Define $A_j$ as the number of sequences of $N$ code words with total length $j$. Then

$$\left(\sum_{i=1}^{K} D^{-n_i}\right)^N = \sum_{j=Nn_1}^{Nn_K} A_j D^{-j}$$

Since the code is uniquely decodable, sequences of $N$ code words and total length $j$ must be distinct. The maximum possible number of sequences of length $j$ is $D^j$; therefore, $A_j \leq D^j$ and

$$\left(\sum_{i=1}^{K} D^{-n_i}\right)^N \leq \sum_{j=Nn_1}^{Nn_K} D^j D^{-j} = N(n_K - n_1) + 1$$

If $\sum_{i=1}^{K} D^{-n_i}$ is greater than unity, the left side of the preceding inequality grows exponentially with $N$, whereas the right side grows linearly. Since $N$ can be arbitrarily large, this cannot happen, and therefore the Kraft inequality must be satisfied.

In conclusion, any uniquely decodable code with word lengths $n_1, \ldots, n_K$ satisfies the Kraft inequality. In Section 3.2 we learned that if integers $n_1, \ldots, n_K$ satisfied the Kraft inequality then a prefix-free code with those lengths could be constructed. Hence

> A uniquely decodable code can always be replaced with a prefix-free code with the same word lengths.

## 3.4 SHANNON–FANO CODING

In this section we establish a lower bound on the average code-word length in terms of the source entropy. We then show that this lower bound can be achieved arbitrarily closely by the Shannon–Fano coding technique.

**Theorem 1.**    Given a source with alphabet $\{a_1, \ldots, a_K\}$ and probabilities $p_1, \ldots, p_K$, the average length $\overline{n}$ of a uniquely decodable code with alphabet size $D$ satisfies the inequality

$$\overline{n} \geq \frac{H(\mathbf{x})}{\log D} \tag{3.2}$$

where $H(\mathbf{x})$ is the source entropy and the base of the logarithm is arbitrary.

*Proof*

$$H(\mathbf{x}) - \overline{n} \ln D = -\sum_{i=1}^{K} p_i \ln p_i - \sum_{i=1}^{K} p_i n_i \ln D = \sum_{i=1}^{K} p_i \ln \frac{D^{-n_i}}{p_i}$$

$$\leq \sum_{i=1}^{K} p_i \left(\frac{D^{-n_i}}{p_i} - 1\right) = \left(\sum_{i=1}^{K} D^{-n_i}\right) - 1$$

Since the code is uniquely decodable, the Kraft inequality must be satisfied. Therefore, $H(\mathbf{x}) - \overline{n} \ln D \leq 0$ and the proof is complete.

*Note:* The equality $\bar{n} = H(\mathbf{x})/\log D$ is achieved iff $p_i = D^{-n_i}$ for all $i$, that is, iff $\log_D^{p_i}$ is an integer for all $i$.

**Theorem 2.** Given a source with alphabet $\{a_1, \ldots, a_K\}$ and probabilities $p_1, \ldots, p_K$, it is possible to construct a prefix-free code from an alphabet of size $D$ such that

$$\bar{n} < \frac{H(\mathbf{x})}{\log D} + 1 \tag{3.3}$$

*Proof.* Choose the length $n_i$ of the code word for $a_i$ according to the rule $n_i = \lceil -\log_D^{p_i} \rceil$, where $\lceil \alpha \rceil$ is the smallest integer greater than or equal to $\alpha$. Now

$$n_i = \lceil -\log_D^{p_i} \rceil \Rightarrow n_i \geq -\log_D^{p_i} \Rightarrow D^{-n_i} \leq p_i \Rightarrow \sum_{i=1}^{K} D^{-n_i} \leq \sum_{i=1}^{K} p_i = 1$$

Since the Kraft inequality is satisfied, it is possible to find a prefix-free code with word lengths $n_1, \ldots, n_K$. Next observe that

$$n_i = \lceil -\log_D^{p_i} \rceil \Rightarrow n_i < -\log_D^{p_i} + 1$$

Therefore,

$$\sum_{i=1}^{K} p_i n_i < -\sum_{i=1}^{K} p_i \log_D^{p_i} + \sum_{i=1}^{K} p_i$$

The last inequality is the same as Eq. (3.3) and the proof is therefore complete.

It is possible to encode a source and to achieve the lower bound $H(\mathbf{x})/\log D$ on $\bar{n}$ as closely as desired. This is done by encoding sequences of $N$ source letters at a time according to the procedure described in Theorem 2. In other words, the source is assumed to have a new alphabet of size $K^N$, each member of which is a sequence of $N$ independently generated letters from $\{a_1, \ldots, a_K\}$. The entropy of the new source is $NH(\mathbf{x})$ (Problem 3.3), and its average code-word length is, by definition, $N$ times the average code-word length for the original source. Applying Theorems 1 and 2 to the new source then yields

$$\frac{NH(\mathbf{x})}{\log D} \leq N\bar{n} < \frac{NH(\mathbf{x})}{\log D} + 1$$

Or, equivalently,

$$\frac{H(\mathbf{x})}{\log D} \leq \bar{n} < \frac{H(\mathbf{x})}{\log D} + \frac{1}{N}$$

Since $N$ can be arbitrarily large, values of $\bar{n}$ that are arbitrarily close to $H(\mathbf{x})/\log D$ can be achieved.

Note that by encoding long sequences at a time one cannot improve the lower bound on $\bar{n}$. However, if, due to the particular distribution of probabilities, the lower bound is not automatically achievable, one may resort to the preceding technique to bring the average code-word length closer to its minimum.

## 3.5 OPTIMUM BINARY CODING: HUFFMAN'S TECHNIQUE

Consider a source $S$ with alphabet $\{a_1, \ldots, a_K\}$ and probability distribution $p_1, \ldots, p_K$. We wish to assign a binary sequence $X_i$ to each source letter $a_i$ to create a uniquely decodable binary code ($D = 2$) with minimum average length $\bar{n}$. Such a code exists since the choice can be confined to a finite number of possibilities. Consequently, a prefix-free code with minimum average length exists.

Let us assume that $p_1 \geq p_2 \cdots \geq p_K$. Let the word lengths of the optimum prefix-free code be $n_1, \ldots, n_K$. If $n_i > n_j$ for some $i < j$, exchange the corresponding code words. The resulting improvement in the average code-word length will be

$$\Delta\bar{n} = p_i n_j + p_j n_i - p_i n_i - p_j n_j = (p_j - p_i)(n_i - n_j)$$

which is less than or equal to zero. But the original code is optimum, which means that its average length cannot be improved by the exchange of two words; therefore, $\Delta\bar{n} = 0$. The new code obtained by the exchange is thus optimum, and it is readily observed that an optimum prefix-free code exists for which $n_1 \leq n_2 \cdots \leq n_K$. For this code we prove the following two theorems.

**Theorem 1.**    $n_K = n_{K-1}$ and the code words $X_K$ and $X_{K-1}$ corresponding to $a_K$ and $a_{K-1}$ differ in only the last digit.

*Proof.* If $n_{K-1} < n_K$, then the last digit of $X_K$ can be dropped without violating the prefix condition. This results in a new code with smaller $\bar{n}$, which is contrary to the assumption that the code under consideration is optimum. Therefore, $n_{K-1} = n_K$.

If $X_K$ and $X_{K-1}$ are identical except for the last digit, the theorem is proved. If not, there may be another code word with length $n_K$ (such as $X_{K-2}$, $X_{K-3}, \ldots$) that differs from $X_K$ in only the last digit. This code word can be exchanged with $X_{K-1}$ and the resulting code will satisfy the theorem. If such a code word does not exist, the last digit of $X_K$ can be dropped without violating the prefix condition. This, however, results in a smaller $\bar{n}$, which contradicts the assumption. Therefore, with proper rearrangement, $X_K$ and $X_{K-1}$ differ in only the last digit.

**Theorem 2.**    Consider a new source $S'$ with alphabet $\{a_1', \ldots, a_{K-1}'\}$ and probability distribution $p_1', \ldots, p_{K-1}'$, where $p_i' = p_i$ for $1 \leq i \leq K - 2$ and $p_{K-1}' = p_{K-1} + p_K$. If $\{X_1', \ldots, X_{K-1}'\}$ is an optimum prefix-free code for $S'$, then the code obtained according to the following rule is optimum for $S$.

$$X_i = X_i', \qquad 1 \le i \le K - 2$$
$$X_{K-1} = X_{K-1}'0$$
$$X_K = X_{K-1}'1$$

*Proof.* Since $n_K = n_{K-1} = 1 + n_{K-1}'$, we have

$$\bar{n} = p_1 n_1 + \cdots + p_K n_K = p_1 n_1' + \cdots + (p_{K-1} + p_K)(1 + n_{K-1}')$$
$$= \bar{n}' + (p_{K-1} + p_K)$$

That is, the difference between $\bar{n}$ and $\bar{n}'$ is a constant. If the optimum code for $S$ is better than the preceding code, the code derived from it for $S'$ must be better than optimum, which is impossible. Therefore, the code obtained for $S$ according to the preceding rule is optimum.

Theorems 1 and 2 reduce the problem of finding an optimum code for a source with $K$ letters to the problem of finding an optimum code for a new source with $K - 1$ letters. The procedure, however, can be repeated until the new source has only two letters, in which case the optimum code is trivial. The procedure of binary Huffman coding is summarized in the following steps.

1. Arrange the source letters in decreasing order of probabilities (i.e., $p_1 \ge p_2 \ge \cdots \ge p_K$).
2. Assign 0 to the last digit of $X_K$ and 1 to the last digit of $X_{K-1}$ (or vice versa).
3. Combine $p_K$ and $p_{K-1}$ to form a new set of probabilities, $p_1, \ldots, p_{K-2}$, $(p_{K-1} + p_K)$.
4. Repeat all the steps for this new set.

**Example 1**

The Huffman coding procedure for a source with a five-letter alphabet is shown in Table 3.2. The optimum code is shown in the rightmost column and its average length is given by

$$\bar{n} = \sum_{i=1}^{5} p_i n_i = 2.2 \text{ bits/source letter}$$

**TABLE 3.2**

| Source Letter | $P(a_i)$ | $P(a_i')$ | $P(a_i'')$ | $P(a_i''')$ | Code Word |
|---|---|---|---|---|---|
| $a_1$ | 0.3 | 0.3 | 0.45 | ①0.55 | 11 |
| $a_2$ | 0.25 | 0.25 | ①0.3 | ⓪0.45 | 10 |
| $a_3$ | 0.25 | ①0.25 | ⓪0.25 | | 01 |
| $a_4$ | ①0.1 | ⓪0.2 | | | 001 |
| $a_5$ | ⓪0.1 | | | | 000 |

Notice that $H(\mathbf{x}) = -\Sigma_{i=1}^{5} p_i \log p_i = 2.1855$ bits/symbol is less than $\bar{n}$; therefore, Eq. (3.2) is satisfied.

If we choose $n_i = \lceil -\log p_i \rceil$ according to the Shannon–Fano scheme, we will have $n_1 = n_2 = n_3 = 2$, $n_4 = n_5 = 4$, and $\bar{n} = 2.4$, which satisfies Eq. (3.3) but is larger than the average code-word length for the Huffman code.

## 3.6 GEOMETRICAL INTERPRETATION OF HUFFMAN'S TECHNIQUE

The concepts of Huffman coding can be easily understood by analyzing a code tree. Consider the tree in Figure 3.2 in which the nodes corresponding to a code word are identified with the probability $p_i$ associated with that word. Since prefix-free codes are being considered, none of the nodes that represent a code word should branch to higher levels. Let us explore the conditions under which the selected nodes would represent an optimum code for the probability distribution $p_1, \ldots, p_6$. To clarify the situation by way of examples, we ask the following questions.

1. Can $p_3$ be larger than $p_1$? The answer is no. If $p_3 > p_1$, then $\bar{n}$ can be reduced by exchanging the corresponding code words. Therefore, longer code words have a probability less than or equal to that of shorter words.

2. Can a free node exist in an intermediate level (levels 1, 2 and 3 in Figure 3.2)? The answer is no. The free node in level 3, for example, can be associated with $p_4$, $p_5$, or $p_6$, resulting in a smaller $\bar{n}$ without violating the prefix condition.

3. Can a free node exist in the final level (level 4 in Figure 3.2)? The answer is no. The branching in level 3 that creates the node associated with $p_6$ and the free node is unnecessary and in fact harmful. $p_6$ should have been assigned to its parent node in level 3 to give a smaller $\bar{n}$ without violating the prefix condition.

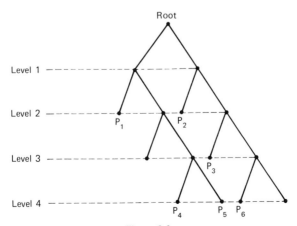

**Figure 3.2**

From the foregoing discussion we conclude that the final level contains the two least-probable code words. These code words have the same parent node and therefore differ in only the last digit. To complete our geometrical interpretation of Huffman coding, we need to know the effect of rearrangement of probabilities on $\bar{n}$. This is the subject of our final question.

4. Can nodes at a given level be exchanged? The answer is yes. The code words associated with the nodes at a given level have the same lengths and, as a result, can be exchanged without increasing $\bar{n}$ or violating the prefix condition. For instance, at level 3 in Figure 3.2 we can exchange the node associated with $p_3$ and the node that is parent to $p_4$ and $p_5$. This kind of rearrangement is essential to Huffman coding since at every stage of the coding process we must be able to shuffle the probabilities until the two smallest ones have the same parent node. Also notice that, once the two smallest probabilities are brought together under the same parent, any reshuffling at a lower level does not destroy this arrangement. For example, any rearrangement at level 1, 2, or 3 cannot assign $p_4$ and $p_5$ to different parents.

## 3.7 GENERALIZATION OF HUFFMAN'S TECHNIQUE

We are now in a position to generalize Huffman's technique to nonbinary situations where the encoder alphabet size $D$ is larger than 2. Visualizing an optimum code tree with $D$ branches stemming from each node, we ask the same four questions as in the previous section. The answers to questions 1, 2, and 4 remain the same. The answer to question 3, however, must be slightly modified since free nodes in the final level can now exist. As long as there is more than one final level code associated with a parent node, that parent node can have other offspring with no code words. The situation for $D = 3$, for example, is shown in Figure 3.3. The free node in the final level cannot be eliminated by assigning $p_5$ or $p_6$ to their parent node since the other probability then remains unassigned.

By exchanging nodes in the final level, all the free nodes should be brought together under the same parent. We then assign zero probabilities to the free nodes and proceed with the general Huffman coding procedure, that is,

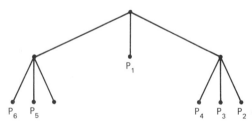

**Figure 3.3**

**TABLE 3.3**

| Source Letter | $P(a_i)$ | $P(a_i')$ | $P(a_i'')$ | Code Word |
|---|---|---|---|---|
| $a_1$ | 0.4 | 0.4 | ⓪0.4 | 0 |
| $a_2$ | 0.3 | 0.3 | ①0.3 | 1 |
| $a_3$ | 0.2 | ⓪0.2 ⎫ | ②0.3 | 20 |
| $a_4$ | 0.05 | ①0.05 ⎬ | | 21 |
| $a_5$ | ⓪0.03 ⎫ | ②0.05 ⎭ | | 220 |
| $a_6$ | ①0.02 ⎬ | | | 221 |
| | ②0 ⎭ | | | |

combining the $D$ smallest probabilities and continuing with a set that has $D - 1$ fewer elements.

With a complete tree, the set of probabilities is reduced by $D - 1$ elements at each stage until $D$ elements remain. Hence, the initial number of elements in the set must be $D + n(D - 1)$, where $n$ is an arbitrary integer. Zeros must therefore be added to the set to bring the total number of elements to $D + n(D - 1)$.

**Example 2**

If $D = 3$, then $D + n(D - 1) = 3 + 2n$, which can be any odd integer. A zero is therefore added to the set of probabilities if the number of elements is even. (If the number is already odd, nothing needs to be done.) The procedure of ternary Huffman coding for a set with six letters is shown in Table 3.3.

## PROBLEMS

**3.1.** A code is not uniquely decodable if there exists a finite sequence of code letters that can be resolved in two different ways into sequences of code words. That is, a situation such as

| $A_1$ | | $A_2$ | | $A_3 \cdots A_m$ | |
|---|---|---|---|---|---|
| $B_1$ | $B_2$ | $B_3$ | | $\cdots$ | $B_n$ |

must occur where each $A_i$ and each $B_j$ is a code word. Note that $B_1$ must be a prefix of $A_1$ with some resulting *dangling suffix*. Each dangling suffix in this sequence in turn must either be a prefix of a code word or have a code word as prefix, resulting in another dangling suffix. Finally, the last dangling suffix in the sequence must itself be a code word. Thus one can set up a test for unique decodability in the following way. Construct a set $S$ of all possible dangling suffixes. The code is uniquely decodable if and only if $S$ contains no code word.
   (a) State the precise rules for building the set $S$.
   (b) Suppose the code word lengths are $n_1, \ldots, n_K$. Find a good upper bound on the number of elements in the set $S$.

**(c)** Determine which of the following codes are uniquely decodable.

$$\{0, 10, 11\} \qquad \{00, 01, 10, 11\} \qquad \{0, 01, 11\} \qquad \{110, 11, 10\}$$

$$\{0, 01, 10\} \qquad \{110, 11, 100, 00, 10\} \qquad \{0, 01\}$$

**(d)** For each uniquely decodable code in part (c), construct, if possible, an infinitely long encoded sequence with known starting point such that it can be resolved into code words in two different ways. (Unique decodability does not always imply finite decodability.) Can this situation arise for a prefix-free code?

**3.2.** A DMS is encoded by a prefix-free ternary code and the average code-word length is found to be $\bar{n} = H_3(\mathbf{x})$ (the subscript 3 indicates the base of the logarithm). Can the source have an even number of letters in its alphabet?

**3.3.** Let a source $S_1$ have alphabet $\{a_1, \ldots, a_K\}$ and probability distribution $p_1, \ldots, p_K$. Construct a new source $S_N$ with alphabet size $K^N$ where each member of the new alphabet is a sequence of $N$ independent, identically distributed letters from $S_1$. Prove that the entropy of $S_N$ is $N$ times the entropy of $S_1$. [*Hint:* Use property (iv) of the function $H(\mathbf{x})$ in Section 2.2.]

**3.4.** Consider the following method of constructing a binary code for a source $S$ with alphabet $\{a_1, \ldots, a_K\}$ and probability distribution $p_1 \geq p_2 \geq \cdots \geq p_K$. Define

$$q_1 = 0, \qquad q_i = \sum_{j=1}^{i-1} p_j, \qquad \text{for } i > 1$$

The code word assigned to $a_i$ is formed by finding the binary expansion of $q_i$ (i.e., $\frac{1}{2} \to 100\ldots, \frac{1}{4} \to 0100\ldots, \frac{5}{8} \to 10100\ldots$) and then truncating this expansion to the first $n_i$ digits, where $n_i = \lceil -\log_2 p_i \rceil$

**(a)** Construct the binary code for an eight-letter source with the probabilities $\frac{1}{4}, \frac{1}{4}, \frac{1}{8}, \frac{1}{8}, \frac{1}{16}, \frac{1}{16}, \frac{1}{16}, \frac{1}{16}.$

**(b)** Prove that the method yields in all cases a prefix-free code whose average length $\bar{n}$ satisfies the inequality $H(\mathbf{x}) \leq \bar{n} < H(\mathbf{x}) + 1$.

**3.5.** Use the concept of code tree in solving this problem: There are $N$ coins of which $N - 1$ are identical and one may have the same weight as others, may be heavier, or may be lighter. A balance and a standard coin (same as the $N - 1$ identical coins) are also available. Each use of the balance can establish a relationship between two groups of coins as to whether one group is equal to, heavier than, or lighter than the other. The goal is to identify the odd coin, if any, and to determine its nature (heavy or light) after $n$ uses of the balance. What is the maximum value of $N$ for a given $n$? Could you solve the problem without the standard coin?

**3.6.** For each of the following discrete memoryless sources, construct a binary and a ternary Huffman code and find the corresponding $\bar{n}$ in each case.

**(a)** A source with a six-letter alphabet and probabilities $0.33, 0.23, 0.12, 0.12, 0.1, 0.1.$

**(b)** A source with a seven-letter alphabet and probabilities $0.35, 0.2, 0.15, 0.15, 0.1, 0.03, 0.02.$

**3.7.** For the source in Problem 3.6(b), construct two different binary Huffman codes with the same (minimum) average length but different variances. Which code is preferable in practice and why?

**3.8.** (a) Give an example in which a source with equiprobable letters is encoded into an optimum (Huffman) code with unequal code-word lengths.

(b) Give an example in which a source with unequiprobable letters is encoded into an optimum (Huffman) code with equal code-word lengths.

**3.9.** Consider a discrete memoryless source with an alphabet of seven letters. The probabilities are 0.3, 0.25, 0.15, 0.1, 0.1, 0.05, 0.05. Find a prefix-free code of minimum average length under the constraint that the first letter of each word must be 0 or 1 and each successive code letter can be 0, 1, or 2. Find a general rule for constructing prefix-free codes of minimum average length with this constraint and outline why it works.

**3.10.** A source with $K$ equiprobable letters is encoded into a binary Huffman code. Let $K = \alpha.2^J$, where $J$ is an integer and $1 \le \alpha < 2$.

(a) Are there any code words with length not equal to either $J$ or $J + 1$?

(b) In terms of $\alpha$ and $J$, how many code words have length $J$?

(c) What is the average code-word length?

**3.11.** (a) A source has five letters with the probabilities 0.3, 0.2, 0.2, 0.15, 0.15. These letters are to be coded into binary digits and transmitted over a channel. It takes 1 second to transmit a 0 and 3 seconds to transmit a 1. Using cut-and-try techniques, find a prefix-free code that minimizes the average transmission time and calculate this minimum average time.

(b) Any such code can be represented by a tree in which the length of a branch is proportional to the time required to transmit the associated digit. Show that, for a code to minimize the average transmission time, the probabilities associated with intermediate and terminal nodes must be nonincreasing with length.

**3.12. Run Length Coding.** A source produces a sequence of independent binary digits with the probabilities $P(0) = 0.9$, $P(1) = 0.1$. We shall encode this sequence in two stages, first counting the number of zeros between successive ones in the source output and then encoding their run lengths into binary code words. The first stage of encoding maps source sequences into intermediate digits by the following rule:

| Source Sequence | Intermediate Digits (no. of zeros) |
|:---:|:---:|
| 1 | 0 |
| 01 | 1 |
| 001 | 2 |
| 0001 | 3 |
| ⋮ | ⋮ |
| 00000001 | 7 |
| 00000000 | 8 |

Thus the following sequence is encoded as

$$1\ 0\ 0\ 1\ 0\ 0\ 0\ 0\ 0\ 0\ 0\ 0\ 0\ 0\ 0\ 1\ 1\ 0\ 0\ 0\ 0\ 1$$
$$0,\quad 2,\qquad\qquad\qquad 8,\quad 2, 0,\qquad\quad 4$$

The final stage of encoding assigns a code word of one binary digit to the intermediate integer 8 and code words of four binary digits to the other intermediate integers.

**(a)** Prove that the overall code is uniquely decodable.

**(b)** Find the average number $\bar{n}_1$ of source digits per intermediate digit.

**(c)** Find the average number $\bar{n}_2$ of encoded binary digits per intermediate digit.

**(d)** Show, by appeal to the law of large numbers, that for a very long sequence of source digits the ratio of the number of encoded binary digits to the number of source digits will, with high probability, be close to $\bar{n}_2/\bar{n}_1$. Compare this ratio to the average number of code letters per source letter for a Huffman code encoding four source digits at a time.

**3.13.** A discrete memoryless source has a six-letter alphabet with probabilities $\{0.3, 0.2, 0.15, 0.15, 0.15, 0.05\}$.

**(a)** Construct an optimum (Huffman) binary code for this source. What is the average code-word length $\bar{n}$?

**(b)** A code is said to satisfy the parity check condition if all its code words have an even (or odd) number of 1's. Does the code in part (a) satisfy the parity check condition? If not, can you construct another Huffman code that does so?

**3.14.** Consider a discrete memoryless source $S$ with alphabet $\{a_1, \ldots, a_K\}$ and probability distribution $\{p_1, \ldots, p_K\}$. A new source $S'$ is formed by adding a zero-probability letter to the alphabet of $S$, forming the alphabet $\{a_1, \ldots, a_{K+1}\}$ with probability distribution $\{p_1, \ldots, p_K, 0\}$. Each source is then encoded into binary digits ($D = 2$) using Huffman's technique. Is it true, in general, that the average code-word lengths of $S$ and $S'$ are the same? If not, which code is better and why?

**3.15.** A pair of independent, honest dice are rolled and the sum of the outcomes is denoted $\sigma$. Obviously, $\sigma$ is a member of the set $S = \{2, 3, 4, \ldots, 11, 12\}$. A student is asked to determine $\sigma$ after asking questions that can be answered Yes or No. If he asked, Is it 2?, Is it 3?, and so on, he would average a little under six questions. It is possible to do better, however.

**(a)** Using the concepts of code tree and Huffman coding, design an optimum strategy for asking questions.

**(b)** What is the minimum average number of questions?

**3.16.** **(a)** Consider a DMS, $S_1$, with probability distribution $\{p_1, \ldots, p_K\}$. Assuming that $p_1 \geq p_2 \geq \cdots \geq p_K$, we divide $p_K$ in two equal halves and form a new source $S_2$ with probability distribution $\{p_1, \ldots, p_{K-1}, 0.5p_K, 0.5p_K\}$. If $\bar{n}_{\text{opt}}$ represents the average code-word length for the binary Huffman code, prove that the redundancy $R = \bar{n}_{\text{opt}} - H(\mathbf{x})$ is the same for both sources $S_1$ and $S_2$.

**(b)** Show that for a source with the two-letter alphabet $\{a_1, a_2\}$ it is possible to find a probability distribution $\{p, 1 - p\}$ such that any amount of redundancy in the range $0 < R < 1$ is achieved.

**(c)** Combining the conclusions in parts (a) and (b), show that it is always possible to find a probability distribution $\{p_1, \ldots, p_K\}$ for a source with a $K$-letter alphabet such that any amount of redundancy in the range $0 < R < 1$ is achieved.

**3.17.** A discrete memoryless source $S_1$ has alphabet $A = \{a_1, a_2, a_3, a_4, a_5\}$ and a certain probability distribution. The following code $C_1$ is suggested for this source.

$$C_1 = \{1, 000, 001, 010, 011\}$$

A second source, $S_2$, has alphabet $B = \{b_1, b_2, b_3, b_4, b_5\}$ and a probability distribution different from that of $S_1$. Two alternative codes $C_2$ and $C_2'$ are suggested for $S_2$, as follows:

$$C_2 = \{1, 01, 001, 0001, 0000\}$$
$$C_2' = \{1, 10, 100, 1000, 0000\}$$

Notice that $C_2$ and $C_2'$ have identical code-word lengths.

**(a)** Prove that all three codes $C_1$, $C_2$, and $C_2'$ are uniquely decodable. Which ones are prefix free?

**(b)** The sources are multiplexed as follows:

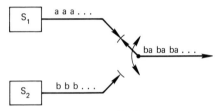

**Figure P3.17**

Here $b$ belongs to $B$ and $a$ belongs to $A$. The initial position of the switch is always fixed. (You can assume that the first letter of the multiplexed sequence is always $b$.) If the multiplexed sequence $bababa\ldots$ is encoded using $C_1$ for $a$ and $C_2$ for $b$, is the resulting code uniquely decodable? What if $C_2'$ is used for $b$?

# 4

# UNIVERSAL SOURCE CODING

**Introduction**  In this chapter we introduce the concept of universal coding. Unlike much of information theory, this is an area that was not pioneered by Shannon himself and represents a fundamentally different approach to source coding. The ideas presented here are due to B. M. Fitingof [9, 10].

Shannon's theory is based on the knowledge of probability distribution functions, without which optimum encoding is impossible. Universal coding, on the other hand, utilizes the structure of the sequences and arrives at the same optimum answer. In situations where the probability distribution functions are not available or the source statistics are time dependent, the universal coding techniques are clearly the right choice.

The material covered in this chapter should serve as an introductory exposition of the idea of universal coding. A growing number of papers are now published in this area each year, and universal coding constitutes an active field of research in information theory.

## 4.1 DISCRETE MEMORYLESS SOURCE WITH UNKNOWN STATISTICS

Consider a source with alphabet $\{a_1, \ldots, a_K\}$ and probability distribution $\{p_1, \ldots, p_K\}$, producing a sequence of independent, identically distributed letters. We assume that the probability distribution $\{p_1, \ldots, p_K\}$ is fixed but unknown to the encoder. All the techniques we have seen so far require the knowledge of the probability distribution in order to achieve optimum or near-optimum encoding. For example, in the block-encoding scheme of Chapter 2, the likely sequences are classified according to their probability of occurrence, and in the Shannon–Fano technique of Chapter 3, the code-word length $n_i$ associated with a given letter (or sequence of letters) is $\lceil \log p_i \rceil$, where $p_i$ is the probability of the letter (or sequence). In practice, however, it is often the case that the probability distribution is not known, or, at best, only an approximation to it is available. It may also happen that the source statistics vary slowly so that for a period of time that is long compared to the block length the statistics are fixed, but change from one period to another. In such situations, a probabilistic coding scheme that is efficient for some time frames will not be so for others.

To appreciate the effect of inexact knowledge of the source statistics on the coding efficiency, consider a binary DMS with probability distribution $P(0) = p$, $P(1) = 1 - p$. If the encoder's approximation to $p$ is denoted by $p_0$, then Shannon–Fano coding of long blocks effectively assigns a code word of length $-\log p_0$ to 0 and a code word of length $-\log(1 - p_0)$ to 1. The average code-word length will then be

$$\bar{n} = -p \log p_0 - (1 - p) \log(1 - p_0)$$

A plot of $\bar{n}$ versus $p$ for a fixed $p_0$ is shown in Figure 4.1. For comparison with the optimum $\bar{n}$ in the case where $p$ is known, a plot of $\bar{n}_{\text{opt}} = -p \log p - (1 - p) \log(1 - p)$ is also shown in the figure. Note that $\bar{n}$ is tangent to $\bar{n}_{\text{opt}}$ at $p = p_0$, but as $p$ deviates from $p_0$, the difference between the two curves increases rather sharply.

In this chapter we develop the basic ideas of universal coding, a scheme that relies not on the probability of the sequences but on their structure. We will show that for any positive number $\varepsilon$ it is possible to encode a source such that $\bar{n}$ is less than or equal to $H(\mathbf{x}) + \varepsilon$ for all possible source statistics $\{p_1, \ldots, p_K\}$. The counterpart of Figure 4.1 for the universal scheme is shown in Figure 4.2. The distance $\varepsilon$ between the upper bound to $\bar{n}$ and $\bar{n}_{\text{opt}}$ can be made as small as desired by choosing a large enough block length.

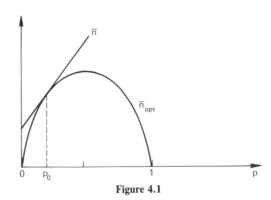

**Figure 4.1**

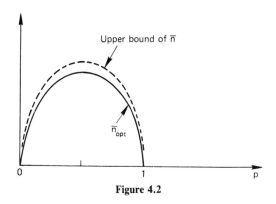

**Figure 4.2**

## 4.2 FREQUENCY VECTORS AND QUASI-ENTROPY

Consider a source sequence $S_i$ of length $N$. Since there are $K$ letters in the source alphabet and individual letters are generated independently, there are $K^N$ sequences of length $N$ and, therefore, the index $i$ of $S_i$ ranges from 1 to $K^N$. We denote the number of appearances of $a_k$ in the sequence $S_i$ by $N_{ki}$ and define the frequency of $a_k$ in $S_i$ by $q_{ki} = N_{ki}/N$. The vector $Q(S_i) = (q_{1i}, \ldots, q_{Ki})$ is the frequency vector associated with $S_i$. It is obvious that $q_{ki}$'s are nonnegative and their sum over $k$ is equal to 1.

**Lemma 1.**    The expected value of $\mathbf{q}_k$ is the probability $p_k$ of $a_k$.

$$E(\mathbf{q}_k) = \sum_{i=1}^{K^N} P(S_i)q_{ki} = p_k$$

*Proof.* Define the random variable $\mathbf{x}_k^{(n)}$ to be equal to $1/N$ if the source outputs the letter $a_k$ as the $n$th letter of the sequence, and equal to zero otherwise. Since the source is memoryless, the sequence $\mathbf{x}_k^{(1)}, \ldots, \mathbf{x}_k^{(N)}$ is independent and identically distributed. The expected value of $\mathbf{x}_k^{(n)}$ is $p_k/N$ for all $n$. Now $\mathbf{q}_k = \sum_{n=1}^{N} \mathbf{x}_k^{(n)}$; therefore

$$E(\mathbf{q}_k) = \sum_{n=1}^{N} E(\mathbf{x}_k^{(n)}) = p_k$$

and the proof is complete.

Each sequence $S_i$ is associated with a frequency vector $Q_i$, but the relationship is not one to one; in other words, a given vector $Q = (q_1, \ldots, q_K)$ may correspond to more than one sequence. Let $\omega(Q)$ denote the number of sequences that have the same frequency vector $Q$ (i.e., sequences in which the number of occurrences of $a_k$ is fixed at $N_k = Nq_k$ for $k = 1, \ldots, K$). It is not difficult to show that

$$\omega(Q) = \frac{N!}{\prod_{k=1}^{K} N_k!}$$

Next we inquire about the total number of different frequency vectors that represent source sequences of length $N$. The number of such vectors is a function of $K$ and $N$ and will be denoted by $\phi(K,N)$. Lemma 2 gives an explicit formula for this function.

**Lemma 2.**    $\phi(K,N) = \binom{N+K-1}{N}$

*Proof.* Consider a row of $N + K - 1$ empty slots. If $N$ identical objects are used to fill $N$ of these slots, $K - 1$ of them remain empty. The empty slots thus divide the $N$ objects into $K$ groups. If the $k$th group contains $N_k$ objects, we identify it by $q_k = N_k/N$. A given distribution of objects therefore corresponds to a vector $Q = (q_1, \ldots, q_K)$. There is a one-to-one correspondence between the set of possible distributions of the objects and the set of possible vectors $Q$, and, since the objects can be distributed in $\binom{N+K-1}{N}$ different ways, the lemma is proved.

The frequency vector $Q(S_i) = (q_{1i}, \ldots, q_{Ki})$ is now used to define the quasi-entropy $\Psi$ of the sequence $S_i$. By definition

$$\Psi(S_i) = -\sum_{k=1}^{K} q_{ki} \log q_{ki}$$

Realizing that $Q_i = (q_{1i}, \ldots, q_{Ki})$ can in fact be a probability vector, one can say that the quasi-entropy $\Psi(Q_i)^{\dagger}$ has all the properties of the entropy function $H(Q_i)$ that depend solely on $Q_i$. For example, $0 \leq \Psi(Q_i) \leq \log K$. Notice, however, that the entropy is a quantity defined for the source and depends on the probability distribution of letters, whereas the quasi-entropy is defined for each source sequence separately and for a given sequence is independent of the probability distribution. The following theorem establishes the connection between the quasi-entropy $\Psi(\mathbf{q}_1, \ldots, \mathbf{q}_K)$ and the source entropy $H(p_1, \ldots, p_K)$.

**Theorem.**    $E(\Psi(\mathbf{Q})) \leq H(p_1, \ldots, p_K)$.

*Proof.*

$$E(\Psi(\mathbf{Q})) = E\left( -\sum_{k=1}^{K} \mathbf{q}_k \log \mathbf{q}_k \right) = \sum_{k=1}^{K} E(-\mathbf{q}_k \log \mathbf{q}_k)$$

The function $-x \log x$ is convex $\cap$ and therefore Jensen's inequality applies. That is,

$$E(-\mathbf{q}_k \log \mathbf{q}_k) \leq -E(\mathbf{q}_k) \log E(\mathbf{q}_k)$$

---

$\dagger$Since $\Psi(S_i)$ is only a function of $Q(S_i)$ or $Q_i$, we use the notations $\Psi(S_i)$ and $\Psi(Q_i)$ interchangeably.

From Lemma 1, we have $E(\mathbf{q}_k) = p_k$. Therefore,

$$E(\Psi(\mathbf{Q})) \le \sum_{k=1}^{K} -p_k \log p_k$$

and the proof is complete.

The concepts developed here will now be used to describe a universal coding scheme and prove its optimality.

## 4.3 A UNIVERSAL ENCODING SCHEME FOR THE DMS

We are now in a position to outline an optimal encoding scheme for the source sequences based on their structure without requiring an a priori knowledge of the probabilities involved. The code for a given sequence $S_i$ is composed of two parts. The first part identifies the frequency vector $Q_i$ associated with $S_i$. The second part identifies $S_i$ among all the sequences that have the same $Q$. Since the total number of different frequency vectors is $\phi(K,N)$, the number of bits required for the first part is $\lceil \log \phi(K,N) \rceil$. Similarly, the number of bits required for the second part is $\lceil \log \omega(Q_i) \rceil$. The base of the logarithm is 2 for a binary encoder and $D$ for an encoder with alphabet size $D$. To prove the optimality of the coding scheme, we need the following lemma.

**Lemma 3**

$$\frac{n!}{\prod_{j=1}^{J} n_j!} \le \frac{n^n}{\prod_{j=1}^{J} n_j^{n_j}}, \qquad \text{where } n_j \ge 0 \quad \text{and} \quad \sum_{j=1}^{J} n_j = n$$

*Proof.* For $J = 1$, the inequality is easily verified. For $J \ge 2$, we use Stirling's formula to obtain

$$\frac{n!}{\prod_{j=1}^{J} n_j!} \le \left[ e^{1-(7J/8)} \left( \frac{n}{\prod_{j=1}^{J} n_j} \right)^{1/2} \right] \cdot \frac{n^n}{\prod_{j=1}^{J} n_j^{n_j}}$$

The proof is complete if it can be shown that the bracketed term is less than or equal to 1. Since $\sum_{j=1}^{J} n_j = n$, at least one of the $n_j$'s is greater than or equal to $n/J$. Consequently, $\prod_{j=1}^{J} n_j \ge n/J$ and

$$e^{1-(7J/8)} \left( \frac{n}{\prod_{j=1}^{J} n_j} \right)^{1/2} \le \sqrt{J} \, e^{1-(7J/8)}$$

It is a trivial matter to prove that the right side of the preceding inequality is less than 1 for $J \ge 2$, and the proof of the lemma is thus complete.

Now let $L(S_i)$ represent the length of the code word assigned to $S_i$. From the previous discussion we have

$$L(S_i) < \log \phi(K,N) + \log \omega(Q_i) + 2$$

But

$$\log \phi(K,N) = \log \frac{(N + K - 1)!}{N!\,(K - 1)!}$$

$$\le \log \frac{(N + K - 1)^{N+K-1}}{N^N \cdot (K - 1)^{K-1}}$$

$$= N \log\left(1 + \frac{K - 1}{N}\right) + (K - 1) \log\left(1 + \frac{N}{K - 1}\right)$$

Similarly,

$$\log \omega(Q_i) = \log \frac{N!}{\prod_{k=1}^{K} N_{ki}!} \le \log \frac{N^N}{\prod_{k=1}^{K} N_{ki}^{N_{ki}}}$$

$$= -N \sum_{k=1}^{K} \frac{N_{ki}}{N} \log \frac{N_{ki}}{N} = N\Psi(S_i)$$

As a result,

$$L(S_i) < N\Psi(S_i) + (K - 1) \log\left(1 + \frac{N}{K - 1}\right) + N \log\left(1 + \frac{K - 1}{N}\right) + 2$$

The expected value of $L(S_i)$ now satisfies

$$E(L(S_i)) < NH(p_1, \ldots, p_K) + (K - 1) \log\left(1 + \frac{N}{K - 1}\right)$$

$$+ N \log\left(1 + \frac{K - 1}{N}\right) + 2$$

The average code-word length per source letter is, by definition, $\bar{n} = E(L(S_i))/N$. Therefore,

$$\bar{n} < H(p_1, \ldots, p_K) + \left[\frac{K - 1}{N} \log\left(1 + \frac{N}{K - 1}\right)\right.$$

$$\left. + \log\left(1 + \frac{K - 1}{N}\right) + \frac{2}{N}\right]$$

The bracketed term in this inequality approaches zero as $N \to \infty$. Thus, for a given $\varepsilon$, it is possible to find $N_0$ such that, for $N > N_0$,

$$\bar{n} < H(p_1, \ldots, p_K) + \varepsilon$$

This completes the proof of universality of the encoding algorithm. Notice that $\varepsilon$ approaches zero as $\log N/N$. This is slow compared to the probabilistic encoding schemes where $\varepsilon$ approaches zero as $1/N$. This is the price one generally has to pay for a universal scheme.

Table 4.1 describes the universal encoding of a binary source in blocks of length 7. There are $\phi(2, 7) = 8$ frequency classes and thus 3 bits are used to

## TABLE 4.1

| $Q_i$ | $\omega(Q_i)$ | $S_i$ | $\Psi(S_i)$ in bits | Code Word |
|---|---|---|---|---|
| $(0, \frac{7}{7})$ | 1 | 1 1 1 1 1 1 1 | 0 | 000 |
| $(\frac{1}{7}, \frac{6}{7})$ | 7 | 1 1 1 1 1 1 0 | 0.592 | 001 000 |
| | | 1 1 1 1 1 0 1 | | 001 001 |
| | | $\vdots$ | | $\vdots$ |
| | | 0 1 1 1 1 1 1 | | 001 110 |
| $(\frac{2}{7}, \frac{5}{7})$ | 21 | 1 1 1 1 1 0 0 | 0.863 | 010 00000 |
| | | 1 1 1 1 0 1 0 | | 010 00001 |
| | | $\vdots$ | | $\vdots$ |
| | | 0 0 1 1 1 1 1 | | 010 10100 |
| $(\frac{3}{7}, \frac{4}{7})$ | 35 | 1 1 1 1 0 0 0 | 0.985 | 011 000000 |
| | | 1 1 1 0 1 0 0 | | 011 000001 |
| | | $\vdots$ | | $\vdots$ |
| | | 0 0 0 1 1 1 1 | | 011 100010 |
| $(\frac{4}{7}, \frac{3}{7})$ | 35 | 1 1 1 0 0 0 0 | 0.985 | 100 000000 |
| | | 1 1 0 1 0 0 0 | | 100 000001 |
| | | $\vdots$ | | $\vdots$ |
| | | 0 0 0 0 1 1 1 | | 100 100010 |
| $(\frac{5}{7}, \frac{2}{7})$ | 21 | 1 1 0 0 0 0 0 | 0.863 | 101 00000 |
| | | 1 0 1 0 0 0 0 | | 101 00001 |
| | | $\vdots$ | | $\vdots$ |
| | | 0 0 0 0 0 1 1 | | 101 10100 |
| $(\frac{6}{7}, \frac{1}{7})$ | 7 | 1 0 0 0 0 0 0 | 0.592 | 110 000 |
| | | 0 1 0 0 0 0 0 | | 110 001 |
| | | $\vdots$ | | $\vdots$ |
| | | 0 0 0 0 0 0 1 | | 110 110 |
| $(\frac{7}{7}, 0)$ | 1 | 0 0 0 0 0 0 0 | 0 | 111 |

encode the frequency vector; these are the first 3 bits in every code word. The remaining bits identify each sequence in a given class.

## PROBLEMS

**4.1.** Consider a binary memoryless source with $P(0) = p_0$ and assume that sequences of length $N$ are encoded according to the Shannon–Fano algorithm. If the source statistics now change so that $P(0) = p$, what can be said about the new average code-word length per source letter?

**4.2.** The vector $n = (n_1, \ldots, n_K)$ consists of integers satisfying $n_k \geq 1$ for $k = 1, \ldots, K$ and $\sum_{k=1}^{K} n_k = N$.
  (a) Show that, for fixed $N$ and $K$, there exist $\binom{N-1}{K-1}$ different vectors $n$.

**(b)** If $n_k$'s are allowed to be zero as well, show that the total number of vectors becomes

$$\sum_{j=1}^{K} \binom{K}{j} \binom{N-1}{j-1}$$

Notice that this must be the same as $\phi(K,N)$ in Lemma 2.

**4.3. (a)** Show that the quasi-entropy $\Psi(Q)$ is a convex $\cap$ function of the frequency vector $Q = (q_1, \ldots, q_K)$.

**(b)** Consider the sequence $S$ of length $N$ composed of letters from an alphabet of size $K$. This sequence is broken into subsequences $s_1, \ldots, s_M$ of lengths $n_1, \ldots, n_M$, where $\sum_{m=1}^{M} n_m = N$. Prove that

$$\sum_{m=1}^{M} \frac{n_m}{N} \Psi(s_m) \leq \Psi(S)$$

**4.4.** In a modified version of the universal encoding algorithm, all frequency classes that correspond to different permutations of the same frequency vector are combined. For example, if $Q(S_i) = (q_1, q_2, q_3)$ and $Q(S_j) = (q_2, q_3, q_1)$, then $S_i$ and $S_j$ belong to the same frequency class.

**(a)** Encode binary sequences of length 7 according to the modified algorithm.

**(b)** Prove that the modified algorithm is universal; that is, for any $\varepsilon > 0$ there exists $N_0$ such that for $N > N_0$ the average code-word length per source letter $\bar{n}$ satisfies the relationship $\bar{n} < H(p_1, \ldots, p_K) + \varepsilon$.

**4.5.** Consider a DMS with alphabet $\{a_1, \ldots, a_K\}$ and unidentified probability distribution $P = \{p_1, \ldots, p_K\}$. $P$ is known, however, to be one of the $M$ distributions $P^{(1)}, \ldots, P^{(M)}$. The $K^N$ sequences $S_i$ of length $N$ are encoded according to the following scheme:

  (i)   Construct $M$ prefix-free codes $C_1, \ldots, C_M$, one code for each distribution $P^{(1)}, \ldots, P^{(M)}$. The length of the code word assigned to $S_i$ in $C_m$ is $\lceil -\log P(S_i|m) \rceil$, where $P(S_i|m)$ is the probability of $S_i$ assuming $P = P^{(m)}$.

  (ii)  Upon observing $S_i$, compare the $M$ codes and choose the one that contains the shortest code word for $S_i$.

  (iii) Identify $S_i$ by an identifier for the chosen code, followed by the code word corresponding to $S_i$ in that code.

Prove that in the limit when $N \to \infty$ this scheme becomes optimum for each of the $M$ possible distributions.

# 5

# MUTUAL INFORMATION, DISCRETE MEMORYLESS CHANNEL, AND CHANNEL CAPACITY

**Introduction**  In this chapter we extend the concept of entropy and introduce an important information theoretic function known as the average mutual information. The immediate application of these new concepts is in the area of communication over noisy channels to which the present chapter and the following chapter are devoted. The ideas, however, are quite general and find application in other areas of information theory.

The simplest class of noisy channels is the class of discrete memoryless channels (DMC) described in Section 5.2. Discrete memoryless channels provide reasonably good models for many practical communication situations; moreover, extensions of the theory to more complicated systems are possible only when this simplest class is well understood. It is for this class that the theory of reliable communication will be developed in this book.

In the remaining part of the chapter, we invoke the concept of equivocation to justify the definition for channel capacity given in Section 5.5. The capacity can be analytically determined only in special cases and, in general, numerical methods must be employed for the calculation of capacity. One such method is described in Chapter 9. The significance of capacity and its role in the theory of reliable communication over noisy channels are the subjects of the next chapter.

## 5.1 CONDITIONAL ENTROPY AND MUTUAL INFORMATION

Consider the random variables $\mathbf{x}$ and $\mathbf{y}$ with joint probability distribution $p(x_i, y_j)$, $1 \le i \le N$, $1 \le j \le M$. The conditional entropy of $\mathbf{x}$ given $\mathbf{y}$ is defined as

$$H(\mathbf{x}|\mathbf{y}) = -\sum_{i=1}^{N} \sum_{j=1}^{M} p(x_i, y_j) \log p(x_i|y_j)$$

$H(\mathbf{x}|\mathbf{y})$ can be interpreted as the average amount of uncertainty about $\mathbf{x}$ after $\mathbf{y}$ has been revealed. In this context, the following version of the same definition is perhaps more informative.

$$H(\mathbf{x}|\mathbf{y}) = \sum_{j=1}^{M} p(y_j) \left[ -\sum_{i=1}^{N} p(x_i|y_j) \log p(x_i|y_j) \right]$$

The inner summation is now a measure of the uncertainty about $\mathbf{x}$ when the outcome of $\mathbf{y}$ is known to be $y_j$. The outer summation is the average of this uncertainty over $\mathbf{y}$. In the following, we derive some important properties of the conditional entropy.

**Theorem 1.**   $H(\mathbf{x}|\mathbf{y}) \le H(\mathbf{x})$ with equality iff $\mathbf{x}$ and $\mathbf{y}$ are independent.

*Proof*

$$H(\mathbf{x}|\mathbf{y}) - H(\mathbf{x}) = -\sum_{i} \sum_{j} p(x_i, y_j) \ln p(x_i|y_j) + \sum_{i} p(x_i) \ln p(x_i)$$

$$= \sum_{i} \sum_{j} p(x_i, y_j) \ln \frac{p(x_i)}{p(x_i|y_j)}$$

The summation is over all pairs $(i, j)$ for which $p(x_i, y_j) \neq 0$. Thus

$$H(\mathbf{x}|\mathbf{y}) - H(\mathbf{x}) \le \sum_{i} \sum_{j} p(x_i, y_j) \left[ \frac{p(x_i)}{p(x_i|y_j)} - 1 \right]$$

$$= \sum_{i} \sum_{j} \left[ p(x_i)p(y_j) - p(x_i, y_j) \right]$$

$$= \sum_{i} \sum_{j} \left[ p(x_i)p(y_j) \right] - 1 \le 0$$

The inequality is therefore proved. Equality holds if two conditions are satisfied. First, $p(x_i) = p(x_i|y_j)$ for all pairs $(i, j)$ such that $p(x_i, y_j) \neq 0$ and, second, the sum of $p(x_i)p(y_j)$ over all such pairs is equal to 1. The second condition will be valid iff $p(x_i)p(y_j) = 0$ whenever $p(x_i, y_j) = 0$. The conclusion is that $H(\mathbf{x}|\mathbf{y}) = H(\mathbf{x})$ iff $\mathbf{x}$ and $\mathbf{y}$ are independent.

**Theorem 2.**   $H(\mathbf{x}, \mathbf{y}) = H(\mathbf{y}) + H(\mathbf{x}|\mathbf{y}) = H(\mathbf{x}) + H(\mathbf{y}|\mathbf{x})$.

*Proof*

$$H(\mathbf{x}, \mathbf{y}) = -\sum_i \sum_j p(x_i, y_j) \log p(x_i, y_j)$$

$$= -\sum_i \sum_j p(x_i, y_j) [\log p(y_j) + \log p(x_i | y_j)]$$

$$= -\sum_j p(y_j) \log p(y_j) - \sum_i \sum_j p(x_i, y_j) \log p(x_i | y_j)$$

$$= H(\mathbf{y}) + H(\mathbf{x} | \mathbf{y})$$

The second part follows from symmetry, completing the proof.

It follows from Theorems 1 and 2 that $H(\mathbf{x}, \mathbf{y}) \le H(\mathbf{x}) + H(\mathbf{y})$ with equality iff $\mathbf{x}$ and $\mathbf{y}$ are independent.

The average amount of information about $\mathbf{x}$ contained in $\mathbf{y}$ can now be defined in terms of the reduction in the uncertainty of $\mathbf{x}$ upon disclosure of $\mathbf{y}$. Denoting this information by $I(\mathbf{x}, \mathbf{y})$, we define

$$I(\mathbf{x}, \mathbf{y}) = H(\mathbf{x}) - H(\mathbf{x} | \mathbf{y})$$

With the aid of Theorem 2, it is easy to show that

$$I(\mathbf{y}, \mathbf{x}) = H(\mathbf{y}) - H(\mathbf{y} | \mathbf{x}) = I(\mathbf{x}, \mathbf{y})$$

That is, the information about $\mathbf{x}$ contained in $\mathbf{y}$ is equal to the information about $\mathbf{y}$ contained in $\mathbf{x}$. For this reason, $I(\mathbf{x}, \mathbf{y})$ is called the average mutual information between $\mathbf{x}$ and $\mathbf{y}$.

From Theorem 1 we observe that $I(\mathbf{x}, \mathbf{y}) \ge 0$ with equality iff $\mathbf{x}$ and $\mathbf{y}$ are independent.

In Problem 5.3 the reader is asked to show that the following relationship is a direct consequence of the definition of $I(\mathbf{x}, \mathbf{y})$:

$$I(\mathbf{x}, \mathbf{y}) = \sum_{i=1}^{N} \sum_{j=1}^{M} p(x_i, y_j) \log \frac{p(x_i, y_j)}{p(x_i) p(y_j)}$$

One can thus interpret the function $\log\{p(x_i, y_j)/[p(x_i)p(y_j)]\}$ as the mutual information between $x_i$ and $y_j$. This function, however, can be positive, zero, or negative, whereas its average, $I(\mathbf{x}, \mathbf{y})$, is always greater than or equal to zero.

## 5.2 DISCRETE MEMORYLESS CHANNEL AND THE CHANNEL MATRIX

A discrete memoryless channel (DMC) is identified by a finite input alphabet $X = \{x_1, \ldots, x_K\}$, a finite output alphabet $Y = \{y_1, \ldots, y_J\}$, and a conditional probability distribution $p(y_j | x_k)$, where $1 \le k \le K$, $1 \le j \le J$. The word memoryless implies that the probability of any sequence of output letters given a sequence of input letters is equal to the product of the conditional probabilities of the individual output letters given the corresponding input letter. In other words,

$$p\{y_{j1}\ldots y_{jN}|x_{k1}\ldots x_{kN}\} = \prod_{n=1}^{N} p(y_{jn}|x_{kn})$$

for any integer $N$. A DMC is therefore completely identified by its channel matrix $[p(y_j|x_k)]$, which is a $K \times J$ matrix. If a probability distribution on $X$ is given, the distribution of $Y$ can be obtained as follows:

$$p(y_j) = \sum_{k=1}^{K} p(x_k)p(y_j|x_k)$$

In the following section we introduce and discuss some special classes of DMC. We then define the rate of transfer of information over a channel, which leads in a natural way to the concept of capacity. Determination of capacity for different channels is then covered in the remainder of the chapter.

## 5.3 SYMMETRIC, LOSSLESS, DETERMINISTIC, AND USELESS CHANNELS

### Symmetric Channel

By definition, a DMC is symmetric if every row of the channel matrix contains the same set of numbers $p'_1,\ldots,p'_J$ and every column contains the same set of numbers $q'_1,\ldots,q'_K$. The following matrices represent symmetric channels.

$$[p(y_j|x_k)] = \begin{pmatrix} 0.2 & 0.2 & 0.3 & 0.3 \\ 0.3 & 0.3 & 0.2 & 0.2 \end{pmatrix}, \quad \begin{matrix} k = 1 \\ k = 2 \end{matrix}$$

with $j = 1 \quad 2 \quad 3 \quad 4$

$$[p(y_j|x_k)] = \begin{pmatrix} 0.2 & 0.3 & 0.5 \\ 0.3 & 0.5 & 0.2 \\ 0.5 & 0.2 & 0.3 \end{pmatrix}$$

$$[p(y_j|x_k)] = \begin{pmatrix} 1-\varepsilon & \varepsilon \\ \varepsilon & 1-\varepsilon \end{pmatrix}, \quad 0 \le \varepsilon \le 1$$

The last example is the binary symmetric channel (BSC), which represents an important practical situation and has been studied extensively. In this channel, either 0 or 1 is transmitted and either 0 or 1 is received. The probability of error is $\varepsilon$ and is the same for both transmitted letters.

An important property of a symmetric channel is that its $H(\mathbf{y}|\mathbf{x})$ is independent of the input distribution and is solely determined by the channel matrix. This can be proved as follows:

$$H(\mathbf{y}\,|\,\mathbf{x}) = -\sum_i \sum_j p(x_i, y_j) \log p(y_j\,|\,x_i)$$

$$= -\sum_i p(x_i) \sum_j p(y_j\,|\,x_i) \log p(y_j\,|\,x_i)$$

$$= -\sum_i p(x_i) \sum_j p_j' \log p_j'$$

Therefore, $H(\mathbf{y}\,|\,\mathbf{x}) = -\sum_{j=1}^{J} p_j' \log p_j'$, independent of input distribution.

### Lossless Channel

Figure 5.1 is a graphical representation of the lossless channel. A connection between $x_k$ and $y_j$ means that $p(y_j\,|\,x_k)$ is nonzero. In a lossless channel the output uniquely specifies the input; therefore, $H(\mathbf{x}\,|\,\mathbf{y}) = 0$.

### Deterministic Channel

In this channel the input uniquely specifies the output (see Figure 5.2); therefore, $H(\mathbf{y}\,|\,\mathbf{x}) = 0$.

### Useless Channel

A channel is useless iff $\mathbf{x}$ and $\mathbf{y}$ are independent for *all* input distributions. For a useless channel, $H(\mathbf{x}\,|\,\mathbf{y}) = H(\mathbf{x})$; that is, knowledge of the output does not reduce the uncertainty about the input. Thus, for the purpose of determining the input, we may ignore the output altogether. In the following we prove that a DMC is useless iff its matrix has identical rows.

   (i) *Proof of sufficiency:*   Assume the matrix has identical rows $p_1', \ldots, p_J'$. Then, for every output $y_j$,

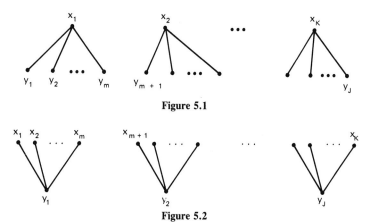

**Figure 5.1**

**Figure 5.2**

$$p(y_j) = \sum_{k=1}^{K} p(x_k, y_j) = \sum_{k=1}^{K} p(x_k)p(y_j \mid x_k) = p_j' \sum_{k=1}^{K} p(x_k) = p_j'$$

For every input–output pair $(x_k, y_j)$,

$$p(x_k, y_j) = p(x_k)p(y_j \mid x_k) = p(x_k)p_j' = p(x_k)p(y_j)$$

Therefore, the input and output are independent, irrespective of the input distribution.

(ii) *Proof of necessity:*   Assume the rows of the matrix are not identical. As a result, there exists a column, say $j_0$, whose elements are not identical. Assume $p(y_{j0} \mid x_{k0})$ is the largest element in this column. Then, for a uniform input distribution,

$$p(y_{j0}) = \sum_{k=1}^{K} p(x_k)p(y_{j0} \mid x_k)$$

$$= \frac{1}{K} \sum_{k=1}^{K} p(y_{j0} \mid x_k) < p(y_{j0} \mid x_{k0})$$

That is, $p(y_{j0}) \neq p(y_{j0} \mid x_{k0})$. Therefore,

$$p(x_{k0}, y_{j0}) = p(x_{k0})p(y_{j0} \mid x_{k0}) \neq p(x_{k0})p(y_{j0})$$

That is, **x** and **y**, at least for the uniform distribution of **x**, are not independent or, what is the same, the channel is not useless.


## 5.4 EQUIVOCATION AND THE RATE OF TRANSFER OF INFORMATION

Consider a binary symmetric channel with crossover probability $\varepsilon$. Assuming that at the input $P(0) = P(1) = \frac{1}{2}$, the rate of generation of input information is equal to $H(\mathbf{x}) = 1$ bit/symbol. A device, called the observer, receives every pair of input/output letters $(x, y)$ and produces an output $z$ that is either 0 (if $x = y$) or 1 (if $x \neq y$), as shown in Figure 5.3. The distribution of **z** is found as follows:

$$P(z = 1) = P(x = 0)P(y = 1 \mid x = 0) + P(x = 1)P(y = 0 \mid x = 1)$$

$$= \frac{\varepsilon}{2} + \frac{\varepsilon}{2} = \varepsilon$$

$$P(z = 0) = 1 - P(z = 1) = 1 - \varepsilon$$

The rate of generation of information by the observer is therefore given by

$$H(\mathbf{z}) = -\varepsilon \log \varepsilon - (1 - \varepsilon) \log(1 - \varepsilon) \quad \text{bits/symbol}$$

For a given output sequence $y^{(1)}y^{(2)} \ldots$, the receiver can exactly reconstruct the input sequence $x^{(1)}x^{(2)} \ldots$ only when the observer output $z^{(1)}z^{(2)} \ldots$ is made available. It is therefore natural to define the rate of transmission of information

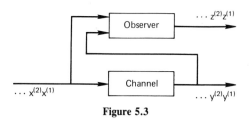

**Figure 5.3**

over the channel $R$ as the rate of generation of information $H(\mathbf{x})$ minus the rate of generation of supplemental information $H(\mathbf{z})$.

$$R = H(\mathbf{x}) - H(\mathbf{z}) \quad \text{bits/symbol}$$

For example, if the input data are generated at the rate of 1000 symbols/second and $\varepsilon = 0.01$, we have

$$H(\mathbf{x}) = 1 \to \text{input data rate} = 1000 \text{ bits/second}$$

$$H(\mathbf{z}) = 0.081 \to \text{supplemental data rate} = 81 \text{ bits/second}$$

$$R = 0.919 \to \text{information transmission rate} = 919 \text{ bits/second}$$

One may argue that in the long run, since $\varepsilon = 0.01$, only 1 percent of the transmitted bits will be in error (with probability close to 1), and therefore the rate of information transmission must be 990 bits/second. The answer is that the knowledge of the number of erroneous bits alone is not sufficient for the reconstruction of the data. One also needs to know the location of the erroneous bits, and for this reason the information transmission rate is actually at the lower value of 919 bits/second.

In the extreme case when $\varepsilon = 0$, we have $H(\mathbf{z}) = 0$ and consequently $R = 1000$ bits/second. On the other hand, if $\varepsilon = \frac{1}{2}$, then $H(\mathbf{z}) = 1$, resulting in zero transmission rate. Both conclusions are consistent with our expectations.

For the binary symmetric channel with equiprobable inputs, it is easy to verify that $H(\mathbf{z}) = H(\mathbf{x}\,|\,\mathbf{y})$. In general, we will show that exact reconstruction of the input sequence from the output sequence is possible only when the observer can generate supplemental information at a rate greater than or equal to $H(\mathbf{x}\,|\,\mathbf{y})$. To see this intuitively, observe that for long sequences of length $N$ there are roughly $2^{NH(\mathbf{x}\,|\,\mathbf{y})}$ input sequences that can produce a particular output sequence. Only when the supplemental information is generated at the rate of $H(\mathbf{x}\,|\,\mathbf{y})$ or faster does it become feasible to distinguish among these possibilities. For this reason, $H(\mathbf{x}\,|\,\mathbf{y})$ is usually referred to as the equivocation of the channel.

The remainder of this section contains a proof of the preceding statements. Specifically, we prove that, in general, exact reconstruction is possible if $H(\mathbf{z})$, the entropy of the supplemental information, is allowed to be larger than $H(\mathbf{x}\,|\,\mathbf{y})$, the equivocation of the channel.

Consider, a DMC with matrix $[p(y_j\,|\,x_k)]$ and input distribution $\{p_1, \ldots, p_K\}$. The observer is capable of observing both the input to the channel $x_k$ and the corresponding output $y_j$. For every output letter, the observer has a code for the input alphabet. Upon observation of $y_j$, the observer transmits the code word for $x_k$, chosen from the code that corresponds to $y_j$. Table 5.1 shows the code-word lengths for all the input–output pairs $(x_k, y_j)$.

Since code words from different codes may now follow each other, it is no longer enough to require that all the $J$ different codes be uniquely decodable. Prefix-free codes, however, are sufficient to guarantee unique decodability of the encoded sequences, and attention will be confined to them in this discussion. The following theorems concern the average code-word length $\bar{n}$ generated by the observer.

**Theorem 1.**   $\bar{n} \geq H(\mathbf{x}|\mathbf{y})/\log D$, where $D$ is the size of the observer's alphabet.

*Proof*

$$H(\mathbf{x}|\mathbf{y}) - \bar{n} \ln D = -\sum_k \sum_j p(x_k, y_j) \ln p(x_k|y_j) - \sum_k \sum_j n_{kj} p(x_k, y_j) \ln D$$

$$= \sum_k \sum_j p(x_k, y_j) \ln \left[ \frac{D^{-n_{kj}}}{p(x_k|y_j)} \right]$$

$$\leq \sum_j \sum_k p(x_k, y_j) \left[ \frac{D^{-n_{kj}}}{p(x_k|y_j)} - 1 \right]$$

$$= \sum_{j=1}^{J} p(y_j) \sum_{k=1}^{K} D^{-n_{kj}} - 1$$

Since all codes are prefix free, they satisfy Kraft's inequality: $\sum_{k=1}^{K} D^{-n_{kj}} \leq 1$ for all $j$. Therefore,

$$H(\mathbf{x}|\mathbf{y}) - \bar{n} \ln D \leq 0$$

completing the proof. Equality holds iff $-\log_D p(x_k|y_j)$ is integer for all $k, j$.

**Theorem 2.**   There exists a set of prefix-free codes for which the average code-word length $\bar{n}$ satisfies

$$\bar{n} < \frac{H(\mathbf{x}|\mathbf{y})}{\log D} + 1$$

**TABLE 5.1**

|       | $y_1$    | $y_2$    | $\cdots$ | $y_J$    |
|-------|----------|----------|----------|----------|
| $x_1$ | $n_{11}$ | $n_{12}$ | $\cdots$ | $n_{1J}$ |
| $x_2$ | $n_{21}$ | $n_{22}$ | $\cdots$ | $n_{2J}$ |
| $\vdots$ | $\vdots$ | $\vdots$ |       | $\vdots$ |
| $x_K$ | $n_{K1}$ | $n_{K2}$ | $\cdots$ | $n_{KJ}$ |

*Proof.* Use base $D$ logarithm and let $n_{kj} = \lceil -\log p(x_k|y_j) \rceil$. Since $n_{kj} \geq -\log p(x_k|y_j)$, we have

$$\sum_k D^{-n_{kj}} \leq \sum_k p(x_k|y_j) = 1$$

for every $j$. Therefore, a prefix-free code can be constructed for each $y_j$. Since $n_{kj} < -\log p(x_k|y_j) + 1$, we have

$$\bar{n} = \sum_k \sum_j p(x_k, y_j) n_{kj}$$

$$< -\sum_k \sum_j p(x_k, y_j) \log p(x_k|y_j) + \sum_k \sum_j p(x_k, y_j)$$

$$= \frac{H(\mathbf{x}|\mathbf{y})}{\log D} + 1$$

and the proof is complete.

The difference between $\bar{n}$ and $H(\mathbf{x}|\mathbf{y})/\log D$ can be arbitrarily reduced provided that long sequences (instead of single letters) are encoded at a time. This yields

$$H_D(\mathbf{x}|\mathbf{y}) \leq \bar{n} < H_D(\mathbf{x}|\mathbf{y}) + \frac{1}{N}$$

where $N$ is the length of the encoded sequences. It is seen therefore that the minimum rate of supplemental information required for exact reconstruction of the input at the receiver is equal to the equivocation $H(\mathbf{x}|\mathbf{y})$ of the channel; this is what we had initially set out to prove.

## 5.5  CHANNEL CAPACITY

In Section 5.4 we saw that the rate of transfer of information over a DMC can be defined as

$$R = H(\mathbf{x}) - H(\mathbf{x}|\mathbf{y})$$

where $H(\mathbf{x})$ is the rate of generation of information at the input and $H(\mathbf{x}|\mathbf{y})$ is the channel's equivocation. It is seen that $R$ is equal to the mutual information $I(\mathbf{x}, \mathbf{y})$ between the input and output of the channel. $I(\mathbf{x}, \mathbf{y})$ is, in general, a function of input probability distribution $\{p_1, \ldots, p_K\}$. It is possible, therefore, to find a distribution that maximizes $I(\mathbf{x}, \mathbf{y})$. [Since the set of possible distributions is closed and bounded, $I(\mathbf{x}, \mathbf{y})$ has a maximum rather than a least upper bound on this set.] The maximum value of $I(\mathbf{x}, \mathbf{y})$ is defined as the channel capacity $C$ and is a function of the channel matrix alone.

$$C = \text{Maximum (over input distributions) } I(\mathbf{x}, \mathbf{y})$$

In general, the problem of calculating the channel capacity in closed form is a difficult problem and one that has not yet been solved. For the channels introduced in Section 5.3, however, simple solutions exist. In the following paragraphs we derive the capacity for these channels.

### Symmetric Channel

For this class of channels, $H(\mathbf{y}\,|\,\mathbf{x})$ was shown to be independent of input distribution. To maximize $I(\mathbf{x}, \mathbf{y}) = H(\mathbf{y}) - H(\mathbf{y}\,|\,\mathbf{x})$, therefore, we have to maximize $H(\mathbf{y})$ over the input distributions. The sample space of $\mathbf{y}$ has $J$ elements, and the maximum possible value of $H(\mathbf{y})$ is $\log J$, which is achieved for uniform distribution of $\mathbf{y}$. This, in turn, is achieved by uniform distribution of $\mathbf{x}$, the reason being that the columns of a symmetric channel's matrix are permutations of the same set of numbers $q'_1, \ldots, q'_K$ and, consequently,

$$p(y_j) = \sum_{k=1}^{K} p(x_k, y_j) = \sum_{k=1}^{K} p(x_k)p(y_j\,|\,x_k) = \frac{1}{K} \sum_{k=1}^{K} q'_k$$

which is a constant, independent of $j$. Therefore, $p(y_j) = 1/J$ for all $j$, and the capacity is given by

$$C = \log J + \sum_{j=1}^{J} p'_j \log p'_j$$

where $p'_1, \ldots, p'_J$ are constituents of the rows of the matrix.

For the special case of a binary symmetric channel with crossover probability $\varepsilon$,

$$C = 1 + \varepsilon \log_2 \varepsilon + (1 - \varepsilon) \log_2(1 - \varepsilon) \quad \text{bits/symbol}$$

Figure 5.4 shows a plot of $C$ versus $\varepsilon$ for the BSC. At $\varepsilon = 0$ the capacity is 1 bit/symbol; that is, all the information is being transferred. As $\varepsilon \to 0.5$ the channel becomes less and less efficient, and the capacity is reduced until at $\varepsilon = 0.5$ the channel becomes useless. For $0.5 < \varepsilon \le 1$, the efficiency increases again, since a channel that lies consistently is just as informative as a consistently honest channel.

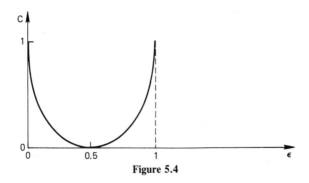

**Figure 5.4**

### Lossless Channel

Here $H(\mathbf{x}\,|\,\mathbf{y}) = 0$. Therefore,

$$C = \text{Max}\{H(\mathbf{x}) - H(\mathbf{x}\,|\,\mathbf{y})\} = \text{Max}\{H(\mathbf{x})\} = \log K$$

where $K$ is the size of the input alphabet. Capacity is achieved for uniform input distribution.

### Deterministic Channel

Here $H(\mathbf{y}\,|\,\mathbf{x}) = 0$. Therefore,

$$C = \text{Max}\{H(\mathbf{y}) - H(\mathbf{y}\,|\,\mathbf{x})\} = \log J$$

where $J$ is the size of the output alphabet. The capacity is achieved by assigning the probabilities $1/J$ to each group of input letters that correspond to the same output letter and distributing this probability arbitrarily among members of each group.

### Useless Channel

Here $H(\mathbf{x}\,|\,\mathbf{y}) = H(\mathbf{x})$. Therefore,

$$C = \text{Max}\{H(\mathbf{x}) - H(\mathbf{x}\,|\,\mathbf{y})\} = \text{Max}\{H(\mathbf{x}) - H(\mathbf{x})\} = 0$$

A useless channel thus has zero capacity, as expected.

As stated earlier, the problem of calculating the capacity $C$ of a general DMC has no simple solution. The convexity of $I(\mathbf{x}, \mathbf{y})$, however, makes the problem amenable to numerical solutions. For a given channel matrix $[p(y_j\,|\,x_k)]$, we now prove that the mutual information $I(\mathbf{x}, \mathbf{y})$ is convex over the space of input distributions $\{p_1, \ldots, p_K\}$. Because of the restrictions $p_k \geq 0$

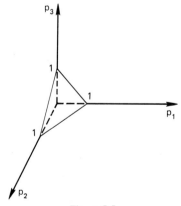

**Figure 5.5**

and $\Sigma_{k=1}^{K} p_k = 1$, the space of input distributions is a subset of the $K$-dimensional Euclidean space. It is not difficult to show that the set of all possible input distributions in this space is a convex set. Figure 5.5 shows this set for the special case of $K = 3$. For simplicity of notation, let us refer to $I(\mathbf{x}, \mathbf{y})$ as $I(P)$, where $P = \{p_1, \ldots, p_K\}$ is a point in the space of input probability distributions. We prove that, for every pair of points $P_1$, $P_2$ and for every real number $\lambda$ in the interval $[0, 1]$, the relationship $I[\lambda P_1 + (1 - \lambda)P_2] \geq \lambda I(P_1) + (1 - \lambda)I(P_2)$ is valid.

*Proof*

$$\lambda I(P_1) + (1 - \lambda)I(P_2) - I[\lambda P_1 + (1 - \lambda)P_2]$$

$$= \lambda \sum_i \sum_j p_1(x_i)p(y_j|x_i) \log \frac{p(y_j|x_i)}{p_1(y_j)}$$

$$+ (1 - \lambda) \sum_i \sum_j p_2(x_i)p(y_j|x_i) \log \frac{p(y_j|x_i)}{p_2(y_j)}$$

$$- \sum_i \sum_j [\lambda p_1(x_i) + (1 - \lambda)p_2(x_i)]p(y_j|x_i) \log \frac{p(y_j|x_i)}{\lambda p_1(y_j) + (1 - \lambda)p_2(y_j)}$$

$$= \lambda \sum_i \sum_j p_1(x_i)p(y_j|x_i) \log \frac{\lambda p_1(y_j) + (1 - \lambda)p_2(y_j)}{p_1(y_j)}$$

$$+ (1 - \lambda) \sum_i \sum_j p_2(x_i)p(y_j|x_i) \log \frac{\lambda p_1(y_j) + (1 - \lambda)p_2(y_j)}{p_2(y_j)}$$

$$\leq \lambda \sum_j p_1(y_j) \left[ \frac{\lambda p_1(y_j) + (1 - \lambda)p_2(y_j)}{p_1(y_j)} - 1 \right]$$

$$+ (1 - \lambda) \sum_j p_2(y_j) \left[ \frac{\lambda p_1(y_j) + (1 - \lambda)p_2(y_j)}{p_2(y_j)} - 1 \right]$$

$$= \lambda^2 + \lambda(1 - \lambda) - \lambda + \lambda(1 - \lambda) + (1 - \lambda)^2 - (1 - \lambda) = 0$$

The proof is thus complete.

The convexity of $I(\mathbf{x}, \mathbf{y})$ in the space of input distributions makes it convenient to use numerical techniques to determine the channel capacity, since any local maximum of a convex function is also its global maximum.

## PROBLEMS

**5.1.** Prove that conditioning cannot increase entropy; that is,

$$H(\mathbf{x}|\mathbf{y}, \mathbf{z}) \leq H(\mathbf{x}|\mathbf{y})$$

You may assume that $\mathbf{x}$, $\mathbf{y}$, and $\mathbf{z}$ are discrete random variables.

**5.2.** Let $\mathbf{x}$ be a discrete random variable and $f(\cdot)$ an arbitrary function. Define the random variable $\mathbf{y}$ as $\mathbf{y} = f(\mathbf{x})$.
(a) Prove that $H(\mathbf{y}\,|\,\mathbf{x}) = 0$.
(b) Show that $H(\mathbf{y}) \leq H(\mathbf{x})$. Under what conditions will equality hold?

**5.3.** Show that $I(\mathbf{x}, \mathbf{y}) = H(\mathbf{x}) - H(\mathbf{x}\,|\,\mathbf{y})$ can also be written as

$$I(\mathbf{x}, \mathbf{y}) = \sum_i \sum_j p(x_i, y_j) \log \frac{p(x_i, y_j)}{p(x_i)p(y_j)}$$

**5.4.** Let $X$, $Y$, and $Z$ be ensembles with two elements in each ensemble so that the eight elements in the joint $XYZ$ ensemble can be taken as the vertices of a unit cube.
(a) Find a joint probability assignment $p(x, y, z)$ such that $I(\mathbf{x}, \mathbf{y}) = 0$ and $I(\mathbf{x}, \mathbf{y}\,|\,\mathbf{z}) = 1$ bit.
(b) Find a joint probability assignment $p(x, y, z)$ such that $I(\mathbf{x}, \mathbf{y}) = 1$ bit and $I(\mathbf{x}, \mathbf{y}\,|\,\mathbf{z}) = 0$.

**5.5.** A source has an alphabet of four letters. The probabilities of the letters and two possible binary codes for the source are given next.

| Letter | $p(a_k)$ | Code I | Code II |
|--------|----------|--------|---------|
| $a_1$ | 0.4 | 1 | 1 |
| $a_2$ | 0.3 | 01 | 10 |
| $a_3$ | 0.2 | 001 | 100 |
| $a_4$ | 0.1 | 000 | 1000 |

For each code, what is the average mutual information provided about the source letter by the specification of the first letter of the code word?

**5.6.** Consider the ensemble of sequences of $N$ binary digits, $\mathbf{x}_1, \ldots, \mathbf{x}_N$. Each sequence containing an even number of 1's has probability $2^{-N+1}$, and each sequence with an odd number of 1's has probability zero. Find the average mutual informations

$$I(\mathbf{x}_2, \mathbf{x}_1), I(\mathbf{x}_3, \mathbf{x}_2\,|\,\mathbf{x}_1), \ldots, I(\mathbf{x}_N, \mathbf{x}_{N-1}\,|\,\mathbf{x}_1, \ldots, \mathbf{x}_{N-2})$$

Check your result for $N = 3$.

**5.7.** Let $\mathbf{y}$ and $\mathbf{z}$ be discrete random variables and define $\mathbf{x} = \mathbf{y} + \mathbf{z}$. Show that, in general, $H(\mathbf{x}\,|\,\mathbf{y}) \leq H(\mathbf{z})$ with equality iff $\mathbf{y}$ and $\mathbf{z}$ are independent. Can we say the same thing about $H(\mathbf{y}\,|\,\mathbf{x})$?

**5.8.** Consider a random variable $\mathbf{x}$ that assumes the values $-2, -1, +1, +2$ with equal probability. A second r.v. $\mathbf{y}$ is defined as $\mathbf{y} = \mathbf{x}^2$.
(a) Find the covariance of $\mathbf{x}$ and $\mathbf{y}$; that is, $\text{Cov}(\mathbf{x}, \mathbf{y}) = E\{(\mathbf{x} - \bar{\mathbf{x}})(\mathbf{y} - \bar{\mathbf{y}})\}$.
(b) Find the average mutual information $I(\mathbf{x}, \mathbf{y})$.
(c) Are $\mathbf{x}$ and $\mathbf{y}$ independent? Is there an inconsistency between the results of parts (a) and (b)?

**5.9.** Consider the following DMC with $p(\mathbf{x} = 0) = \frac{2}{3}$ and $p(\mathbf{x} = 1) = \frac{1}{3}$.

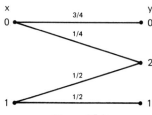

**Figure P5.9**

(a) Compute $H(\mathbf{x})$, $H(\mathbf{x}\,|\,\mathbf{y} = 0)$, $H(\mathbf{x}\,|\,\mathbf{y} = 1)$, $H(\mathbf{x}\,|\,\mathbf{y} = 2)$, and $H(\mathbf{x}\,|\,\mathbf{y})$.

(b) If you have not made any mistakes your results must indicate that $H(\mathbf{x}\,|\,\mathbf{y} = 2) > H(\mathbf{x})$; that is, the uncertainty about $\mathbf{x}$ becomes larger after $\mathbf{y}$ is observed to be equal to 2. Does this represent an inconsistency in information theory?

**5.10.** For each of the following classes of channels, give an example of the channel matrix and calculate the capacity.

(a) Lossless but *not* deterministic and *not* symmetric.

(b) Deterministic but *not* lossless and *not* symmetric.

(c) Lossless *and* deterministic.

(d) Symmetric *and* lossless but *not* deterministic.

(e) Useless *and* deterministic.

**5.11.** Consider a DMC with $\mathbf{x}$ and $\mathbf{y}$ as the input and output random variables, respectively. Show that $H(\mathbf{y})$, the entropy of the output, is a convex $\cap$ function of the input probability distribution and that $H(\mathbf{y}\,|\,\mathbf{x})$, the conditional entropy of the output given the input, is a linear function of the input probability distribution. Combining these results, show that $I(\mathbf{x}, \mathbf{y})$ is convex $\cap$ on the space of the input probability distribution.

# 6

# CHANNEL THEOREMS

**Introduction** In this chapter we discuss some of the most important properties of the discrete memoryless channel. The culmination of the chapter is in the last three sections when these properties are put together to prove the noisy channel theorem, which is perhaps the most basic and surprising result in information theory. The noisy channel theorem states that, at rates below capacity, information can be transmitted over the channel with negligible probability of error. The converse theorem states that, at rates above capacity, arbitrarily accurate communication is impossible. The noisy channel theorem and its converse thus give the concept of capacity its practical significance.

## 6.1 CONDITIONAL MUTUAL INFORMATION AND CAPACITY

The conditional mutual information $I(x_k, \mathbf{y})$ ia defined as

$$I(x_k, \mathbf{y}) = \sum_{j=1}^{J} p(y_j | x_k) \log \frac{p(y_j | x_k)}{p(y_j)}$$

It is the information between the output and a particular input letter $x_k$ of a DMC. The conditional mutual information is a function of both the channel matrix and the input distribution, and its average over all input letters is equal to $I(\mathbf{x}, \mathbf{y})$; that is,

$$I(\mathbf{x}, \mathbf{y}) = \sum_{k=1}^{K} p(x_k) I(x_k, \mathbf{y})$$

In this section we derive a useful relationship between the channel capacity $C$ and the conditional mutual information. The following theorem is helpful in this derivation.

**Theorem 1.**   Let $f(P)$ be a convex $\cap$ function of $P = (p_1, \ldots, p_K)$, where $P$ is a probability vector. Assuming that the partial derivatives $\partial f(P)/\partial p_k$ are continuous, the necessary and sufficient conditions for a vector $P^*$ to maximize $f(P)$ are

$$\frac{\partial f(P^*)}{\partial p_k} = \gamma, \qquad \text{for all } k \text{ such that } p_k^* \neq 0$$

$$\frac{\partial f(P^*)}{\partial p_k} \leq \gamma, \qquad \text{for all } k \text{ such that } p_k^* = 0$$

where $\gamma$ is an arbitrary constant.

*Proof*
(i) *Sufficiency:* Assume that for some $P^*$ and $\gamma$ the preceding relations are satisfied. We show for every $P$ that $f(P) - f(P^*) \leq 0$ and therefore prove that $P^*$ maximizes $f(P)$. From convexity

$$\lambda f(P) + (1 - \lambda)f(P^*) \leq f[\lambda P + (1 - \lambda)P^*]$$

Therefore,

$$f(P) - f(P^*) \leq \frac{f[P^* + \lambda(P - P^*)] - f(P^*)}{\lambda}$$

for all $\lambda$ in the interval $[0, 1]$. In the limit when $\lambda \to 0$,

$$f(P) - f(P^*) \leq \sum_{k=1}^{K} \frac{\partial f(P^*)}{\partial p_k} (p_k - p_k^*)$$

Now, if $p_k^* \neq 0$, by assumption $\partial f(P^*)/\partial p_k = \gamma$. If $p_k^* = 0$, then $\partial f(P^*)/\partial p_k \leq \gamma$ and $p_k - p_k^* \geq 0$, yielding $(\partial f(P^*)/\partial p_k)(p_k - p_k^*) \leq \gamma(p_k - p_k^*)$. Consequently,

$$f(P) - f(P^*) \leq \sum_{k=1}^{K} \gamma(p_k - p_k^*) = \gamma \left( \sum_{k=1}^{K} p_k - \sum_{k=1}^{K} p_k^* \right) = 0$$

(ii) *Necessity:* Let $P^*$ maximize the function $f(P)$. Then for every $P$ and every $\lambda$ in the interval $[0, 1]$

$$f[P^* + \lambda(P - P^*)] - f(P^*) \leq 0$$

In the limit when $\lambda \to 0$, this inequality yields

$$\sum_{k=1}^{K} \frac{\partial f(P^*)}{\partial p_k} (p_k - p_k^*) \leq 0$$

Since $P^*$ is a probability vector, at least one of its components must be strictly positive. For simplicity of notation, let $p_1^* > 0$. Let $P = (p_1^* - \varepsilon, p_2^*, \ldots, p_{k0}^* + \varepsilon, \ldots, p_K^*)$; that is, $P$ differs from $P^*$ in only $p_1$ and $p_{k0}$. Any $\varepsilon$ satisfying $-p_{k0}^* \leq \varepsilon \leq p_1^*$ is acceptable. Now

$$\sum_{k=1}^{K} \frac{\partial f(P^*)}{\partial p_k} (p_k - p_k^*) = -\varepsilon \frac{\partial f(P^*)}{\partial p_1} + \varepsilon \frac{\partial f(P^*)}{\partial p_{k0}} = \varepsilon \left( \frac{\partial f(P^*)}{\partial p_{k0}} - \frac{\partial f(P^*)}{\partial p_1} \right) \leq 0$$

If $p_{k0}^* > 0$, then $\varepsilon$ could be either positive or negative, in which case we must have

$$\frac{\partial f(P^*)}{\partial p_{k0}} = \frac{\partial f(P^*)}{\partial p_1}$$

If $p_{k0}^* = 0$, then $\varepsilon$ must be positive, in which case we must have

$$\frac{\partial f(P^*)}{\partial p_{k0}} \leq \frac{\partial f(P^*)}{\partial p_1}$$

Taking $\gamma = \partial f(P^*)/\partial p_1$, we see that the conditions of the theorem are satisfied. The proof is thus complete.

Theorem 1 is now applied to the mutual information $I(\mathbf{x}, \mathbf{y})$ between the input and output of a DMC. $I(\mathbf{x}, \mathbf{y})$ is a convex $\cap$ function of the input distribution $P = (p_1, \ldots, p_K)$, and its partial derivative with respect to $p_k$ is obtained as follows:

$$\frac{\partial I(P)}{\partial p_k} = \frac{\partial}{\partial p_k} \sum_{i=1}^{K} \sum_{j=1}^{J} p(x_i, y_j) \log \frac{p(y_j|x_i)}{p(y_j)}$$

$$= \frac{\partial}{\partial p_k} \sum_{i=1}^{K} p_i \sum_{j=1}^{J} p(y_j|x_i) \log \frac{p(y_j|x_i)}{\sum_m p_m p(y_j|x_m)}$$

$$= \sum_{j=1}^{J} p(y_j|x_k) \log \frac{p(y_j|x_k)}{p(y_j)} - \sum_{i=1}^{K} p_i \sum_{j=1}^{J} p(y_j|x_i) \frac{p(y_j|x_k) \log e}{\sum_m p_m p(y_j|x_m)}$$

$$= \sum_{j=1}^{J} p(y_j|x_k) \log \frac{p(y_j|x_k)}{p(y_j)} - \sum_{j=1}^{J} p(y_j) \frac{p(y_j|x_k) \log e}{p(y_j)}$$

$$= I(x_k, \mathbf{y}) - \log e$$

The maximizing distribution must therefore have the following property:

$$I(x_k, \mathbf{y}) = \gamma', \qquad \text{for all } k \text{ such that } p_k^* \neq 0$$

$$I(x_k, \mathbf{y}) \leq \gamma', \qquad \text{for all } k \text{ such that } p_k^* = 0$$

Here $\gamma' = \gamma + \log e$ is a constant. Moreover, for the maximizing distribution, $I(\mathbf{x}, \mathbf{y}) = \sum p_k^* I(x_k, \mathbf{y}) = \gamma'$. Therefore, $\gamma' = C$. These results are summarized in the following theorem.

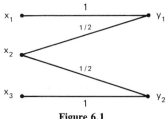

**Figure 6.1**

**Theorem 2.** A necessary and sufficient condition for an input distribution $\{p_1, \ldots, p_K\}$ to achieve capacity is that, for some number $C$,

$$I(x_k, \mathbf{y}) = C, \quad \text{for all } k \text{ such that } p_k \neq 0$$

$$I(x_k, \mathbf{y}) \leq C, \quad \text{for all } k \text{ such that } p_k = 0$$

$C$ is then the capacity of the channel.

**Example**

For the channel shown in Figure 6.1, it is reasonable to assume that $\{p(x_1) = 0.5, p(x_2) = 0, p(x_3) = 0.5\}$ is a good choice for the maximizing input distribution, since $x_2$ seems to be a poor choice for transmission. Straightforward calculations then yield

$$I(x_1, \mathbf{y}) = 1 \text{ bit}$$

$$I(x_2, \mathbf{y}) = 0$$

$$I(x_3, \mathbf{y}) = 1 \text{ bit}$$

Since $I(x_2, \mathbf{y}) < I(x_1, \mathbf{y}) = I(x_3, \mathbf{y})$, the conditions of theorem 2 are satisfied. The assumed distribution therefore achieves capacity.

## 6.2 CASCADED CHANNELS

Consider a DMC with input alphabet $\{x_1, \ldots, x_K\}$, output alphabet $\{y_1, \ldots, y_J\}$, and channel matrix $[p(y_j|x_k)]$. A second DMC with input alphabet $\{y_1, \ldots, y_J\}$, output alphabet $\{z_1, \ldots, z_M\}$, and channel matrix $[p(z_m|y_j)]$ is cascaded with the first channel, as shown in Figure 6.2. DMC2 may be considered as a signal-processing unit operating on the output of DMC1, but in general it can be any channel. In the following we prove that the processing of $\mathbf{y}$ does not increase the mutual information between the input and output of a channel; that is, $I(\mathbf{x}, \mathbf{y}) \geq I(\mathbf{x}, \mathbf{z})$ for all input distributions $\{p(x_1), \ldots, p(x_K)\}$. A consequence of this result is that the channel capacity does not increase by processing the output.

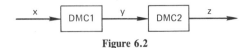

**Figure 6.2**

$$I(\mathbf{x}, \mathbf{z}) - I(\mathbf{x}, \mathbf{y}) = \sum_k \sum_j \sum_m p(x_k, y_j, z_m) \ln \frac{p(x_k \mid z_m)}{p(x_k)}$$

$$- \sum_k \sum_j \sum_m p(x_k, y_j, z_m) \ln \frac{p(x_k \mid y_j)}{p(x_k)}$$

$$= \sum_k \sum_j \sum_m p(x_k, y_j, z_m) \ln \frac{p(x_k \mid z_m)}{p(x_k \mid y_j)}$$

$$\leq \sum_k \sum_j \sum_m p(x_k \mid y_j, z_m) p(y_j, z_m) \frac{p(x_k \mid z_m)}{p(x_k \mid y_j)} - 1$$

Now $p(x_k \mid y_j, z_m) = p(x_k \mid y_j)$ since the knowledge of $z_m$ does not provide additional information about $x_k$ once $y_j$ is identified. This is a consequence of the definition of cascaded channels. Therefore,

$$I(\mathbf{x}, \mathbf{z}) - I(\mathbf{x}, \mathbf{y}) \leq \sum_j \sum_m p(y_j, z_m) \sum_k p(x_k \mid z_m) - 1 = 1 - 1 = 0$$

Equality holds iff $p(x_k \mid y_j) = p(x_k \mid z_m)$ for all triplets $(x_k, y_j, z_m)$ with nonzero joint probability. If the second channel is lossless, this requirement is obviously satisfied, making $I(\mathbf{x}, \mathbf{y}) = I(\mathbf{x}, \mathbf{z})$. Losslessness, however, is not a necessary condition for the equality of $I(\mathbf{x}, \mathbf{y})$ and $I(\mathbf{x}, \mathbf{z})$, as shown in the following example.

**Example**

For the cascaded channels in Figure 6.3

$$p(x_1 \mid y_1) = p(x_1 \mid z_1) = 1, \quad \text{if } p(x_1) \neq 0$$

Also,

$$p(x_1 \mid y_2) = \frac{p(x_1) p(y_2 \mid x_1)}{p(x_1) p(y_2 \mid x_1) + p(x_2) p(y_2 \mid x_2)}$$

$$= \frac{(\frac{1}{3}) p(x_1)}{(\frac{1}{3}) p(x_1) + (\frac{1}{2}) [1 - p(x_1)]}$$

$$= \frac{2 p(x_1)}{3 - p(x_1)}$$

$$p(x_1 \mid z_2) = \frac{p(x_1, y_2, z_2) + p(x_1, y_3, z_2)}{p(x_1, y_2, z_2) + p(x_1, y_3, z_2) + p(x_2, y_2, z_2) + p(x_2, y_3, z_2)}$$

$$= \frac{p(x_1) [(\frac{1}{3})(\frac{2}{3}) + (\frac{1}{3})(\frac{1}{3})]}{(\frac{1}{3}) p(x_1) + [1 - p(x_1)] [(\frac{1}{2})(\frac{2}{3}) + (\frac{1}{2})(\frac{1}{3})]}$$

$$= \frac{2 p(x_1)}{3 - p(x_1)}$$

Therefore, $p(x_1 \mid y_2) = p(x_1 \mid z_2)$. Other equalities can be checked similarly. Note that in this example $I(\mathbf{x}, \mathbf{y}) = I(\mathbf{x}, \mathbf{z})$ for all input distributions. There are examples where the equality holds for only some of the distributions.

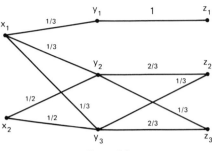

**Figure 6.3**

## 6.3 REDUCED CHANNELS AND SUFFICIENT REDUCTIONS

In many practical situations it is desired to reduce the number of output letters of a channel to simplify the processing of data. A reduction can be considered as cascading with a deterministic channel. An elementary reduction is defined as a reduction in which two output letters are combined to form a single letter. In this case the matrix of the new channel can be obtained from the matrix of the original channel by adding the columns that correspond to the combined letters. If the original matrix is

$$
\begin{bmatrix}
p_{1,1} & \cdots & p_{1,j} & p_{1,j+1} & \cdots & p_{1,J} \\
p_{2,1} & \cdots & p_{2,j} & p_{2,j+1} & \cdots & p_{2,J} \\
\vdots & & \vdots & \vdots & & \vdots \\
p_{K,1} & \cdots & p_{K,j} & p_{K,j+1} & \cdots & p_{K,J}
\end{bmatrix}
$$

and if the elementary reduction is applied to letters $y_j$ and $y_{j+1}$, the matrix of the reduced channel will be

$$
\begin{bmatrix}
p_{1,1} & \cdots & p_{1,j} + p_{1,j+1} & \cdots & p_{1,J} \\
p_{2,1} & \cdots & p_{2,j} + p_{2,j+1} & \cdots & p_{2,J} \\
\vdots & & \vdots & & \vdots \\
p_{K,1} & \cdots & p_{K,j} + p_{K,j+1} & \cdots & p_{K,J}
\end{bmatrix}
$$

Since any reduction can be achieved by successive application of elementary reductions, we confine our analysis here to elementary reductions.

Figure 6.4 shows an elementary reduction where $y_1$ and $y_2$ are combined into $z_1$. From the discussion of cascaded channels in Section 6.2, we know that $I(\mathbf{x}, \mathbf{z}) \leq I(\mathbf{x}, \mathbf{y})$ with equality iff $p(x_k | y_j) = p(x_k | z_m)$ for all $(x_k, y_j, z_m)$, where $p(x_k, y_j, z_m) \neq 0$. For the elementary reduction of Figure 6.4, equality holds iff

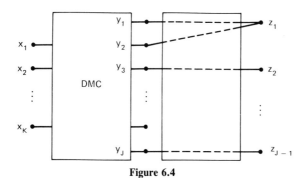

**Figure 6.4**

$p(x_k|y_1) = p(x_k|z_1)$ for all $x_k$ that can reach $y_1$, and $p(x_k|y_2) = p(x_k|z_1)$ for all $x_k$ that can reach $y_2$. Now

$$p(x_k|z_1) = \frac{p(x_k)p(z_1|x_k)}{p(z_1)} = \frac{p(x_k)[p(y_1|x_k) + p(y_2|x_k)]}{p(y_1) + p(y_2)}$$

$$= \frac{p(y_1)p(x_k|y_1) + p(y_2)p(x_k|y_2)}{p(y_1) + p(y_2)}$$

It is now easy to see that $I(\mathbf{x}, \mathbf{y}) = I(\mathbf{x}, \mathbf{z})$ iff $p(x_k|y_1) = p(x_k|y_2)$ for all $k$.

*Note:* The reason that $p(x_k|y_1)$ and $p(x_k|y_2)$ must be equal for all $x_k$, and not just the ones that can reach both $y_1$ and $y_2$, is as follows: If $x_k$ does not reach $y_1$ and $y_2$, then $p(x_k|y_1) = p(x_k|y_2) = 0$ and the equality is satisfied. If an $x_k$ exists that reaches $y_1$ but not $y_2$, then, in general, $p(x_k|z_1) \neq p(x_k|y_1)$ and the reduction does not preserve information.

The preceding results are summarized by the following statement:

The outputs $y_{j1}$ and $y_{j2}$ of a DMC with given input distribution $\{p(x_1), \ldots, p(x_K)\}$ can be combined without loss of average mutual information between input and output iff $p(x_k|y_{j1}) = p(x_k|y_{j2})$ for all $x_k$.

A reduction in which $I(\mathbf{x}, \mathbf{y})$ is preserved for all input distributions is called a sufficient reduction. Considering that

$$p(x_k|y_j) = \frac{p(x_k)p(y_j|x_k)}{\Sigma_i p(x_i)p(y_j|x_i)}$$

equality of $p(x_k|y_1)$ and $p(x_k|y_2)$ requires that

$$\frac{p(y_1|x_k)}{p(y_2|x_k)} = \frac{\Sigma_i p(x_i)p(y_1|x_i)}{\Sigma_i p(x_i)p(y_2|x_i)}$$

It is easy to verify that this relation will hold for all input distributions iff $p(y_1|x_k)/p(y_2|x_k)$ is a constant for all $k$, that is, iff columns 1 and 2 of the channel matrix differ by a multiplicative constant. The two columns can then be combined and the resulting reduction is a sufficient one.

**Example**

The matrix

$$\begin{bmatrix} \frac{1}{6} & \frac{1}{3} & \frac{1}{2} & 0 \\ \frac{1}{12} & \frac{1}{6} & \frac{1}{4} & \frac{1}{2} \end{bmatrix}$$

can be reduced to

$$\begin{bmatrix} \frac{1}{2} & \frac{1}{2} & 0 \\ \frac{1}{4} & \frac{1}{4} & \frac{1}{2} \end{bmatrix}$$

and then to

$$\begin{bmatrix} 1 & 0 \\ \frac{1}{2} & \frac{1}{2} \end{bmatrix}$$

Both reductions are sufficient, and therefore the final two-output channel is as good as the original four-output channel.

## 6.4 FANO'S BOUND ON EQUIVOCATION

Consider the cascade of two discrete memoryless channels shown in Figure 6.5. The second channel is a special channel whose output alphabet Z has a one-to-one correspondence with the first channel's input alphabet X. DMC2 can be interpreted as a decision device, which, upon observation of $y_j$, decides which input letter $x_k$ has been transmitted. In general, the decision is not free from errors, and the probability of error $P_E$ is given by

$$P_E = \sum_{k=1}^{K} \sum_{\substack{m=1 \\ m \neq k}}^{K} p(x_k, z_m)$$

According to Fano, the following inequality is always satisfied.

$$H(\mathbf{x} \mid \mathbf{y}) \leq H(P_E) + P_E \log(K - 1)$$

where $H(P_E) = -P_E \log P_E - (1 - P_E) \log(1 - P_E)$. Since $H(\mathbf{x} \mid \mathbf{z}) \geq H(\mathbf{x} \mid \mathbf{y})$, it is sufficient to prove Fano's inequality for $H(\mathbf{x} \mid \mathbf{z})$.

*Proof*

$$H(\mathbf{x} \mid \mathbf{z}) - H(P_E) - P_E \log(K - 1)$$

$$= -\sum_{k=1}^{K} \sum_{m=1}^{K} p(x_k, z_m) \log p(x_k \mid z_m) + \sum_{k=1}^{K} \sum_{\substack{m=1 \\ k \neq m}}^{K} p(x_k, z_m) \log P_E$$

$$+ \sum_{k=1}^{K} p(x_k, z_k) \log(1 - P_E) - \sum_{k=1}^{K} \sum_{\substack{m=1 \\ k \neq m}}^{K} p(x_k, z_m) \log(K - 1)$$

$$= \sum_{k=1}^{K} \sum_{\substack{m=1 \\ m \neq k}}^{K} p(x_k, z_m) \log \frac{P_E}{(K - 1)p(x_k \mid z_m)} + \sum_{k=1}^{K} p(x_k, z_k) \log \frac{1 - P_E}{p(x_k \mid z_k)}$$

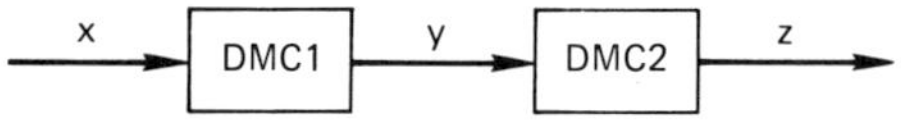

**Figure 6.5**

$$\leq \sum_{\substack{k=1 \\ k \neq m}}^{K} \sum_{m=1}^{K} p(x_k, z_m) \left[ \frac{P_E}{(K-1)p(x_k \mid z_m)} - 1 \right] + \sum_{k=1}^{K} p(x_k, z_k) \left[ \frac{1 - P_E}{p(x_k \mid z_k)} - 1 \right]$$

$$= \frac{P_E}{K-1} \sum_{\substack{k=1 \\ k \neq m}}^{K} \sum_{m=1}^{K} p(z_m) + (1 - P_E) \sum_{k=1}^{K} p(z_k) - \sum_{k=1}^{K} \sum_{m=1}^{K} p(x_k, z_m)$$

$$= \frac{P_E}{K-1} (K-1) \sum_{m=1}^{K} p(z_m) + (1 - P_E) - 1 = 0$$

The proof is now complete.

Notice that Fano's inequality is independent of the decision scheme being employed. $P_E$ is, of course, a function of the decision scheme, and the bound on equivocation can be improved by reducing the probability of error. $P_E$ can be minimized by assigning to each $y_j$ the input letter $x_k$ that maximizes $p(x_k \mid y_j)$.

There is an intuitive justification for the validity of Fano's inequality. Consider an observer that has access to both **x** and **z** and provides supplemental information to the receiver by transmitting a signal to indicate whether an error has occurred and another signal, in case of error, to identify the correct input. Since the probability of error is $P_E$, the first signal requires a rate of at least $H(P_E)$. For the second signal, the observer treats all the input letters equally and encodes them into equal-length code words. Since the letter to be identified in the case of an incorrect transmission is among the $K - 1$ remaining letters, the code-word lengths must be $\log(K - 1)$. These code words are transmitted with probability $P_E$, and therefore the total rate of supplemental information is $H(P_E) + P_E \log(K - 1)$, which must be larger than or equal to the channel equivocation $H(\mathbf{x} \mid \mathbf{y})$, since equivocation is the minimum rate at which complete supplemental information can be provided. Fano's inequality is thus justified.

## 6.5 IMPROVING CHANNEL RELIABILITY

Consider a binary symmetric channel (BSC) with crossover probability $\varepsilon = 0.01$, where data are transmitted at the rate of 1 bit/second. If each bit is repeated three times during transmission, the useful rate will obviously drop to 1 bit every 3 seconds but the error rate will improve. This scheme is capable of correcting for one transmission error if the receiver applies the majority rule in decoding 3-bit sequences. The majority rule is to decide 1 if the majority of bits are 1's and to decide 0 otherwise. The probability of error per information bit is now $3(1 - \varepsilon)\varepsilon^2 + \varepsilon^3 = 2.98 \times 10^{-4}$, which is better than the original value of 0.01. It is possible to improve the error rate even further by repeating each letter $2N + 1$ times, but in the limit when $N$ becomes large the rate approaches zero and the communication system becomes useless.

The Hamming distance between two equal-length binary sequences is defined as the number of positions in which the sequences differ from each other. The distance between 001011 and 001101, for example, is 2. The important feature of the repetition scheme just described is that the input letters, 0 and 1, which have a distance of 1 from each other, are replaced with input sequences 11...1 and 00...0, which are a distance of $2N + 1$ apart. This feature allows the channel to commit a maximum of $N$ transmission errors without hindering the ability of the receiver to make a correct decision. The setback is, of course, the reduced transmission rate.

The essence of the noisy channel theorem of the next section is that it is not necessary to have excessively small data rates in order to have arbitrarily accurate communication. The trick is to handpick a set of appropriate sequences from the input alphabet and to confine transmitted signals to these sequences. The distance between each and every pair of selected sequences must be large to ensure that a large number of transmission errors can be tolerated. At the same time, the number of these sequences must also be large so that a reasonable data rate is maintained.

The probability of error is a function of the decision scheme used at the receiver. This is a decision as to which input sequence should be assigned to a given received sequence. Before proceeding to the noisy channel theorem, it is appropriate to say a few words about the decision schemes. Let $W_i = x_{i1}x_{i2}\ldots x_{iN}$ and $V_j = y_{j1}y_{j2}\ldots y_{jN}$ represent the input and output sequences, respectively. $W_i$ must belong to the set of selected code words, whereas $V_j$ can be any output sequence. The optimum decision scheme upon observation of $V_j$ is to choose the particular $W_i$ that maximizes the backward channel probability $p(W_i \mid V_j)$. This, however, requires the knowledge of the input distribution $\{p(W_i)\}$. A suboptimum scheme that is generally used, known as the maximum likelihood (ML) scheme, chooses the sequence $W_i$ that maximizes the forward channel probability $p(V_j \mid W_i)$. Since $p(W_i \mid V_j) = p(W_i)p(V_j \mid W_i)/p(V_j)$, it is easy to show that the ML rule is optimum in the special case where the $W_i$'s are equally likely.

For the BSC with crossover probability $\varepsilon < 0.5$,

$$p(V_j \mid W_i) = \varepsilon^D(1 - \varepsilon)^{N-D}$$

where $D$ is the number of positions in which $W_i$ and $V_j$ differ (i.e., the Hamming distance between them). Consequently, the ML rule requires minimization of $D$ (i.e., choosing the code word $W_i$ that is closest to the received sequence $V_j$ in the Hamming sense). Although this is not an optimum decision rule, it is sufficiently good for the fulfillment of the promise of the noisy channel theorem.

## 6.6 NOISY CHANNEL THEOREM FOR THE BSC

Consider a BSC with crossover probability $p$. The channel capacity in units of bits/symbol is $C = 1 - H(p)$, where $H(p) = -p \log p - (1 - p) \log(1 - p)$. Assuming that each symbol has duration $\tau$, the capacity in bits/second is $C = [1 - H(p)]/\tau$. Consider a source that creates information at the rate of $R$ bits/second for transmission over the channel. The noisy channel theorem states that, as long as $R$ is less than $C$, communication with negligible error rate is possible. This is achieved by encoding sequences of data into certain sequences (code words) from the channel input alphabet and treating the code words as elementary channel inputs. Any degree of reliability is obtained provided that these code words are (1) long enough and (2) far from each other in the Hamming sense.

The first step in the proof of the theorem is the derivation of error probability $P_e$ for a given set of code words $\{W_1, \ldots, W_M\}$. Each word has length $N$, and the total number of words is given by

$$M = 2^{NR\tau}$$

The justification for the preceding equation is that each word has duration $N\tau$, and therefore the total number of bits produced by the source in this interval is $NR\tau$. This corresponds to $2^{NR\tau}$ source sequences, each of which must be assigned a unique $W_i$.

In the second step, $P_e$ is averaged over all possible code-word sets of length $N$ and size $M$ to yield $\overline{P}_e$. This is equivalent to randomly selecting $M$ code words from the set of $2^N$ possible binary sequences and calculating the corresponding error probability. The random coding argument enables us to obtain a closed form for $\overline{P}_e$, which is then used to identify the conditions under which $\overline{P}_e$ can be made arbitrarily small. Finally, we argue that, since $\overline{P}_e$ is the average error probability over the set of all possible codes $\{W_1, \ldots, W_M\}$, there must exist at least one code for which $P_e$ is less than or equal to $\overline{P}_e$. We thus conclude that under certain conditions a set of code words exists for which the probability of error is arbitrarily small. These steps are now described in detail.

Assume the code $\{W_1, \ldots, W_M\}$, consisting of code words of length $N$, is used over a BSC with crossover probability $p$. Since the channel is memoryless, the average number of transmission errors for each $W_i$ is $Np$. Given two arbitrary positive numbers $\varepsilon$ and $\delta$, the law of large numbers asserts that for sufficiently large $N$ the probability of receiving a sequence $V_j$ whose distance from $W_i$ is larger than $N(p + \varepsilon)$ is less than $\delta$. Define the test set as the set of all binary sequences of length $N$ whose distance from $V_j$ is less than $N(p + \varepsilon)$. The decision strategy is the following: If a code word such as $W_i$ belongs to the test set and no other code word is in the test set, announce $W_i$ as the transmitted sequence; otherwise, announce that an error has occurred. An error thus occurs if (1) the transmitted word $W_i$ is not in the test set or (2) if some other code word, say $W_j$, is in the test set. An upper bound on error probability $P_e$ is therefore given by

$$P_e \leq \delta + \sum_{\substack{j=1 \\ j \neq i}}^{M} P\{W_j \text{ belongs to test set}\}$$

The average of $P_e$ over all possible codes of length $N$ and size $M$ can now be calculated using the random coding argument. Assume the code words $W_1, \ldots, W_M$ are chosen independently and with equal probability from the set of all possible sequences of $N$ binary digits. (The random selection is done with replacement; therefore, the possibility of two or more identical code words in a given code exists.) The probability that $W_j$ belongs to the test set is now equal to the number of sequences in the test set divided by the total number of sequences of length $N$, the reason being that $W_j$ is selected independently of $W_i$ and according to a uniform distribution.

$$\overline{P}\{W_j \text{ belongs to test set}\} = \frac{\sum_{k=0}^{N(p+\varepsilon)} \binom{N}{k}}{2^N}$$

The summation on the right side gives the number of sequences of length $N$ that differ from a given sequence in at most $N(p + \varepsilon)$ places. Noting that the preceding is independent of $j$, the upper bound on the average error probability can be written as

$$\overline{P}_e \leq \delta + (M - 1)\frac{\sum_{k=0}^{N(p+\varepsilon)} \binom{N}{k}}{2^N}$$

Using the following well-known inequality (see the Appendix),

$$\sum_{k=0}^{N\alpha} \binom{N}{k} \leq 2^{NH(\alpha)}, \qquad \alpha < 0.5$$

we have

$$\overline{P}_e \leq \delta + M \cdot 2^{-N[1 - H(p+\varepsilon)]}$$

Replacing for $M$ in this equation then yields

$$\overline{P}_e \leq \delta + 2^{-N[1 - H(p+\varepsilon) - R\tau]}$$

Since $\varepsilon$ and $\delta$ can be arbitrarily small, it is seen that, as long as $R$ is less than $[1 - H(p)]/\tau$, the average error probability can be made arbitrarily small by increasing $N$. As we have argued earlier, a small $\overline{P}_e$ means that at least one code exists that has a small error probability $P_e$. The proof is thus complete.

## 6.7 NOISY CHANNEL THEOREM FOR THE GENERAL DMC

Consider a DMC with input alphabet $\{x_1, \ldots, x_K\}$, output alphabet $\{y_1, \ldots, y_J\}$, transition matrix $[p(y_j | x_k)]$, and capacity $C$. All input–output letters have equal duration $\tau$. The input distribution that achieves capacity is denoted $P_x^*$ and, without loss of generality, we assume that $p^*(x_k) \neq 0$ for $1 \leq k \leq K$. [If $p^*(x_i) = 0$ for some letter, omit $x_i$ from the list of the input alphabet. The omission is of no consequence since the promise of the noisy channel theorem can still be fulfilled.] The output distribution corresponding to $P_x^*$ is denoted $P_y^*$. If an information source generates data at the rate of $R$ bits/second with $R < C$, then the noisy channel theorem states that the data can be transmitted over the channel with negligible probability of error. The proof is similar to the one given for the BSC in Section 6.6, and only major differences are outlined in this section.

First, a general distance between sequences must be defined since the Hamming distance is only applicable to the binary case. The maximum likelihood rule compares $p(V_j | W_i)$ for all code words $W_i$ upon arrival of $V_j$ and chooses the code word with the largest forward probability. The following definition for the distance between $W_i$ and $V_j$ therefore seems reasonable:

$$D(W_i, V_j) = \log \frac{p^*(V_j)}{p(V_j | W_i)}$$

$p^*(V_j)$ is the probability of $V_j$ when the input letters are chosen independently and according to the capacity-achieving distribution $P_x^*$. The reason for the appearance of $p^*(V_j)$ in this definition will become clear later. As far as the ML rule is concerned, however, $p^*(V_j)$ is a constant and does not affect the decision scheme. Since logarithm is a monotonically increasing function, the inequality $p(V_j | W_i) \geq p(V_j | W_k)$ is equivalent to $D(W_i, V_j) \leq D(W_k, V_j)$. Therefore, the ML rule yields the minimum distance decision scheme in this case.

Assuming that a given code word $W_{i0}$ has been transmitted, the average distance between $W_{i0}$ and the received sequence $V_j$ is

$$\overline{D(W_{i0}, V_j)} = \sum_j p(V_j | W_{i0}) D(W_{i0}, V_j)$$

$$= -\sum_j p(V_j | W_{i0}) \log \frac{p(V_j | W_{i0})}{p^*(V_j)}$$

The summation is over all output sequences $V_j = (y_{j1}, \ldots, y_{jN})$. Since the channel is memoryless,

$$p(V_j | W_{i0}) = \prod_{n=1}^{N} p(y_{jn} | x_{in})$$

and since $p^*(V_j)$ is obtained by independent selection of input letters,

$$p^*(V_j) = \prod_{n=1}^{N} p^*(y_{jn})$$

Therefore,

$$\overline{D(W_{i0}, V_j)} = -\sum_{n=1}^{N} \sum_{j=1}^{J} p(y_j | x_{in}) \log \frac{p(y_j | x_{in})}{p^*(y_j)}$$

$x_{in}$ is the $n$th letter of $W_{i0}$, and $J$ is the size of the output alphabet. The inner summation is the conditional mutual information for $x_{in}$ and, according to a previous theorem, is equal to $C$, independent of $x_{in}$. Thus

$$\overline{D(W_{i0}, V_j)} = -NC$$

for all $i_0$. The following decision scheme is now equivalent to the one used in Section 6.6. Given a received sequence $V_j$, calculate the distance between $V_j$ and each code word $W_i$. If there is one and only one code word with a distance less than $-NC + N\varepsilon$ from $V_j$, choose it as the transmitted sequence. Otherwise, announce that an error has occurred. The probability of error $P_e$ upon transmission of $W_i$ is now written as

$$P_e \leq \delta + \sum_{\substack{j=1 \\ j \neq i}}^{M} P\{W_j \text{ closer than } -N(C - \varepsilon) \text{ to the received sequence}\}$$

Using the random coding argument, $P_e$ can now be averaged over all possible code-word sets. The random selection of code words, however, is according to the capacity-achieving distribution $P_x^*$.

$$\overline{P}\{W_j \text{ closer than } -N(C - \varepsilon) \text{ to the received sequence}\}$$

$$= \sum_{\text{all } V} p^*(V) \sum_{\substack{\text{all } W \text{ with} \\ D(W, V) < -N(C-\varepsilon)}} p^*(W)$$

$$= \sum_{\substack{\text{all pairs } (W, V) \text{ with} \\ D(W, V) < -N(C-\varepsilon)}} p^*(V) p^*(W)$$

All pairs $(W, V)$ with $D(W, V) < -N(C - \varepsilon)$ satisfy the following:

$$\log \frac{p^*(V)}{p(V | W)} < -N(C - \varepsilon)$$

Therefore,

$$p^*(V) < p(V | W) \cdot 2^{-N(C-\varepsilon)}$$

Consequently,

$$\sum_{\text{all pairs} \ldots} p^*(V) p^*(W) < 2^{-N(C-\varepsilon)} \sum_{\text{all pairs} \ldots} p^*(W, V) \leq 2^{-N(C-\varepsilon)}$$

Combining all the results, we conclude that

$$\overline{P}_e \leq \delta + M \cdot 2^{-N(C-\varepsilon)} = \delta + 2^{-N(C-\varepsilon-R\tau)}$$

Since $\varepsilon$ and $\delta$ can be arbitrarily small, the average probability of error approaches zero with increasing $N$, provided that $R\tau < C$. A small $\overline{P}_e$ means that at least one appropriate code exists, and thus the proof is complete.


## 6.8 CONVERSE THEOREM

The noisy channel theorem states that a source that generates information at a rate below channel capacity can be transmitted with negligible error probability. The converse theorem is concerned with the opposite situation and states that at rates above channel capacity arbitrarily accurate communication is impossible. There are several versions of the converse theorem in the literature. The strong converse theorem asserts that at rates above capacity the probability of message error approaches 1 with increasing length of the message sequences. This version has only been proved for block codes and, in addition, does not provide any information about the probability of single-letter errors. Another version of the theorem states that the average probability of error per source letter is bounded away from zero when the source maintains a rate above channel capacity. In other words, the probability of error per source letter (on the average) cannot be made to go to zero no matter what coding technique is employed.

These theorems will not be proved here. Instead, we consider a simple version of the converse theorem that is based on Fano's inequality. Consider $M$ messages $W_1, \ldots, W_M$ of length $N$ that are used with equal probability for transmission over a DMC. If the input ensemble is $\mathbf{W}$ and the output ensemble is $\mathbf{V}$, then

$$H(\mathbf{W} \mid \mathbf{V}) = -I(\mathbf{W}, \mathbf{V}) + H(\mathbf{W}) = -I(\mathbf{W}, \mathbf{V}) + \log M$$

But

$$I(\mathbf{W}, \mathbf{V}) = H(\mathbf{V}) - H(\mathbf{V} \mid \mathbf{W}) = H(\mathbf{V}) - \sum_{n=1}^{N} H(\mathbf{y}^{(n)} \mid \mathbf{x}^{(n)})$$

$$\leq \sum_{n=1}^{N} H(\mathbf{y}^{(n)}) - \sum_{n=1}^{N} H(\mathbf{y}^{(n)} \mid \mathbf{x}^{(n)})$$

$$= \sum_{n=1}^{N} I(\mathbf{x}^{(n)}, \mathbf{y}^{(n)}) \leq NC$$

Therefore,

$$H(\mathbf{W} \mid \mathbf{V}) \geq -NC + \log M$$

On the other hand, according to Fano's inequality,

$$H(\mathbf{W} \mid \mathbf{V}) \leq P_e \log(M - 1) - P_e \log P_e - (1 - P_e) \log(1 - P_e)$$

Therefore,

$$-NC + \log M \leq P_e \log(M - 1) + H(P_e) \leq P_e \log M + \log 2$$

Replacing $M$ with $2^{NR\tau}$ yields,

$$P_e \geq 1 - \frac{C}{R\tau} - \frac{1}{NR\tau}$$

It is readily observed that, for $R\tau > C$ and sufficiently large $N$, the probability of error is bounded away from zero. This completes the proof of the converse theorem.

## PROBLEMS

**6.1.** The channel shown in Figure P6.1 is known as the binary erasure channel. (A bit transmitted through this channel may be erased but can never be received in error.) Asuming that $P(\mathbf{x} = 0) = p_0$, calculate $I(\mathbf{x}, \mathbf{y})$ in terms of $p_0$. What is the channel capacity?

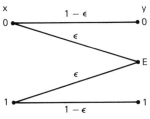

**Figure P6.1**

**6.2.** Suppose that the transmitter in the binary erasure channel of Problem 6.1 is connected to the receiver via a feedback loop and can repeat the erased bits until they are correctly received. Assuming that the input stream of data is i.i.d., determine the average number of transmitted information bits per use of the channel.

**6.3.** Find a discrete memoryless channel together with an input distribution such that the sequence of outputs $\mathbf{y}^{(1)} \dots \mathbf{y}^{(N)}$ is independent even though the corresponding sequence of inputs $\mathbf{x}^{(1)} \dots \mathbf{x}^{(N)}$ might be dependent.

**6.4.** In a joint ensemble $XY$, the mutual information $I(x_i, y_j) = \log[p(x_i, y_j)/p(x_i)p(y_j)]$ is a random variable. In this problem we are concerned with the variance of that random variable.
    **(a)** Prove that $\text{Var}[I(x_i, y_j)] = 0$ iff there is a constant $\alpha$ such that, for all $x_i, y_j$ with $p(x_i, y_j) \neq 0$,

$$p(x_i, y_j) = \alpha p(x_i)p(y_j)$$

    **(b)** Express $I(\mathbf{x}, \mathbf{y})$ in terms of $\alpha$ and interpret the special case $\alpha = 1$.
    **(c)** For each of the channels in Figure P6.4, find an input distribution such that $I(\mathbf{x}, \mathbf{y}) \neq 0$ and $\text{Var}[I(x_i, y_j)] = 0$. Calculate $I(\mathbf{x}, \mathbf{y})$.

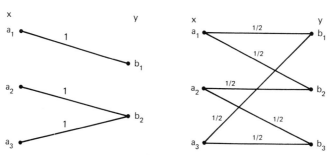

**Figure P6.4**

**6.5.** A DMC is called additive modulo $K$ if it has the input and output alphabet $0, 1, \ldots, K - 1$ and the output $y$ is given in terms of the input $x$ and a noise variable $z$ by $y = x \oplus z$. The noise variable takes on values $0, 1, \ldots, K - 1$ and is statistically independent of the input, and the addition $x \oplus z$ is taken modulo $K$ (i.e., as $x + z$ or $x + z - K$, whichever is between 0 and $K - 1$).
(a) Show that $I(\mathbf{x}, \mathbf{y}) = H(\mathbf{y}) - H(\mathbf{z})$.
(b) Find the capacity in terms of $H(\mathbf{z})$ and find the maximizing input distribution.

**6.6.** Two discrete memoryless channels $A$ and $B$ are connected in cascade. Assuming that $M_A$ and $M_B$ are the individual channel matrices, determine the matrix of the cascade channel.

**6.7.** Consider a DMC with input alphabet $\{x_1, \ldots, x_K\}$ and output alphabet $\{y_1, \ldots, y_J\}$. Given the input distribution $p(x_k)$ for $1 \leq k \leq K$ and the channel transition matrix $[p(y_j|x_k)]$, the optimum detection rule is as follows: For a received letter $y_j$, choose $x_k$ such that $p(x_k|y_j)$ is maximum. Let $P(E|y_j)$ be the probability of error when $y_j$ is received.
(a) Express $P(E|y_j)$ in terms of the backward channel probabilities $p(x_k|y_j)$.
(b) Show that $H(\mathbf{x}|y_j) \geq 2P(E|y_j)$ when entropy is in bits [see Problem 2.7(d)].
(c) Prove the following upper bound on the total probability of error, $P(E)$, in terms of equivocation:

$$P(E) \leq 0.5H(\mathbf{x}|\mathbf{y}) \qquad \text{(in bits)}$$

**6.8.** A DMC is characterized by the matrix

$$
\begin{array}{c}
\begin{array}{ccc} \phantom{x_1} & y_1 \quad y_2 \quad y_3 \end{array} \\
\begin{array}{c} x_1 \\ x_2 \\ x_3 \end{array}
\begin{bmatrix}
\frac{1}{2} & \frac{1}{3} & \frac{1}{6} \\
\frac{1}{6} & \frac{1}{2} & \frac{1}{3} \\
\frac{1}{3} & \frac{1}{6} & \frac{1}{2}
\end{bmatrix}
\end{array}
$$

If $p(x_1) = \frac{1}{2}$ and $p(x_2) = p(x_3) = \frac{1}{4}$, find the optimum decision scheme and calculate the associated probability of error.

**6.9.** A source produces statistically independent, equally probable letters from an alphabet $(a_1, a_2)$ at a rate of one letter each 3 seconds. These letters are transmitted over a binary symmetric channel that is used once each second by encoding the source letter $a_1$ into the code word 000 and encoding $a_2$ into the code word 111. If, in the corresponding 3-second interval at the channel output, any of the sequences 000, 001, 010, 100 is received, $a_1$ is decoded; otherwise, $a_2$ is decoded. Let $\varepsilon < 0.5$ be the channel crossover probability.

(a) For each possible received three-digit sequence in the interval corresponding to a given source letter, find the probability that $a_1$ came out of the source given that received sequence.

(b) Using part (a), show that the preceding decoding rule minimizes the probability of an incorrect decision.

(c) Find the probability of an incorrect decision [using part (a) is not the easy way here].

(d) Suppose the source is slowed down to produce one letter each $2n + 1$ seconds, $a_1$ being encoded into $2n + 1$ zeros and $a_2$ into $2n + 1$ ones. What decision rule minimizes the probability of an incorrect decision at the decoder? Find this probability of incorrect decision in the limit as $n \to \infty$. (*Hint:* Use the law of large numbers.)

**6.10.** Let the discrete memoryless channels $A$ and $B$ have matrices $M_A$ and $M_B$ and capacities $C_A$ and $C_B$, respectively.

(a) The sum of the channels is a new channel with the following matrix:

$$\begin{bmatrix} M_A & 0 \\ 0 & M_B \end{bmatrix}$$

It is operated by choosing either $A$ or $B$ at a given time and transmitting a letter through it. The channel used can always be identified by the input–output symbols. Show that the capacity $C$ of the sum channel is given by

$$2^C = 2^{C_A} + 2^{C_B}$$

(b) The product of the channels is defined as the channel whose inputs are the pairs $(x_{ia}, x_{jb})$ and whose outputs are the pairs $(y_{ma}, y_{nb})$, where $x_{ia}$ and $y_{ma}$ are the input and output letters of channel $A$, while $x_{jb}$ and $y_{nb}$ are the input and output letters of channel $B$. The elements of the channel matrix are given by

$$p(y_{ma}, y_{nb} \mid x_{ia}, x_{jb}) = p(y_{ma} \mid x_{ia}) p(y_{nb} \mid x_{jb})$$

The product channel is thus operated by using the two channels simultaneously for each transmission. Show that the capacity of the product channel is $C = C_A + C_B$.

**6.11.** For each of the following channels, determine the capacity and a maximizing input distribution.

(a) $\begin{pmatrix} 1-p & p & 0 \\ p & 1-p & 0 \\ 0 & 0 & 1 \end{pmatrix}$

(b) $\begin{pmatrix} \dfrac{p}{2} & \dfrac{p}{2} & \dfrac{(1-p)}{2} & \dfrac{(1-p)}{2} \\ \dfrac{(1-p)}{2} & \dfrac{(1-p)}{2} & \dfrac{p}{2} & \dfrac{p}{2} \end{pmatrix}$

(c) $\begin{pmatrix} 1-\alpha-\beta & \beta & \alpha \\ \alpha & \beta & 1-\alpha-\beta \end{pmatrix}$

**(d)** $\begin{pmatrix} 1 & 0 & 0 \\ \frac{1}{2} & \frac{1}{4} & \frac{1}{4} \\ 0 & \frac{1}{2} & \frac{1}{2} \end{pmatrix}$

**(e)** $\begin{pmatrix} 1-\alpha & \alpha & 0 \\ 0 & 1-\alpha & \alpha \\ \alpha & 0 & 1-\alpha \end{pmatrix}$

**(f)** $\begin{pmatrix} \frac{3}{4} & \frac{1}{4} & 0 \\ \frac{1}{3} & \frac{1}{3} & \frac{1}{3} \\ 0 & \frac{1}{4} & \frac{3}{4} \end{pmatrix}$

**(g)** $\begin{pmatrix} \frac{1}{3} & \frac{1}{3} & 0 & \frac{1}{3} \\ 0 & \frac{1}{3} & \frac{1}{3} & \frac{1}{3} \\ \frac{1}{3} & 0 & \frac{1}{3} & \frac{1}{3} \end{pmatrix}$

**6.12.** Consider a BSC with crossover probability $\varepsilon$ and a DMS that produces binary data at the rate of $R = 3$ bits per channel symbol $[p(0) = p(1) = \frac{1}{2}]$. The following two strategies for the reproduction of source data at the channel output are suggested:

(i) Of every 3 bits produced by the source, transmit 1 bit and at the channel output reconstruct the other 2 bits by coin flipping.

(ii) For every 3-bit block of source data, transmit 1 bit that represents the majority and at the channel output repeat each received bit three times.

Compute the average probability of error in each case and compare the two strategies. Which is better?

**6.13** **(a)** Find the capacity of the channel of Figure P6.13.

**(b)** If the code words $W_1 = x_1$, $W_2 = x_3$ constitute the set of permissible code words for this channel, determine the probability of error per message (i.e., per code word). What is the rate of generation of information $R$ (in bits per channel symbol) that could be transmitted over this channel with the preceding choice of code words?

**(c)** Same as part (b) except for the code words. The code in this case consists of $W_1 = x_1 x_1$, $W_2 = x_2 x_3$, $W_3 = x_3 x_5$, $W_4 = x_4 x_2$, and $W_5 = x_5 x_4$.

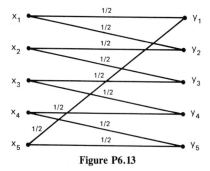

**Figure P6.13**

**6.14.** Consider a binary channel in which noise affects the input in blocks of seven symbols. A block of seven is either transmitted without error or exactly one symbol out of seven is incorrect. These eight possibilities are equally likely. Define $W$ and $V$ as ensembles of the 7-bit input and output sequences, respectively.

(a) Calculate $H(V \mid W)$.

(b) What is the maximum value of $I(W, V)$?

(c) What is the capacity of the original binary channel?

**6.15.** Consider all binary sequences of length $n = 7$. We wish to choose $M$ code words $W_1, \ldots, W_M$ for use on a binary channel. To correct all single errors that occur during transmission, the Hamming distance between all code words $W_i$ and $W_j$, $i \neq j$, must be $\geq 3$.

(a) How many binary sequences have a distance less than or equal to 1 from a given sequence $W_i$?

(b) What is the maximum possible value of $M$?

(c) Assuming that the maximum value of $M$ can be achieved, what is the rate of generation of information that can be transmitted over the channel?

# 7

# RATE-DISTORTION THEORY

**Introduction**  In Chapters 2 and 3 we studied the problem of source coding for discrete memoryless sources and learned that the minimum rate at which data could be accurately reproduced was the source entropy $H(\mathbf{x})$. In this chapter we address the problem of source coding with a fidelity criterion. Here a distortion measure is defined and, accordingly, the deviation of the reproduced data from the original (source) data is quantified. The problem is then to minimize the data rate for a given level of distortion or, what amounts to the same thing, to minimize the level of distortion for a given data rate. It turns out that, for a broad class of sources and corresponding distortion measures, a rate-distortion function $R(D)$ can be obtained that has the following properties:

(i)  For any given level of distortion $D$, it is possible to find a coding scheme with rate arbitrarily close to $R(D)$ and average distortion arbitrarily close to $D$.

(ii)  It is impossible to find a code that achieves reproduction with fidelity $D$ (or better) at a rate below $R(D)$.

In the following discussion we confine our attention to discrete memoryless sources and single-letter fidelity criteria for which the rate-distortion function can be easily defined and its properties are easy to prove. The results, however, are applicable to a wide variety of sources, and the interested reader is referred to the vast literature on rate-distortion theory for further details [3, 5, 7, 8].

## 7.1 SOURCE CODING WITH A FIDELITY CRITERION

Consider a DMS with alphabet $\{a_1, \ldots, a_K\}$ and probability distribution $\{p_1, \ldots, p_K\}$. Sequences of length $N$ from this source will be encoded into sequences of length $N$ from the reproducing alphabet $\{b_1, \ldots, b_J\}$. The single-letter distortion measure is defined as $d(a_k, b_j)$, which assigns a real, nonnegative value to every pair $(a_k, b_j)$. Let $W_i = a_{i1}a_{i2} \ldots a_{iN}$ be a source sequence whose reproduced version in a given encoding scheme is $V_j = b_{j1}b_{j2} \ldots b_{jN}$. The distortion per letter of $W_i$ is then given by

$$d(W_i, V_j) = \frac{1}{N} \sum_{n=1}^{N} d(a_{in}, b_{jn}) \tag{7.1}$$

The average distortion will then be the statistical average of $d(W_i, V_j)$ over all source sequences; that is,

$$\overline{d} = \sum_{\text{all } W_i} p(W_i) d(W_i, V_j) \tag{7.2}$$

In general, a code consists of $M$ code words $\{V_1, \ldots, V_M\}$, and each $W_i$ is assigned a code word $V_j$ such that $d(W_i, V_j)$ is minimized. The average distortion is given by Eq. (7.2), and the rate of the code is defined as

$$R = \frac{1}{N} \log_2 M \tag{7.3}$$

in bits per source letter. A code is said to be $D$-admissible if the average distortion $\overline{d}$ associated with the code is less than or equal to $D$. The smallest value of $R$ among all $D$-admissible codes is denoted $R(D)$ and is known as the rate-distortion function.

The minimum distortion is achieved if each letter $a_k$ is assigned a letter $b_{j0}$ with the property that $d(a_k, b_{j0}) \leq d(a_k, b_j)$ for all $j$. The minimum distortion is then given by

$$\overline{d}_{\min} = \sum_{k=1}^{K} p(a_k) d(a_k, b_{j0}) \tag{7.4}$$

$\overline{d}_{\min}$ will be zero if for every $a_k$ there exists at least one $b_j$ such that $d(a_k, b_j) = 0$; otherwise, $\overline{d}_{\min}$ will be strictly positive. In any event, $R(D)$ is defined only for $D \geq \overline{d}_{\min}$. For $D = \overline{d}_{\min}$, each letter $a_k$ is assigned a certain $b_{j0}$. In the worst case, all the $b_{j0}$ will be different and the code will have a rate equal to the source entropy. Thus, in general,

$$R(\overline{d}_{\min}) \leq -\sum_{k=1}^{K} p_k \log p_k \tag{7.5}$$

The function $R(D)$ is a nonincreasing function of $D$. To see this, let $D_1 > D_2 \geq \overline{d}_{\min}$. Then the set of $D_2$-admissible codes will be a subset of the set of $D_1$-admissible codes and, consequently, $R(D_1) \leq R(D_2)$.

As $D$ increases, the function $R(D)$ decreases until at some value of D, say $\overline{d}_{max}$, it becomes equal to zero and remains zero afterward. To determine the value of $\overline{d}_{max}$, we notice in Eq. (7.3) that $R = 0$ if $M = 1$. Therefore, we must look for a code with a single code word that has the smallest distortion among all codes of size $M = 1$. Let us call this code word $V_0 = b_{01}b_{02}\ldots b_{0N}$. The average distortion associated with $\{V_0\}$ is given by

$$\overline{d} = \sum_{\text{all } W_i} p(W_i)d(W_i, V_0) = \frac{1}{N} \sum_{\text{all } W_i} p(a_{i1}\ldots a_{iN}) \sum_{n=1}^{N} d(a_{in}, b_{0n})$$

$$= \frac{1}{N} \sum_{n=1}^{N} \sum_{k=1}^{K} p(a_k)d(a_k, b_{0n}) \tag{7.6}$$

To minimize $\overline{d}$, one must minimize the inner sum in Eq. (7.6) by choosing the proper $b_{0n}$. This choice is independent of $n$, however, and thus the minimum value of $\overline{d}$ for a code of size $M = 1$ is

$$\min_j \sum_{k=1}^{K} p(a_k)d(a_k, b_j) \tag{7.7}$$

This is the smallest value of $D$ at which $R(D)$ becomes equal to zero, and we denote it by $\overline{d}_{max}$.

From the foregoing discussion it is concluded that the rate-distortion function $R(D)$ is a nonincreasing function of $D$, and the interval $[\overline{d}_{min}, \overline{d}_{max}]$ whose boundaries are defined by Eqs. (7.4) and (7.7) is the range of interest.

**Example 1**

Consider a memoryless binary source with alphabet $\{0, 1\}$ and probability distribution $\{p_0, 1 - p_0\}$, where $p_0 \leq \frac{1}{2}$. The reproducing alphabet is also $\{0, 1\}$, and the distortion measure is given in Figure 7.1. The minimum distortion is achieved when 0 is mapped to 0 and 1 mapped to 1; thus $\overline{d}_{min} = 0$. This is obviously the case of perfect reconstruction, and therefore

$$R(\overline{d}_{min}) = H(p_0) = -p_0 \log p_0 - (1 - p_0) \log(1 - p_0)$$

$\overline{d}_{max}$ is obtained from Eq. (7.7) by noting that

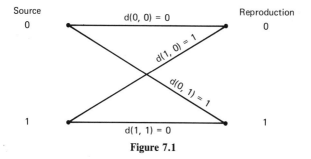

**Figure 7.1**

$$\sum_{k=1}^{2} p(a_k)d(a_k, b_j) = \begin{cases} p_0 \times 0 + (1 - p_0) \times 1 = 1 - p_0, & b_j = 0 \\ p_0 \times 1 + (1 - p_0) \times 0 = p_0, & b_j = 1 \end{cases}$$

Since $p_0 \leq \frac{1}{2} \leq 1 - p_0$, we conclude that $\overline{d}_{\max} = p_0$.

We are not yet in a position to calculate $R(D)$ for values of $D$ in the interval $[\overline{d}_{\min}, \overline{d}_{\max}]$, but we shall give an example of methods that are generally used in data compression. This example will bring out the essence of source coding with a fidelity criterion and will shed light on the intimate relation between the noisy channel theorem of Chapter 6 and the fundamental theorem of the rate-distortion theory. The method is based on the $(7, 4)$ Hamming error-correcting-code, and we digress at this point to introduce this code.

### The $(7, 4)$ Hamming Code

Consider the circle diagram in Figure 7.2 where the three circles are drawn such that their intersections create the regions numbered 1 through 7. Using this diagram, it is possible to construct 16 binary sequences of length 7 according to the following rules: (1) Bits 1, 2, 3, and 4 are chosen arbitrarily and placed in the corresponding regions of the circle diagram, regions 1 to 4. (2) Bits 5, 6, and 7 are chosen such that when placed in the corresponding regions of the diagram the total number of 1's in each circle becomes an even number. These are thus the parity check bits.

We now show that the 16 sequences constructed according to these rules form a single-error-correcting code. If a code word were transmitted over a BSC and the received sequence satisfied all the parity checks, we would say that no errors have occurred. A single error in bits 5, 6, or 7 would violate one of the parity checks, a single error in bits 2, 3, or 4 would violate two parity checks, while an error in bit 1 would violate all three parity checks. In each case it is possible to detect the erroneous bit by consulting the circle diagram. Thus, whether the received sequence is error free or contains a single error, it is always possible to recover the transmitted sequence.

Now consider the space of all binary sequences of length 7. There are $2^7 = 128$ points in this space. The 16 code words of the Hamming code can be considered as the centers of 16 nonoverlapping spheres of radius 1 in this space. Each sphere contains the code word plus seven other sequences that have a unit distance from it. The total number of points covered by the spheres is $16 \times 8 = 128$, which is all the points that belong to the space. Therefore the spheres cover the entire space.

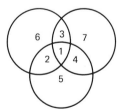

**Figure 7.2**

Let us now go back to the source introduced in example 1 and encode source sequences of length $N = 7$ into code words of the $(7, 4)$ Hamming code. Since spheres of unit radius around the code words cover the entire space, each source sequence is reproduced with at most one error. For $p_0 = 0.5$, the average distortion per letter will be given by

$$\bar{d} = \frac{1}{7} \times \left[ \frac{16}{128} \times 0 + \frac{112}{128} \times 1 \right] = \frac{1}{8}$$

The rate is obtained from Eq. (7.3) with $N = 7$ and $M = 16$. Thus $R \approx 0.571$ bit/source letter.

The rate distortion function for this problem is known to be (see Problem 7.1)

$$R(D) = H(p_0) - H(D), \qquad 0 \le D \le p_0 \qquad (7.8)$$

Thus, for $p_0 = 0.5$, we have $R(1/8) = 0.456$ bit/source letter, which is somewhat better than that achieved by the $(7, 4)$ Hamming code

**Example 2**

Consider a DMS with alphabet $\{a_1, a_2, a_3\}$ and probability distribution $p_1 = p_2 = p_3 = \frac{1}{3}$. The reproducing alphabet is $\{b_1, b_2\}$, and the distortion measure is given in Figure 7.3. The minimum distortion is achieved by assigning $a_1$ to $b_1$, $a_2$ to $b_2$, and $a_3$ to either $b_1$ or $b_2$. The average distortion is then given by $\bar{d}_{\min} = 1$. To obtain $\bar{d}_{\max}$, observe that

$$\sum_{k=1}^{K} p(a_k) d(a_k, b_j) = \begin{cases} \frac{1}{3} \times 1 + \frac{1}{3} \times 1 + \frac{1}{3} \times 2 = \frac{4}{3}, & b_j = b_1 \\ \frac{1}{3} \times 2 + \frac{1}{3} \times 1 + \frac{1}{3} \times 1 = \frac{4}{3}, & b_j = b_2 \end{cases}$$

and thus $\bar{d}_{\max} = 4/3$ according to Eq. (7.7). The rate-distortion function for this source is known to be (see Problem 7.5)

$$R(D) = \frac{2}{3}\left[ 1 - H\left( \frac{3(D-1)}{2} \right) \right], \qquad 1 \le D \le \frac{4}{3}$$

in bits per source symbol. Notice that $R(\bar{d}_{\min}) = \frac{2}{3}$ is much less than $H(\frac{1}{3}) = 0.9183$, which one would obtain by assigning $a_1$ to $b_1$, $a_2$ to $b_2$, and $a_3$ to $b_1$.

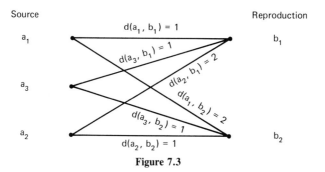

**Figure 7.3**

## 7.2 RATE-DISTORTION FUNCTION AND ITS PROPERTIES

In this section we define the rate-distortion function from a completely different point of view. It turns out, however, that the definition given here will result in the same function $R(D)$ as described in Section 7.1. We continue to use the notations $\overline{d}$ and $R(D)$ for the average distortion and the rate-distortion function, respectively, but the reader should bear in mind that these quantities are now defined from a new perspective and may or may not have the previous connotations.

Consider a discrete memoryless channel with input alphabet $\{a_1, \ldots, a_K\}$, input probability distribution $\{p_1, \ldots, p_K\}$, and output alphabet $\{b_1, \ldots, b_J\}$. Let an arbitrary set of transition probabilities $[p(b_j \mid a_k)]$ be assigned to the channel. We define the average distortion $\overline{d}$ associated with this channel in the following way:

$$\overline{d} = \sum_{k=1}^{K} \sum_{j=1}^{J} p(a_k)p(b_j \mid a_k)d(a_k, b_j) \tag{7.9}$$

A channel matrix is said to be $D$-admissible if the average distortion $\overline{d}$ associated with that matrix is less than or equal to $D$.

With each channel matrix is associated an average mutual information $I(\mathbf{a}, \mathbf{b})$ between the channel input and output. We define the rate-distoration function $R(D)$ as the minimum of $I(\mathbf{a}, \mathbf{b})$ over all $D$-admissible channel matrices; that is,

$$R(D) = \min_{\text{all } D\text{-admissible channels}} \{I(\mathbf{a}, \mathbf{b})\} \tag{7.10}$$

Since the set of $D$-admissible channel matrices is a closed and bounded set and since $I(\mathbf{a}, \mathbf{b})$ is a real-valued, continuous, and bounded function of $[p(b_j \mid a_k)]$, the minimum indicated in Eq. (7.10) exists.

It is not difficult to show that the minimum achievable $\overline{d}$ in Eq. (7.9) is the same as $\overline{d}_{\min}$ in Eq. (7.4). Therefore, $R(D)$ is only defined for $D \geq \overline{d}_{\min}$. Moreover, since $I(\mathbf{a}, \mathbf{b}) \leq H(\mathbf{a})$, we have

$$R(\overline{d}_{\min}) \leq -\sum_{k=1}^{K} p_k \log p_k \tag{7.11}$$

similar to Eq. (7.5). $R(D)$ is a nonincreasing function of $D$ because the set of $D$-admissible channels can only expand with increasing $D$. The following theorem establishes the smallest value of $D$ at which $R(D)$ becomes equal to zero.

**Theorem 1.** Let $\overline{d}_{\max}$ be defined as follows:

$$\overline{d}_{\max} = \min_{j} \sum_{k=1}^{K} p(a_k)d(a_k, b_j) \tag{7.12}$$

Then $R(D) = 0$ for $D \geq \overline{d}_{\max}$ and $R(D) > 0$ otherwise.

*Proof:* Let $j_0$ achieve the minimum in Eq. (7.12); then the deterministic channel that connects all $a_k$ to $b_{j_0}$ has distortion equal to $\overline{d}_{max}$ and $I(\mathbf{a}, \mathbf{b}) = 0$. Since zero is the smallest value that the average mutual information can assume, we conclude that $R(\overline{d}_{max}) = 0$. Conversely, let $R(D) = 0$ for some value of $D$. Then there must exist a $D$-admissible channel for which $I(\mathbf{a}, \mathbf{b}) = 0$. This is equivalent to the statement that $\mathbf{a}$ and $\mathbf{b}$ are independent random variables; consequently

$$\overline{d} = \sum_{k=1}^{K} \sum_{j=1}^{J} p(a_k, b_j) d(a_k, b_j) = \sum_{j=1}^{J} p(b_j) \sum_{k=1}^{K} p(a_k) d(a_k, b_j)$$

$$\geq \sum_{j=1}^{J} p(b_j) \overline{d}_{max} = \overline{d}_{max}$$

But the channel is $D$-admissible; therefore, $D \geq \overline{d}_{max}$ and the proof is thus complete.

The next theorem shows that $R(D)$ is a convex $\cup$ function. Convexity implies continuity at all points except possibly at $D = \overline{d}_{min}$. [It has been shown however that $R(D)$ is also continuous at $D = \overline{d}_{min}$.] The fact that $R(D)$ is a nonincreasing convex function of $D$ also implies that it is strictly decreasing. Therefore, the general behavior of $R(D)$ is similar to the function shown in Figure 7.4.

**Theorem 2.**    $R(D)$ is a convex $\cup$ function of $D$.

*Proof:* Let $\lambda \in [0, 1]$ and $D_1, D_2$ belong to $[\overline{d}_{min}, \overline{d}_{max}]$. We will show that

$$R[\lambda D_1 + (1 - \lambda)D_2] \leq \lambda R(D_1) + (1 - \lambda)R(D_2) \tag{7.13}$$

Let $[p_1(b_j \mid a_k)]$ be the $D_1$-admissible channel with $I_1(\mathbf{a}, \mathbf{b}) = R(D_1)$ and, similarly, let $[p_2(b_j \mid a_k)]$ be the $D_2$-admissible channel with $I_2(\mathbf{a}, \mathbf{b}) = R(D_2)$. Consider a new channel matrix defined as

$$[p(b_j \mid a_k)] = \lambda[p_1(b_j \mid a_k)] + (1 - \lambda)[p_2(b_j \mid a_k)] \tag{7.14}$$

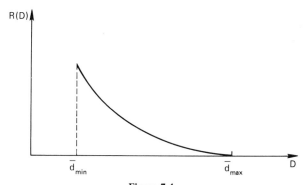

**Figure 7.4**

It is easy to show that this new channel is $\lambda D_1 + (1 - \lambda)D_2$-admissible. If the mutual information between the input and output of the new channel is $I(\mathbf{a}, \mathbf{b})$, then

$$R[\lambda D_1 + (1 - \lambda)D_2] \leq I(\mathbf{a}, \mathbf{b}) \qquad (7.15)$$

But the average mutual information is a convex $\cup$ function of the transition matrix (see Problem 7.2); therefore,

$$I(\mathbf{a}, \mathbf{b}) \leq \lambda I_1(\mathbf{a}, \mathbf{b}) + (1 - \lambda)I_2(\mathbf{a}, \mathbf{b}) \qquad (7.16)$$

Combining Eqs. (7.15) and (7.16) and replacing $I_1(\mathbf{a}, \mathbf{b})$ and $I_2(\mathbf{a}, \mathbf{b})$ with $R(D_1)$ and $R(D_2)$, we obtain Eq. (7.13), thus completing the proof.

As was mentioned earlier, convexity implies that $R(D)$ is a strictly decreasing function of $D$. This, in turn, implies that the channel matrix that achieves $R(D)$ for a given $D$ is not merely $D$-admissible, but its average distortion $\bar{d}$ is exactly equal to $D$; for if $\bar{d}$ were less than $D$, then the rate-distortion function would have been constant on the interval $[\bar{d}, D]$.

## 7.3 FUNDAMENTAL THEOREM OF RATE-DISTORTION THEORY

In this section we establish the relationship between the rate-distoriton function, which was formally defined in Section 7.2, and its practical, more intuitive version, which was described in Section 7.1. In particular, we will show that for every $D$ in the interval $[\bar{d}_{min}, \bar{d}_{max}]$ there exists a source code $\{V_1, \ldots, V_M\}$ whose average distortion $\bar{d}$ is arbitrarily close to $D$ and whose rate $R$ is arbitrarily close to $R(D)$. The concept of random coding, which was central to the proof of the noisy channel theorem, will again be used here, and by showing that the average distortion over all randomly selected codes of rate less than $R(D) + \varepsilon$ is less than $D + \varepsilon$, we will establish the existence of at least one code with the desired properties.

Consider the discrete memoryless channel that achieves the minimum in Eq. (7.10), and let its matrix be $[p(b_j | a_k)]$. From the discussions of Section 7.2 we know that

$$\bar{d} = \sum_{k=1}^{K} \sum_{j=1}^{J} p(a_k)p(b_j | a_k)d(a_k, b_j) = D \qquad (7.17)$$

$$I(\mathbf{a}, \mathbf{b}) = \sum_{k=1}^{K} \sum_{j=1}^{J} p(a_k)p(b_j | a_k) \log \frac{p(b_j | a_k)}{p(b_j)} = R(D) \qquad (7.18)$$

If the source produces a sequence of length $N$ and this sequence is transmitted over the channel, the probability of the received sequence $V_j = b_{j1} \ldots b_{jN}$ will be given by

$$p(V_j) = \prod_{n=1}^{N} \left( \sum_{k=1}^{K} p(a_k)p(b_{jn} | a_k) \right) \qquad (7.19)$$

This will be the probability distribution for random coding; in other words, the M code words will be selected independently and according to the probability distribution in Eq. (7.19).

Now consider a source sequence $W_i = a_{i1}a_{i2}\ldots a_{iN}$ and define the set $S_i$ as the set of all sequences $V_j$ such that $d(W_i, V_j) < D + \varepsilon$. If $S_i$ happens to contain at least one of the code words $V_1, \ldots, V_M$, then the distortion associated with $W_i$ will be less than $D + \varepsilon$. We are therefore interested in the probability that a code word, chosen randomly according to the probability distribution of Eq. (7.19), belongs to $S_i$. We call this probability $P(S_i)$:

$$P(S_i) = \sum_{V_j \in S_i} p(V_j) \qquad (7.20)$$

We also define the set $T_i$ as the set of all sequences $V_j$ such that

$$(1/N) \log_2[p(V_j \mid W_i)/p(V_j)] < R(D) + \varepsilon.$$

Thus

$$p(V_j) > 2^{-N[R(D)+\varepsilon]} p(V_j \mid W_i), \qquad \text{for } V_j \in T_i \qquad (7.21)$$

Now

$$P(S_i) \geq P(S_i \cap T_i) = \sum_{V_j \in S_i \cap T_i} p(V_j) > 2^{-N[R(D)+\varepsilon]} \sum_{V_j \in S_i \cap T_i} p(V_j \mid W_i) \quad (7.22)$$

and we will show that $\sum_{V_j \in S_i \cap T_i} p(V_j \mid W_i)$ is arbitrarily close to 1, provided that $N$ is sufficiently large. In fact, this is a consequence of the law of large numbers. If $W_i$ is transmitted and $V_j$ received, then $d(W_i, V_j) = (1/N)\sum_{n=1}^{N} d(a_{in}, b_{jn})$ is the time average of the r.v. $d(a_k, b_j)$ and must therefore be close to the statistical average $D$ of the r.v. [see Eq. (7.17)] with probability close to 1. Consequently, when $W_i$ is transmitted, the probability of $V_j$ belonging to $S_i$ will be close to 1. Similarly, the probability of $V_j$ belonging to $T_i$ will be close to 1, because $(1/N) \log[p(V_j \mid W_i)/p(V_j)] = (1/N)\sum_{n=1}^{N} \log[p(b_{jn} \mid a_{in})/p(b_{jn})]$ is the time average of a random variable whose statistical average is $R(D)$ according to Eq. (7.18). Thus we conclude that, when $W_i$ is transmitted, the received sequence $V_j$ will be in $S_i \cap T_i$ with probability close to unity. Therefore,

$$\sum_{V_j \in S_i \cap T_i} p(V_j \mid W_i) \approx 1 \qquad (7.23)$$

If the code words are randomly selected and at least one of them belongs to $S_i$, the average distortion for $W_i$ will be less than $D + \varepsilon$. The probability that none of the M code words belongs to $S_i$ is given by

$$[1 - P(S_i)]^M < \left[1 - 2^{-N[R(D)+\varepsilon]} \sum_{V_j \in S_i \cap T_i} p(V_j \mid W_i)\right]^M \qquad (7.24)$$

where the upper bound is a direct consequence of Eq. (7.22). We can further upper bound Eq. (7.24) by using the following inequality:

$$(1 - \alpha\beta)^M \leq 1 - \beta + e^{-M\alpha}, \qquad 0 \leq \alpha, \beta \leq 1 \qquad (7.25)$$

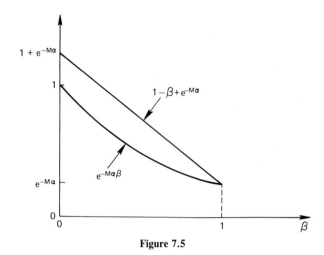

**Figure 7.5**

which is obtained from

$$(1 - \alpha\beta)^M = e^{M \ln(1-\alpha\beta)} \le e^{-M\alpha\beta} \le 1 - \beta + e^{-M\alpha}$$

The last inequality is obtained by examining Figure 7.5.

Using Eq. (7.25) in Eq. (7.24), we will have

$$[1 - P(S_i)]^M < 1 - \sum_{V_j \in S_i \cap T_i} p(V_j \mid W_i) + e^{-M \cdot 2^{-N[R(D)+\varepsilon]}} \qquad (7.26)$$

Now if $M = 2^{N[R(D)+2\varepsilon]}$, the last term in Eq. (7.26) can be made extremely small for sufficiently large $N$. Similarly, the second term can be made arbitrarily close to 1 according to Eq. (7.23). Consequently, the probability of having no code words in $S_i$ is arbitrarily small. In such situations where $W_i$ has to be encoded into some $V_j$ outside of $S_i$, the distortion, although larger than $D + \varepsilon$, will still remain below some finite value. [The maximum possible distortion is given by $\max_{k,j}\{d(a_k, b_j)\}$.] Therefore, the contribution to the average distortion by codes that have no code words in $S_i$ can be made less than $\varepsilon$. From the foregoing discussion, we conclude that for $M = 2^{N[R(D)+2\varepsilon]}$, or equivalently for $R = R(D) + 2\varepsilon$, there exists at least one code whose average distortion is less than $D + 2\varepsilon$. The proof is thus complete.

## 7.4 CONVERSE THEOREM

The converse to the fundamental theorem states that no $D$-admissible code can have a rate less than $R(D)$. To prove this, let $\{V_1, \ldots, V_M\}$ be a $D$-admissible code and consider a deterministic channel that assigns to each $W_i$ the closest $V_j$ in the code. Obviously, $H(\mathbf{V} \mid \mathbf{W}) = 0$, and consequently

$$I(\mathbf{W}, \mathbf{V}) = H(\mathbf{V}) - H(\mathbf{V} \mid \mathbf{W}) = H(\mathbf{V}) \le \log M \qquad (7.27)$$

On the other hand,

$$I(\mathbf{W}, \mathbf{V}) = H(\mathbf{W}) - H(\mathbf{W}|\mathbf{V}) = \sum_{n=1}^{N} H(\mathbf{a}^{(n)}) - H(\mathbf{W}|\mathbf{V}) \tag{7.28}$$

Now

$$H(\mathbf{W}|\mathbf{V}) = H(\mathbf{a}^{(1)} \ldots \mathbf{a}^{(N)} | \mathbf{b}^{(1)} \ldots \mathbf{b}^{(N)}) \le \sum_{n=1}^{N} H(\mathbf{a}^{(n)} | \mathbf{b}^{(1)} \ldots \mathbf{b}^{(N)})$$

$$\le \sum_{n=1}^{N} H(\mathbf{a}^{(n)} | \mathbf{b}^{(n)}) \tag{7.29}$$

Therefore,

$$I(\mathbf{W}, \mathbf{V}) \ge \sum_{n=1}^{N} I(\mathbf{a}^{(n)}, \mathbf{b}^{(n)}) \tag{7.30}$$

Combining Eqs. (7.27) and (7.30), we obtain

$$R = \frac{1}{N} \log M \ge \frac{1}{N} \sum_{n=1}^{N} I(\mathbf{a}^{(n)}, \mathbf{b}^{(n)}) \tag{7.31}$$

Let $\overline{d}_n$ be the average distortion with which $\mathbf{a}^{(n)}$ is reproduced; then

$$R(\overline{d}_n) \le I(\mathbf{a}^{(n)}, \mathbf{b}^{(n)}) \tag{7.32}$$

and consequently

$$R \ge \frac{1}{N} \sum_{n=1}^{N} R(\overline{d}_n) \ge R\left(\frac{1}{N} \sum_{n=1}^{N} \overline{d}_n\right) \tag{7.33}$$

The last inequality is a consequence of the fact that $R(D)$ is a convex $\cup$ function. Now the average distortion $\overline{d}$ is equal to $(1/N)\sum_{n=1}^{N} \overline{d}_n$, and since the code is $D$-admissible by definition, we have $\overline{d} \le D$. From Eq. (7.33) and the fact that $R(D)$ is a decreasing function of $D$, we conclude that $R \ge R(D)$. The proof is thus complete.

## PROBLEMS

**7.1.** A discrete memoryless source has alphabet $\{0, 1\}$ and probability distribution $\{p_0, 1 - p_0\}$. The reproducing alphabet is also $\{0, 1\}$, and the distortion measure is $d(0, 0) = d(1, 1) = 0$ and $d(0, 1) = d(1, 0) = 1$. Show that the rate-distortion function is given by $R(D) = H(p_0) - H(D)$ for $0 \le D \le p_0$.

**7.2.** Prove that the average mutual information $I(\mathbf{x}, \mathbf{y})$ between the input and output of a DMC is convex $\cup$ in the transition probability matrix $[p(y_j | x_k)]$.

**7.3.** A source produces independent, equiprobable binary digits. The reproducing alphabet is ternary, and the distortion measure is shown in Figure P7.3 (omitted transitions in the diagram correspond to infinite distortion).
   **(a)** Find and sketch the rate-distortion function $R(D)$.
   **(b)** Find a simple encoding scheme that achieves any desired rate $R$ at the distortion level $D$ determined from $R = R(D)$.

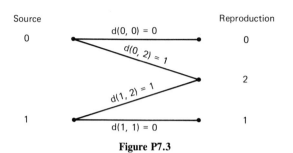

**Figure P7.3**

**7.4.** A source produces independent equiprobable letters from an alphabet of five letters. The distortion measure is as shown in Figure P7.4 (omitted transitions correspond to infinite distortion and included transitions to zero distortion). Find the
rate-distortion function for this source and distortion measure.

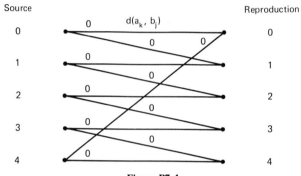

**Figure P7.4**

**7.5.** For the source of Example 2 in Section 7.1:
  **(a)** Calculate and plot the rate-distortion function $R(D)$.
  **(b)** Let the source code have length $N = 2$ and consist of two code words $b_1b_2$
and $b_2b_1$. Find the average distortion $\overline{d}$ and the rate $R$ for this code. Compare $R$
with $R(\overline{d})$ obtained in part (a).

**7.6.** Consider a DMS with alphabet $\{a_1, \ldots, a_K\}$ and uniform distribution $p_1 = p_2 =
\cdots = 1/K$. The reproducing alphabet is also $\{a_1, \ldots, a_K\}$ and the distortion mea-
sure is given by

$$d(a_k, a_j) = \begin{cases} 0, & k = j \\ 1, & k \neq j \end{cases}$$

What is the rate-distortion function $R(D)$ for this source? [*Hint:* You may use
Fano's inequality to bound $R(D)$.]

# 8

# LINEAR ERROR-CORRECTING CODES FOR THE BINARY SYMMETRIC CHANNEL

**Introduction**     In this chapter we introduce some elementary concepts from the theory of error-correcting codes. We do not intend to get involved in a detailed study of the techniques that have been developed over the past four decades for encoding and decoding of information. Rather, we want to introduce the reader to the practical problems involved in achieving the promise of information theory. Shannon's idea of random coding has been instrumental in proving the existence of good codes, but it does not help us find codes that can be implemented on systems with speed and memory constraints. The problem is that a randomly selected code, which with a high probability is a good code, lacks any useful structure that can be utilized for encoding and decoding purposes. Consequently, the brute-force method of looking up a table is about the best technique for its implementation. But to achieve significant improvements in performance, one must use long codes; the resulting tables will then be excessively large and the search times impractically long.

By imposing various constraints on the code, researchers have been able to develop highly structured and yet powerful error-correcting codes. The most significant of these constraints is the constraint of linearity, which will be discussed throughout this chapter in the context of codes for the binary symmetric channel. More general treatments of the subject, as well as detailed description of various error-correcting codes, can be found in the extensive literature of coding theory.

It has been shown that linear codes fulfill the promise of Shannon's theory; that is, the noisy channel theorem can be proved even when the randomly selected code words are confined to the class of linear codes. The price one generally pays for the convenience of linearity is the longer code words one has to use for a given error-correcting power. Many classes of linear error-correcting codes have been found to date, but unfortunately a general technique of designing good codes for arbitrary channels is yet to be discovered.

Our discussion of linear block codes for the binary symmetric channel begins with the introduction of linear block codes, also known as parity check codes. We discuss methods for encoding and decoding arbitrary parity check codes and study their error-correcting power. Later in the chapter, we introduce the idea of convolutional coding and describe an algorithm, known as the Viterbi algorithm, for decoding linear convolutional codes. Both block and convolutional codes are widely used in practice, and the decision as to which code is more appropriate in a given application depends on the specific problem at hand, as well as the cost/performance requirements.

## 8.1 HAMMING DISTANCE AND ERROR-CORRECTING POWER

Consider a binary symmetric channel with crossover probability $\varepsilon < 0.5$. Let a code of block length $N$ consisting of code words $W_1, \ldots, W_M$ be chosen for use over this channel. We saw in Section 6.5 that if a sequence $V_j$ is received at the output the maximum likelihood receiver decodes it as $W_i$, where $W_i$ is the closest code word to $V_j$ in the Hamming sense. For example, if the code words are $W_1 = 00000$, $W_2 = 10011$, $W_3 = 11100$, and $W_4 = 01111$, then $V_j = 01011$ is decoded as $W_4$ since $D(W_4, V_j) = 1$ and $D(W_i, V_j) > 1$ for $i \neq 4$. Similarly, $V_j = 00110$ may be decoded as either $W_1$ or $W_4$ since $D(W_1, V_j) = D(W_4, V_j) = 2$ and $D(W_2, V_j) = D(W_3, V_j) = 3$.*

*From R. Asn, *Information Theory*. New York: Interscience, 1965, p. 88. Reprinted by permission of John Wiley & Sons, Inc.

The Hamming distance has the characteristic properties of a distance function. For arbitrary sequences $V_1$, $V_2$, $V_3$, the properties are as follows:

(i)   $D(V_1, V_2) \geq 0$ with equality iff $V_1 = V_2$.

(ii)  $D(V_1, V_2) = D(V_2, V_1)$.

(iii) $D(V_1, V_2) \leq D(V_1, V_3) + D(V_3, V_2)$   (triangle inequality).

Another useful property is the following: $D(V_1, V_2) = D(V_1 \oplus V_3, V_2 \oplus V_3)$, where $\oplus$ is modulo 2 addition. For example, if $V_1 = 0111$, $V_2 = 1010$, and $V_3 = 1100$, then $V_1 \oplus V_3 = 1011$ and $V_2 \oplus V_3 = 0110$. It is easy to check that $D(0111, 1010) = D(1011, 0110) = 3$. The proof of the preceding relations is simple and the reader can take them up as an exercise.

The following theorem relates the error-correcting power of a code to the minimum Hamming distance between its code words.

**Theorem 1.**   Let $W_1, \ldots, W_M$ be binary code words of length $N$, and assume that a positive integer $v$ exists such that, for all $i \neq j$,

$$D(W_i, W_j) \geq 2v + 1 \qquad (8.1)$$

Then the code can correct all errors of magnitude $\leq v$. Conversely, any code with this error-correcting power must satisfy Eq. (8.1).

*Proof.*   Assume some code word, say $W_{i_0}$, is transmitted. If the magnitude of error is $\leq v$, the received sequence $V_j$ satisfies the relation $D(W_{i_0}, V_j) \leq v$. By the triangle inequality, we then have, for all $i \neq i_0$,

$$D(W_{i_0}, W_i) \leq D(W_{i_0}, V_j) + D(W_i, V_j)$$

Consequently,

$$D(W_i, V_j) \geq D(W_{i_0}, W_i) - D(W_{i_0}, V_j) \geq 2v + 1 - v = v + 1$$

Thus $W_{i_0}$ is closest to $V_j$ and as a result $V_j$ is decoded as $W_{i_0}$. All errors of magnitude $\leq v$ are thus correctable.

Conversely, assume that two code words, say $W_1$ and $W_2$, have a distance less than $2v + 1$ [i.e., $D(W_1, W_2) \leq 2v$]. Upon transmission of $W_1$, an error pattern of magnitude $v$ that only affects the positions where $W_1$ and $W_2$ differ will result in a received sequence $V_j$, where $D(W_2, V_j) \leq v$. Therefore, in this case at least, an error of magnitude $v$ cannot be corrected. The proof is now complete.

The next theorem is similar to the previous one, and its proof is left as an exercise.

**Theorem 2.**   Let $W_1, \ldots, W_M$ be binary code words of length $N$, and assume that a positive integer $v$ exists such that, for all $i \neq j$,

$$D(W_i, W_j) \geq 2v \qquad (8.2)$$

Then the code can correct all errors of magnitude $\leq \nu - 1$ and detect all errors of magnitude $\nu$. Conversely, any code with this error correcting/detecting capability must satisfy Eq. (8.2).

## 8.2 HAMMING UPPER BOUND ON THE NUMBER OF CODE WORDS

The following theorem is due to Hamming.

**Theorem.** If the code $\{W_1, \ldots, W_M\}$ consisting of binary sequences of length $N$ corrects all errors of magnitude $\nu$ and less, then the number of code words $M$ must satisfy the following inequality:

$$M \leq \frac{2^N}{\sum_{k=0}^{\nu} \binom{N}{k}} \tag{8.3}$$

*Proof.* For each code word $W_i$, define a set $B_i$ as the set of all sequences $V_j$ that differ from $W_i$ in at most $\nu$ places. The total number of sequences in $B_i$ is then given by

$$1 + N + \binom{N}{2} + \cdots + \binom{N}{\nu} = \sum_{k=0}^{\nu} \binom{N}{k}$$

Since the code is capable of correcting all errors of magnitude $\nu$ and less, the sets $B_1, \ldots, B_M$ corresponding to the code words $W_1, \ldots, W_M$ must be disjoint. The reason is that if $B_i$ and $B_j$ have a common element $V$ then $D(W_i, W_j) \leq D(W_i, V) + D(W_j, V) \leq \nu + \nu = 2\nu$, contradicting Theorem 1 of the previous section. The total number of elements in the sets $B_1, \ldots, B_M$ must now be less than or equal to the total number of sequences of length $N$; that is,

$$M \sum_{k=0}^{\nu} \binom{N}{k} \leq 2^N$$

which is equivalent to Eq. (8.3). The proof is thus complete.

The Hamming upper bound in Eq. (8.3) is a necessary but not sufficient condition. For instance, if $N = 4$ and $\nu = 1$, then $M = 3$ satisfies the Hamming condition. However, no single-error-correcting code of length $N = 4$ and size $M = 3$ exists. The reason is that the distance between all pairs of code words in such a code must be greater than or equal to $2\nu + 1 = 3$, and with sequences of length 4, three such code words are impossible to find. The maximum possible value of $M$ for the preceding values of $N$ and $\nu$ is 2.

## 8.3 PARITY CHECK CODES

So far in our discussions of coding we have not addressed the practical problems of encoding and decoding. We have assumed that a "table" or "code book" exists that at the transmitter associates a code word with every source sequence, and at the receiver associates every received sequence with a code word. In the case of minimum-distance decoding, for instance, every received sequence is associated with the closest code word in the Hamming sense. In general, when the code words are long, the storage and processing of data become excessively prohibitive. We now introduce the class of parity check codes that, thanks to their structure, have substantially improved the efficiency of encoding and decoding procedures.

Assuming that $r_1, r_2, \ldots, r_N$ represent the digits of a binary sequence of length $N$, a linear (parity check) code is defined as one whose code words are solutions of the following set of simultaneous linear equations:

$$a_{11}r_1 + a_{12}r_2 + \cdots + a_{1N}r_N = 0$$
$$\vdots \tag{8.4}$$
$$a_{m1}r_1 + a_{m2}r_2 + \cdots + a_{mN}r_N = 0$$

The coefficients $a_{ij}$ are given binary numbers (either 0 or 1), and the additions and multiplications are all modulo 2 operations. All solutions of Eqs. (8.4) must be included in the code.

**Example**

Consider the set of simultaneous linear equations*

$$\begin{aligned}
r_1 \quad\quad + r_4 + r_5 \quad\quad &= 0 \\
r_2 + r_3 + r_4 \quad\quad + r_6 &= 0 \quad (\text{mod } 2) \\
r_1 \quad + r_3 + r_4 \quad + r_6 &= 0
\end{aligned} \tag{8.5}$$

Any sequence of binary digits $r_1 r_2 \ldots r_6$ that satisfies these equations will be an acceptable code word. For instance, $W_1 = 001001$ and $W_2 = 111010$ are acceptable code words, whereas the sequence 101101 is not.

In Eqs. (8.4), if an equation is a linear combination of others, it may be deleted without affecting the solutions. The reason is that any solution that satisfies a certain set of equations will also satisfy linear combinations of those equations. We thus assume, without loss of generality, that the equations that describe a parity check code are linearly independent.

An immediate consequence of the preceding definition is that the sequence with $r_1 = r_2 = \cdots = r_N = 0$ always satisfies the equations. Therefore, a parity check code will always contain the trivial code word $W = 000 \ldots 0$.

*From R. Ash, *Information Theory*. New York: Interscience, 1965, p. 164. Reprinted by permission of John Wiley & Sons, Inc.

Using the notation of linear algebra, Eqs. (8.4) can be written as

$$
\begin{pmatrix} a_{11} & a_{12} & \cdots & a_{1N} \\ & \vdots & & \\ a_{m1} & a_{m2} & \cdots & a_{mN} \end{pmatrix} \begin{pmatrix} r_1 \\ \vdots \\ r_N \end{pmatrix} = 0 \qquad (\text{mod } 2) \qquad (8.6)
$$

The $m$ by $N$ matrix $A = [a_{ij}]$ is called the parity check matrix; it identifies the code uniquely, although it is not the only matrix that could give rise to the same code. Properties of the parity check matrix are discussed in the following section.

## 8.4 PROPERTIES OF THE PARITY CHECK MATRIX

Some important properties of the parity check matrix $A$ that will be useful later in the chapter are as follows:

(i)   No row of $A$ is entirely zero. If such a row exists, it could be eliminated without affecting the code.

(ii)  No row of $A$ is a linear combination of other rows. This is a consequence of the linear independence of Eqs. (8.4) discussed in the previous section. The rank of $A$ is equal to $m$, the number of linearly independent rows of the matrix. According to a well-known theorem of linear algebra, the number of linearly independent columns of $A$ is also equal to $m$. A proof of this theorem will be given later in this section.

(iii) The rows of $A$ could be arbitrarily rearranged without affecting the code. This should be obvious considering the fact that the solution of a set of simultaneous equations is independent of the order in which the equations are arranged.

(iv)  Any pair of rows could be combined (modulo 2 addition) and the resulting vector could replace either one of the rows. This will leave the code intact, since every solution of the new set of equations satisfies the old set, and vice versa. As an example, consider the matrix corresponding to the set of Eqs. (8.5):

$$
A = \begin{pmatrix} 1 & 0 & 0 & 1 & 1 & 0 \\ 0 & 1 & 1 & 1 & 0 & 1 \\ 1 & 0 & 1 & 1 & 0 & 1 \end{pmatrix} \qquad (8.7)
$$

Upon adding the first row to the third row, we obtain

$$A' = \begin{pmatrix} 1 & 0 & 0 & 1 & 1 & 0 \\ 0 & 1 & 1 & 1 & 0 & 1 \\ 0 & 0 & 1 & 0 & 1 & 1 \end{pmatrix} \tag{8.8}$$

Although $A$ and $A'$ are different in appearance, they represent the same code. This could be checked by finding all the solutions of the equations $AW^T = 0$ and $A'W^T = 0$ and verifying that the two sets of solutions are indeed the same. ($W$ is a $1 \times N$ row vector and $T$ denotes the transpose.)

(v)  A solution $W = (r_1, r_2, \ldots, r_N)$ represents a linear dependence among the columns of the matrix $A$. For example, if the nonzero elements of $W$ are $r_1, r_2, r_3$, and $r_5$, then the sum of columns $C_1, C_2, C_3$, and $C_5$ is equal to zero. On the other hand, if a group of columns is linearly independent, then no solution can express a linear dependence among them. As an example, consider the matrix $A$ in Eq. (8.7). Columns 1, 2, and 3 of this matrix are linearly independent; consequently, none of the sequences 100000, 010000, 001000, 110000, 101000, 011000, 111000 are solutions of $AW^T = 0$.

(vi)  By definition, variants of a matrix are those obtained by rearranging the rows [property (iii)] and/or combining the rows [property (iv)] in any order any number of times. The code that corresponds to the matrix $A$ is the same as the code corresponding to any of its variants. Since the rows of $A$ are linearly independent, we can easily show that the rows of any variant of $A$ are also linearly independent. Furthermore it is possible to show, using property (v), that any linear dependence or independence of the columns of $A$ remains valid for all its variants.

(vii)  Triangular variants of the parity check matrix are useful in explaining several properties of the codes. A triangular variant of $A$ can be constructed as follows:

(a)  Start with the first column. If the column has all 0's skip it. If the first element of the first column is not a 1, rearrange the rows such that the first element becomes a 1.

(b)  If the first column contains 1's other than the first element, make them equal to 0 by adding the first row to the corresponding rows.

(c)  Eliminate the first row and the first column from consideration. Repeat steps (a) and (b) for the remaining $(m - 1) \times (N - 1)$ matrix.

**Example**

The following sequence shows the process of constructing a triangular variant.

$$A = \begin{bmatrix} 0 & 0 & 1 & 0 & 1 & 0 \\ 1 & 1 & 0 & 1 & 1 & 0 \\ 1 & 0 & 0 & 0 & 0 & 1 \\ 0 & 0 & 1 & 0 & 0 & 1 \end{bmatrix}$$

Move second row to the top.

$$A_1 = \begin{bmatrix} 1 & 1 & 0 & 1 & 1 & 0 \\ 0 & 0 & 1 & 0 & 1 & 0 \\ 1 & 0 & 0 & 0 & 0 & 1 \\ 0 & 0 & 1 & 0 & 0 & 1 \end{bmatrix}$$

Add first row to third row.

$$A_2 = \begin{bmatrix} 1 & 1 & 0 & 1 & 1 & 0 \\ 0 & 0 & 1 & 0 & 1 & 0 \\ 0 & 1 & 0 & 1 & 1 & 1 \\ 0 & 0 & 1 & 0 & 0 & 1 \end{bmatrix} \qquad (8.9)$$

Exchange second and third rows.

$$A_3 = \begin{bmatrix} 1 & 1 & 0 & 1 & 1 & 0 \\ 0 & 1 & 0 & 1 & 1 & 1 \\ 0 & 0 & 1 & 0 & 1 & 0 \\ 0 & 0 & 1 & 0 & 0 & 1 \end{bmatrix}$$

Add third row to fourth row.

$$A_4 = \begin{bmatrix} 1 & 1 & 0 & 1 & 1 & 0 \\ 0 & 1 & 0 & 1 & 1 & 1 \\ 0 & 0 & 1 & 0 & 1 & 0 \\ 0 & 0 & 0 & 0 & 1 & 1 \end{bmatrix}$$

$A_4$ is now a triangular matrix. Its lower left triangle is all 0's, and its columns $C_1$, $C_2$, $C_3$, and $C_5$ are linearly independent. This is due to the fact that these columns have the "diagonal" elements of the triangular matrix. If, for some set of numbers $a$, $b$, $c$, $d$, we happen to have

$$a \begin{bmatrix} 1 \\ 0 \\ 0 \\ 0 \end{bmatrix} + b \begin{bmatrix} 1 \\ 1 \\ 0 \\ 0 \end{bmatrix} + c \begin{bmatrix} 0 \\ 0 \\ 1 \\ 0 \end{bmatrix} + d \begin{bmatrix} 1 \\ 1 \\ 1 \\ 1 \end{bmatrix} = \begin{bmatrix} 0 \\ 0 \\ 0 \\ 0 \end{bmatrix} \qquad (8.10)$$

then $d = 0$ because of the last row. Consequently, $c = 0$ from the third row, $b = 0$ from the second row, and, eventually, $a = 0$ from the first row. Since Eq. (8.10) is only valid for $a = b = c = d = 0$, we conclude that the preceding columns of the matrix are linearly independent. This is obviously quite general and applies to triangular variants of any matrix. Also observe that the remaining columns $C_4$ and $C_6$ of $A_4$ can be obtained by a linear combination of $C_1$, $C_2$, $C_3$, and $C_5$. To obtain $C_6$, for example we write

$$a \begin{bmatrix} 1 \\ 0 \\ 0 \\ 0 \end{bmatrix} + b \begin{bmatrix} 1 \\ 1 \\ 0 \\ 0 \end{bmatrix} + c \begin{bmatrix} 0 \\ 0 \\ 1 \\ 0 \end{bmatrix} + d \begin{bmatrix} 1 \\ 1 \\ 1 \\ 1 \end{bmatrix} = \begin{bmatrix} 0 \\ 1 \\ 0 \\ 1 \end{bmatrix} \tag{8.11}$$

and find that $d = 1$, $c = 1$, $b = 0$, and $a = 1$; that is, $C_6$ is the sum of $C_1$, $C_3$, and $C_5$. Again, this is quite general and could be applied to triangular variants of any matrix. Using these results together with property (vi), we conclude that the number of independent columns of the matrix $A$ is exactly equal to $m$, the number of (independent) rows of the matrix.

## 8.5  CONSTRUCTION OF PARITY CHECK CODES FROM THE MATRIX

The $m \times N$ matrix $A$ has $m$ independent columns, say, $C_{j1}, C_{j2}, \ldots, C_{jm}$. All other columns can be expressed as linear combinations of the independent columns. To determine the solutions $W = (r_1, r_2, \ldots, r_N)$ of the equation $AW^T = 0$, let us define the elements $r_{j1}, r_{j2}, \ldots, r_{jm}$ as check digits and the remaining $r$'s as information digits. We can then choose the information digits arbitrarily and solve the $m$ independent equations for the $m$ remaining unknowns (i.e., the $m$ check digits). In general there are $N - m$ information digits and hence $2^{N-m}$ code words. The rate of transfer of information is thus given by $R = 1 - (m/N)$ bits/symbol.

**Example**

Consider the $3 \times 6$ matrix

$$A = \begin{pmatrix} 1 & 0 & 0 & 1 & 1 & 0 \\ 0 & 1 & 1 & 1 & 0 & 1 \\ 1 & 0 & 1 & 1 & 0 & 1 \end{pmatrix} \tag{8.12}$$

Since columns $C_1$, $C_2$, and $C_3$ are linearly independent, we choose $r_1$, $r_2$, and $r_3$ as check digits. $r_4$, $r_5$, and $r_6$ will then be information digits and can be chosen arbitrarily. There are eight possible choices for the sequence $r_4 r_5 r_6$, and therefore there are eight code words altogether, as follows:*

*From R. Ash, *Information Theory*. New York: Interscience, 1965, p. 93. Reprinted by permission of John Wiley & Sons, Inc.

|       | $r_1$ | $r_2$ | $r_3$ | $r_4$ | $r_5$ | $r_6$ |
|-------|-------|-------|-------|-------|-------|-------|
| $W_1$ | 0 | 0 | 0 | 0 | 0 | 0 |
| $W_2$ | 0 | 0 | 1 | 0 | 0 | 1 |
| $W_3$ | 1 | 1 | 1 | 0 | 1 | 0 |
| $W_4$ | 1 | 1 | 0 | 0 | 1 | 1 |
| $W_5$ | 1 | 1 | 0 | 1 | 0 | 0 |
| $W_6$ | 1 | 1 | 1 | 1 | 0 | 1 |
| $W_7$ | 0 | 0 | 1 | 1 | 1 | 0 |
| $W_8$ | 0 | 0 | 0 | 1 | 1 | 1 |

## 8.6 EQUIVALENCE OF GROUP CODES AND PARITY CHECK CODES

A binary group code is a code $\{W_1, \ldots, W_M\}$ whose code words are binary sequences of equal length that form an algebraic group under modulo 2 addition.

**Definition.**   A group is a set $G$ with an operation, usually referred to as addition, defined on the set. A group must have the following properties:

(i) *Closure:* If $\alpha$ and $\beta$ belong to $G$, then $\alpha + \beta$ must belong to $G$.

(ii) *Associativity:* For all $\alpha$, $\beta$, $\gamma$ belonging to $G$, we must have $(\alpha + \beta) + \gamma = \alpha + (\beta + \gamma)$.

(iii) *Identity element:* There exists an element $\theta$ in $G$ such that, for all $\alpha$ in $G$, $\alpha + \theta = \theta + \alpha = \alpha$.

(iv) *Inverse:* For each $\alpha$ in $G$, there exists an element $\alpha'$ in $G$ such that $\alpha + \alpha' = \alpha' + \alpha = \theta$. $\alpha'$ is called the inverse of $\alpha$.

If the group has the additional property that $\alpha + \beta = \beta + \alpha$ for all $\alpha$, $\beta$ in $G$, then the group is said to be Abelian or commutative.

The set of integers (positive, zero, and negative) under ordinary addition forms an Abelian group, as does the set of all binary sequences of fixed length under modulo 2 addition.

The following theorems establish the equivalence of group codes and parity check codes.

**Theorem 1.**   The set $S$ of code words of a parity check code is an Abelian group under modulo 2 addition.

*Proof.* Let $A$ be the matrix of the code. If $W_i$ and $W_j$ belong to $S$, then $AW_i^T = AW_j^T = 0$. Consequently, $A(W_i^T \oplus W_j^T) = AW_i^T \oplus AW_j^T = 0$; that is, the modulo 2 sum of $W_i$ and $W_j$ is itself a code word and thus belongs to $S$ (closure). Associativity and commutativity follow from the definition of modulo 2 addition. The word $W = 000\ldots0$ is the identity element, and each element $W_i$ is its own inverse (i.e., $W_i \oplus W_i = 0$). $S$ is therefore an Abelian group.

**Theorem 2.**    The set $S$ of $M$ binary sequences of length $N$ that forms a group under modulo 2 addition is a parity check code; that is, there exists a parity check matrix for $S$.

*Proof.* Arrange the code words in an $M \times N$ matrix where each row is a code word of the group code $S$. Assuming that the matrix has rank $K$, there will be $K$ independent rows (columns). All other rows (columns) can be expressed as a linear combination of the $K$ independent rows (columns). For simplicity of notation, we assume that the independent rows are $W_1, W_2, \ldots, W_K$. Since $S$ is a group code, every linear combination of its code words must be a code word; that is, $W = \lambda_1 W_1 \oplus \lambda_2 W_2 \oplus \cdots \oplus \lambda_K W_K$, where $\lambda_i$'s are binary constants, must be a row of the matrix. On the other hand, every row of the matrix must be expressible as a linear combination of $W_1, \ldots, W_K$. Since every distinct choice of $(\lambda_1, \ldots, \lambda_K)$ results in a distinct code word (a consequence of linear independence of $W_1, \ldots, W_K$), we conclude that the total number of code words $M$ is $2^K$.

To prove that $S$ is a parity check code, we must find the parity check Eqs. (8.4). If we find a set of equations satisfied by $W_1, \ldots, W_K$, then all other code words will also satisfy the equations because they are linear combinations of the first $K$ code words. Now consider the $K \times N$ matrix whose rows are $W_1, \ldots, W_K$. This is usually known as the generator matrix. Since there are $K$ independent rows, there are $K$ independent columns. The remaining $N - K$ columns can be expressed as linear combinations of the $K$ independent columns. This will give us $N - K$ equations that are simultaneously satisfied by the columns or, equivalently, by $r_1, r_2, \ldots, r_N$. These equations are linearly independent since each contains an element $r_j$ that does not appear in any other equation. Since the total number of solutions to these equations is $2^{N-m} = 2^{N-(N-K)} = 2^K$ and there are $2^K$ code words in $S$, the equations cannot have a solution outside $S$. Therefore, the parity check code obtained from the equations and the group code $S$ are equivalent.

**Example**

Consider the group code $S$ whose code words are as follows (you can check that the code words indeed form a group).

|       | $r_1$ | $r_2$ | $r_3$ | $r_4$ | $r_5$ | $r_6$ |
|-------|-------|-------|-------|-------|-------|-------|
| $W_1$ | 1     | 0     | 1     | 0     | 0     | 1     |
| $W_2$ | 1     | 1     | 0     | 0     | 1     | 0     |
| $W_3$ | 0     | 1     | 0     | 1     | 0     | 1     |
| $W_4$ | 0     | 1     | 1     | 0     | 1     | 1     |
| $W_5$ | 1     | 1     | 1     | 1     | 0     | 0     |
| $W_6$ | 1     | 0     | 0     | 1     | 1     | 1     |
| $W_7$ | 0     | 0     | 1     | 1     | 1     | 0     |
| $W_8$ | 0     | 0     | 0     | 0     | 0     | 0     |

There are eight code words; therefore, there must be three independent rows. It can easily be checked that $W_1$, $W_2$, and $W_3$ are linearly independent. Therefore, we must find a set of linear equations for $r_1, r_2, \ldots, r_6$ that is satisfied by $W_1$, $W_2$, and $W_3$. Observe that in the generating matrix

|       | $r_1$ | $r_2$ | $r_3$ | $r_4$ | $r_5$ | $r_6$ |
|-------|-------|-------|-------|-------|-------|-------|
| $W_1$ | 1     | 0     | 1     | 0     | 0     | 1     |
| $W_2$ | 1     | 1     | 0     | 0     | 1     | 0     |
| $W_3$ | 0     | 1     | 0     | 1     | 0     | 1     |

columns 4, 5, and 6 are independent. Therefore, columns 1, 2, and 3 can be expressed in terms of the independent columns as follows:

$$r_1 + r_4 + r_5 + r_6 = 0$$
$$r_2 + r_4 + r_5 = 0$$
$$r_3 + r_4 + r_6 = 0$$

The parity check matrix is thus given by

$$A = \begin{pmatrix} 1 & 0 & 0 & 1 & 1 & 1 \\ 0 & 1 & 0 & 1 & 1 & 0 \\ 0 & 0 & 1 & 1 & 0 & 1 \end{pmatrix}$$

## 8.7 DECODING OF PARITY CHECK CODES: DECODING SETS

Consider the set $S$ of the code words $W_1, W_2, \ldots, W_M$ of a parity check code with matrix $A$. The matrix is $m \times N$, and therefore all code words have length $N$ with $M = 2^{N-m}$. Consider an arbitrary binary sequence $Z$ of length $N$ and form the set $Z \oplus S \overset{\triangle}{=} \{Z \oplus W_1, Z \oplus W_2, \ldots, Z \oplus W_M\}$. The set $Z \oplus S$ has the following properties:

(i)  $Z$ itself belongs to $Z \oplus S$. The reason is that the trivial code word $W_i = 000\ldots0$ is always a member of $S$ and $Z \oplus 000\ldots0 = Z$.

(ii) If $Z$ belongs to $S$ (i.e., if $Z$ is a code word itself), then $Z \oplus S = S$. The reason is that the modulo 2 sum of any two code words must be a code word. Moreover, $Z \oplus W_i \neq Z \oplus W_j$ if $W_i \neq W_j$; therefore, no two elements of $Z \oplus S$ can be identical.

(iii) If $V$ belongs to $Z \oplus S$, then $V \oplus S = Z \oplus S$. The reason is that $V = Z \oplus W_i$ for some code word $W_i$. Therefore, $V \oplus S = Z \oplus W_i \oplus S$. But $W_i \oplus S = S$; therefore, $V \oplus S = Z \oplus S$.

(iv) If $V$ does not belong to $Z \oplus S$, then $V \oplus S$ and $Z \oplus S$ are disjoint. The reason is that if the two sets were not disjoint there would be a sequence $U$ belonging to both. Then $U \oplus S = Z \oplus S$ and $U \oplus S = V \oplus S$ from property (iii). Therefore, $Z \oplus S$ and $V \oplus S$ must be equal. But $V$ belongs to $V \oplus S$ from property (i) and does not belong to $Z \oplus S$ by assumption. This is a contradiction, and thus $Z \oplus S$ and $V \oplus S$ must be disjoint.

For reasons to become clear later, the set $Z \oplus S$ is called a decoding set. Using the terminology of group theory, $Z \oplus S$ is sometimes referred to as the coset of $Z$ with respect to $S$. For a given code $S$, one can construct several distinct cosets. Such cosets are mutually disjoint and, since every binary sequence of lengh $N$ must belong to one coset or another, the total number of cosets is equal to $2^N/M = 2^N/2^{N-m} = 2^m$, where $M$ is the number of elements of each coset and $m$ is the rank of the parity check matrix.

The minimum-distance decoding scheme for parity check codes is intimately related to the concept of cosets. Consider a sequence $V_j$ of length $N$ at the receiving end of the channel. To compare $V_j$ with the code word $W_i$, we can form the error-pattern vector $V_j \oplus W_i$. The error-pattern vector is zero at positions where $V_j$ and $W_i$ are the same and is 1 where $V_j$ and $W_i$ are different. For example, if $V_j = 01011$ and $W_i = 10010$, then the error-pattern vector would be $V_j \oplus W_i = 11001$. The number of 1's in the error-pattern vector is the distance between $V_j$ and $W_i$. In the preceding example, the distance between $V_j$ and $W_i$ is 3. The minimum-distance decoding can thus be described as follows: Given a received sequence $V_j$, (1) form all the sequences $V_j \oplus W_i$ (i.e., form the coset $V_j \oplus S$). (2) Choose the member of this coset with the least number of 1's; this member is known as the coset leader. (3) Announce the transmitted sequence as $Z \oplus V_j$, where $Z$ is the coset leader.

Obviously, the coset leader is the error-pattern vector that the minimum-distance decoder associates with $V_j$. Remember that all members of the coset $V_j \oplus S$ have the same coset as $V_j$ (property iii). Therefore, all members of a coset are associated with the same error-pattern vector by the minimum-distance decoder. It is now clear why the cosets are called decoding sets. The decoder does not have to know everything about the received sequence $V_j$; all it needs is the knowledge of the coset (or decoding set) to which $V_j$ belongs. Since each coset is associated with a unique error-pattern vector (coset leader), the decoder can then add the proper error pattern to $V_j$ to obtain the transmitted code word.

**Example**

Consider the following parity check matrix:

$$A = \begin{pmatrix} 1 & 0 & 1 & 0 \\ 0 & 1 & 1 & 1 \end{pmatrix} \tag{8.13}$$

The code words associated with $A$ are $W_1 = 0000$, $W_2 = 0101$, $W_3 = 1110$, and $W_4 = 1011$. All cosets of this code are listed next and the coset leaders are underlined.

$$S = \{\underline{0000}, 0101, 1110, 1011\}$$

$$S_1 = \{0001, \underline{0100}, 1111, 1010\}$$

$$S_2 = \{1001, 1100, 0111, \underline{0010}\}$$

$$S_3 = \{0110, 0011, \underline{1000}, 1101\}$$

Notice that in the case of $S_1$ we have a choice between 0001 and 0100 for the coset leader. As far as the decoding algorithm is concerned, there is no difference between the two and we could have selected either.

It is seen that the cosets are disjoint and, together, they contain all possible sequences of length 4. If the sequence $V_j = 0111$, for example, is received, the decoder must somehow realize that $V_j$ belongs to $S_2$. Once this is achieved, the corresponding error sequence 0010 will be added to $V_j$ and the decision announced as $0010 \oplus 0111 = 0101 = W_2$. You can check that $W_2$ is in fact the closest code word to $V_j$.

We now turn our attention to the problem of identification of the coset for a received sequence $V_j$. Obviously, this can be done through a table lookup, which is a slow and usually impractical technique. Fortunately, there is an easier way. It turns out that each coset is uniquely identified by an $m \times 1$ vector called the corrector.[†] The corrector $C_j$ for a given $V_j$ is defined as $C_j = AV_j^T$. The same corrector belongs to other members of the coset $V_j \oplus S$ since

$$A(V_j^T \oplus W_i^T) = AV_j^T \oplus AW_i^T = AV_j^T = C_j$$

Thus all elements of $V_j \oplus S$ have the same corrector $C_j$. On the other hand, if $V_k$ does not belong to $V_j \oplus S$, then $C_j = AV_j^T$ is different from $C_k = AV_k^T$; for if $C_j = C_k$, then $A(V_j^T \oplus V_k^T) = 0$, which means that $V_j \oplus V_k = W_i$ or $V_k = V_j \oplus W_i$ (i.e., $V_k$ belongs to $V_j \oplus S$) which is a contradiction.

The corrector vectors are binary sequences of length $m$ ($m$ is the rank of $A$) and there are $2^m$ such sequences. The number of cosets associated with the matrix $A$ was also found to be $2^m$. Therefore, there is a one-to-one correspondence between the cosets of the code associated with $A$ and all binary sequences of length $m$.

The parity check decoder must keep a table that associates all binary sequences of length $m$ (the correctors) with the corresponding error-pattern

[†]In the literature, the corrector is also known as syndrome.

vectors (coset leaders). Upon receiving a sequence $V_j$, the decoder computes its corrector $C_j = AV_j^T$. It then searches the table to find the error-pattern vector $Z_j$ corresponding to the corrector $C_j$. The minimum-distance decision will then be the code word $W_i = V_j \oplus Z_j$.

The amount of storage for the preceding decoding technique is on the order of $2^m$, which could be significantly lower than $2^N$, the storage needed for a direct table-lookup approach.

For the code corresponding to the matrix $A$ in Eq. (8.13), the correctors and their error-pattern vectors are as follows:

| C | Z |
|---|---|
| 00 | 0000 |
| 01 | 0100 |
| 10 | 1000 |
| 11 | 0010 |

This code can thus correct some of the single errors. All other errors will be neither detected nor corrected.

**Example**

Consider the parity check matrix

$$A = \begin{pmatrix} 1 & 0 & 0 & 0 & 1 & 1 \\ 0 & 1 & 0 & 0 & 1 & 0 \\ 0 & 0 & 1 & 0 & 1 & 1 \\ 0 & 0 & 0 & 1 & 0 & 1 \end{pmatrix} \qquad (8.14)$$

The code words are $W_1 = 000000$, $W_2 = 111010$, $W_3 = 101101$, and $W_4 = 010111$. The cosets associated with this code are listed in Table 8.1. The coset leaders are all in the leftmost column. The correctors associated with the cosets are shown on the right. Note that this code is capable of correcting all single errors along with some (but not all) double and triple errors. If this code were used on a binary symmetric channel with crossover probability $\varepsilon$, the probability of message error $P_E$ would have been obtained from

$$1 - P_E = (1 - \varepsilon)^6 + 6\varepsilon(1 - \varepsilon)^5 + 7\varepsilon^2(1 - \varepsilon)^4 + 2\varepsilon^3(1 - \varepsilon)^3 \qquad (8.15)$$

Here $1 - P_E$ is the probability of correct detection, the first term on the right side is the probability of correct detection corresponding to correct transmission, the second term is the probability of correct detection corresponding to single errors in transmission, the third term is the probability of correct detection corresponding to double errors in transmission, and so on. If coding is not used, the transmission of four messages requires 2 bits and the probability of correct transmission would be

$$1 - P_E = (1 - \varepsilon)^2 \qquad (8.16)$$

For $\varepsilon = 0.01$, Eq. (8.15) yields $P_E = 7.86 \times 10^{-4}$, whereas from Eq. (8.16), $P_E = 1.99 \times 10^{-2}$. This improvement in error probability is achieved at the cost of reducing the data rate to one-third.

TABLE 8.1

| Code<br>Words | 000000 | 111010 | 101101 | 010111 | Correctors<br>0000 |
|---|---|---|---|---|---|
| Single<br>errors | 100000 | 011010 | 001101 | 110111 | 1000 |
| | 010000 | 101010 | 111101 | 000111 | 0100 |
| | 001000 | 110010 | 100101 | 011111 | 0010 |
| | 000100 | 111110 | 101001 | 010011 | 0001 |
| | 000010 | 111000 | 101111 | 010101 | 1110 |
| | 000001 | 111011 | 101100 | 010110 | 1011 |
| Double<br>errors | 110000 | 001010 | 011101 | 100111 | 1100 |
| | 101000 | 010010 | 000101 | 111111 | 1010 |
| | 100100 | 011110 | 001001 | 110011 | 1001 |
| | 100010 | 011000 | 001111 | 110101 | 0110 |
| | 100001 | 011011 | 001100 | 110110 | 0011 |
| | 010100 | 101110 | 111001 | 000011 | 0101 |
| | 010001 | 101011 | 111100 | 000110 | 1111 |
| Triple<br>errors | 110100 | 001110 | 011001 | 100011 | 1101 |
| | 110001 | 001011 | 011100 | 100110 | 0111 |

*Source:* R. Ash, *Information Theory,* Wiley-Interscience, New York, 1965.

## 8.8 ERROR-CORRECTING POWER OF
## PARITY CHECK CODES

In Section 8.1 we saw that to correct all errors of magnitude $\nu$ and less, a code $\{W_1, \ldots, W_M\}$ must satisfy

$$D(W_i, W_j) \geq 2\nu + 1, \qquad \text{for all } i \neq j$$

For parity check codes, this condition can be stated in terms of the minimum code-word weight, where the weight of a code word is the number of 1's in it. For instance, the weight of $W_i = 1001100$ is 3.

The minimum distance between code words of a parity check code is equal to the weight of the code word with the least number of 1's (excluding the trivial word $W = 000 \ldots 0$). The reason is that, if the distance between $W_i$ and $W_j$ is $D$, then the code word $W_k = W_i \oplus W_j$ has a weight equal to $D$ that cannot be less than the minimum weight. On the other hand, the minimum-weight code word itself has a distance from the trivial code word equal to its own weight. As an example, consider the parity check code $\{0000, 0101, 1110, 1011\}$. The minimum-weight code word is 0101, which has a weight of 2, and the minimum distance is indeed equal to 2.

In light of the preceding result, Theorem 1 of Section 8.1 can be stated as follows: A necessary and sufficient condition for a parity check code to correct all errors of magnitude $\nu$ and less is to have a minimum weight greater than or equal to $2\nu + 1$.

If the code word with minimum weight has at least $2\nu + 1$ ones, then no code word (except the trivial one) can have $2\nu$ or less 1's. Since the 1's in a code word represent a linear dependence among the columns of the matrix $A$ [see Section 8.4, property (v)], the preceding theorem can be restated as follows: A necessary and sufficient condition for a parity check code to correct all errors of magnitude $\nu$ and less is that every set of $2\nu$ columns of the matrix $A$ be linearly independent.

**Example**

The following parity check matrix represents a double-error-correcting code with seven check digits and three information digits.

$$
A = \begin{bmatrix}
1 & 0 & 0 & 0 & 0 & 0 & 0 & 1 & 0 & 1 \\
0 & 1 & 0 & 0 & 0 & 0 & 0 & 0 & 0 & 1 \\
0 & 0 & 1 & 0 & 0 & 0 & 0 & 1 & 0 & 1 \\
0 & 0 & 0 & 1 & 0 & 0 & 0 & 0 & 1 & 1 \\
0 & 0 & 0 & 0 & 1 & 0 & 0 & 1 & 1 & 0 \\
0 & 0 & 0 & 0 & 0 & 1 & 0 & 0 & 1 & 0 \\
0 & 0 & 0 & 0 & 0 & 0 & 1 & 1 & 1 & 0
\end{bmatrix}
\tag{8.17}
$$

It may be verified that any four columns of this matrix are linearly independent.*

## 8.9 HAMMING LOWER BOUND ON THE NUMBER OF CHECK DIGITS

The following theorem is due to Hamming:

**Theorem.**    If a parity check code of block length $N$ corrects all errors of magnitude $\nu$ and less, then the number of check digits $m$ must satisfy the following inequality:

$$
2^m \geq \sum_{k=0}^{\nu} \binom{N}{k}
\tag{8.18}
$$

*Proof.* To correct an error pattern $Z$, we must have a distinct corrector $C = AZ^T$ corresponding to that error pattern. To correct all errors of magnitude $k$, we need $\binom{N}{k}$ distinct correctors. To correct all errors of magnitude $\nu$ and less, we need $\sum_{k=0}^{\nu} \binom{N}{k}$ distinct correctors. But there are $2^m$ correctors altogether; therefore inequality (8.18) must be satisfied. The proof is now complete.

Notice that the preceding lower bound on $m$ is necessary but not sufficient. For instance, if $N = 10$ and $\nu = 2$, we find from Eq. (8.18) that $m \geq 6$

*From R. Ash, *Information Theory*. New York: Interscience, 1965, p. 183. Reprinted by permission of John Wiley & Sons, Inc.

is necessary. However, it may be verified (by trial and error, for example) that the smallest number of check digits for a double-error-correcting parity check code of block length 10 is $m = 7$.

The Hamming lower bound on the number of check digits for a parity check code is, in fact, identical to the Hamming upper bound on the number of code words for a general binary code, which was described in Section 8.2. To see this, observe that $M = 2^{N-m}$ and therefore inequalities (8.3) and (8.18) are equivalent.

## 8.10 VARSHARMOV–GILBERT UPPER BOUND ON THE NUMBER OF CHECK DIGITS

**Theorem.** A sufficient condition for the constructability of a parity check code with block length $N$ that corrects all errors of magnitude $\nu$ and less is that $m$, the number of check digits, satisfy the strict inequality

$$2^m > \sum_{k=0}^{2\nu-1} \binom{N-1}{k} \tag{8.19}$$

*Proof.* We describe a construction procedure for the parity check matrix and show that a $\nu$-error-correcting code can be constructed if Eq. (8.19) is satisfied. The construction procedure consists of selecting successive columns of the matrix $A$ in a way that makes every set of $2\nu$ columns linearly independent. As we have shown in Section 8.8, a matrix with this property corresponds to a $\nu$-error-correcting code. Obviously, none of the columns can be entirely zero; otherwise, a single error will be confused with correct transmission. The first column $C_1$ is thus chosen arbitrarily from the set of all nonzero vectors of length $m$. The second column $C_2$ is chosen such that $C_2 \neq 0$ and $C_2 \neq C_1$. This can be done provided $2^m > 2$. The third column $C_3$ is chosen such that $C_3 \neq 0$, $C_3 \neq C_1$, and $C_3 \neq C_2$. If $\nu \geq 2$, then we must also have $C_3 \neq C_1 + C_2$ to assure that the three columns are linearly independent. This can be done provided $2^m > 4$. The procedure continues until all columns are selected. Each column is chosen with the aid of the previously selected columns in such a way that all combinations of $2\nu$ columns are forced to be linearly independent. At each stage of the process, the previously selected columns bar a number of vectors from candidacy for the next selection. The excluded vectors increase in number as we proceed; therefore, in the last stage, when we must choose $C_N$, the number of excluded vectors is the largest, and if at least one vector is still left to choose for $C_N$, the process will end successfully. The excluded vectors for the final stage are as follows:

$C_N \neq 0,$

$C_N \neq C_i,$        $i = 1, 2, \ldots, N - 1$

$C_N \neq C_i + C_j,$      $i, j = 1, 2, \ldots, N - 1$   and   $i \neq j$

$C_N \neq C_i + C_j + C_k,$    $i, j, k = 1, 2, \ldots, N - 1$   and

           $i, j, k$ distinct

$$\vdots$$

$C_N \neq C_{i_1} + C_{i_2} + \cdots + C_{i_{2\nu-1}}, \quad i_1, i_2, \ldots, i_{2\nu-1} = 1, 2, \ldots, N - 1$   and

              $i_1, i_2, \ldots, i_{2\nu-1}$ distinct

At worst, all these combinations will be distinct, in which case the total number of excluded vectors will be

$$1 + \binom{N-1}{1} + \binom{N-1}{2} + \cdots + \binom{N-1}{2\nu-1} = \sum_{k=0}^{2\nu-1} \binom{N-1}{k}$$

Since there are $2^m$ vectors of length $m$, we can choose the last column $C_N$ if Eq. (8.19) is satisifed. The proof is thus complete.

**Example**

If $N = 10$ and $\nu = 2$, the upper bound for $m$ is 8, which means that for $m \geq 8$ and $N = 10$ a double-error-correcting parity check matrix can be constructed. The preceding theorem does not exclude, however, the possibility of finding a parity check code with $m < 8$. From the Hamming bound, we know that $m$ must be larger than or equal to 6. In fact, a double-error-correcting parity check code of length $N = 10$ exists with $m = 7$ check digits. [See the matrix in Eq. (8.17).]

We close our discussion of parity check codes by noting that in the special case of $\nu = 1$ (single-error-correcting codes) the Hamming lower bound is $2^m \geq 1 + N$ and the Varsharmov–Gilbert upper bound is $2^m > N$. Since $2^m$ is an integer, the two bounds are equal, and the minimum value of $m$ is uniquely determined by $m = \lceil \log_2(N + 1) \rceil$. This can be seen in a much simpler way by observing that the columns of a single-error-correcting code must satisfy only two requirements: (1) all columns are distinct and (2) no column is entirely zero. For a further discussion of single-error-correcting codes, see Problem 8.1.

## 8.11 CONVOLUTIONAL ENCODER

In the remaining part of this chapter we will discuss convolutional codes, which are different from block codes in the sense that here one cannot divide the stream of data into separate blocks and associate independent code words with them. The distinction will become clear once we introduce a convolutional encoder later in the section. The mapping of the entire sequence of data into a

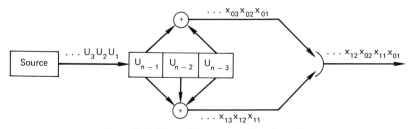

**Figure 8.1**   Linear binary convolutional encoder.

code sequence, however, can be thought of as one giant block code, and it is in this sense that linear convolutional codes and linear block codes are similar. Convolutional codes are powerful error-correcting codes with relatively simple encoding and decoding schemes and have found application in many communication systems. We introduce the concept of convolutional codes by means of simple examples and describe an optimum decoding technique known as the Viterbi algorithm. We will not discuss topics such as the error-correcting power of convolutional codes and sequential decoding techniques; the interested reader is referred to the vast literature on coding theory for further information [3, 5].

The following example of a linear binary convolutional code will bring out the important features of the convolutional technique. Consider a sequence of binary information digits $U_1 U_2 U_3 \ldots$ at the output of an information source, with $\tau_s$ being the fixed duration of each digit. The information sequence enters a three-digit shift register as shown in Figure 8.1. The shift register is initially reset to 000. At $t = (n - 1)\tau_s$, the $n$th information digit $U_n$ enters the shift register and creates two code letters $X_{0n} = U_n \oplus U_{n-2}$ and $X_{1n} = U_n \oplus U_{n-1} \oplus U_{n-2}$, which are then transmitted during the time intervals $[(n - 1)\tau_s, (n - 0.5)\tau_s]$ and $[(n - 0.5)\tau_s, n\tau_s]$, respectively. Since for every information digit there are two code digits, this code is a (2, 1) convolutional code; in other words, the rate of the code is $R = \frac{1}{2}$. Since at every stage the encoder remembers the previous two input letters, the code is said to have a memory or constraint length of 3. Notice that the stream of data cannot be partitioned into nonoverlapping blocks with each block corresponding to a block of code letters. It is in this respect that convolutional codes differ from block codes.

## 8.12 STATE AND LADDER DIAGRAMS

A convolutional encoder can be identified with a state diagram. In Figure 8.1 the contents of the leftmost two registers, $U_{n-1}$ and $U_{n-2}$, determine the state of the encoder in the time interval $(n - 2)\tau_s < t < (n - 1)\tau_s$; thus the state is $U_{n-1} U_{n-2}$ just before $U_n$ arrives, and upon arrival of $U_n$ the state moves to $U_n U_{n-1}$. The knowledge of the previous state and the present state is therefore sufficient information for determining the encoder input and output at each stage. Figure 8.2 shows the state diagram of the encoder of Figure 8.1. There are four

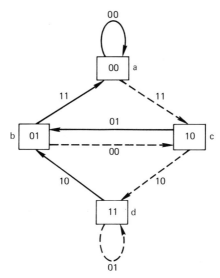

**Figure 8.2**    State diagram. (From R. J. McEliece, *The Theory of Information and Coding,* Addison-Wesley, Reading, Mass., 1977.)

states corresponding to four different values of $U_{n-1} U_{n-2}$; these states are labeled $a$, $b$, $c$, $d$ and are represented by boxes in Figure 8.2. The lines that join these boxes show possible transitions from state to state upon arrival of a new information digit. A solid line represents a 0 input, while a broken line represents a 1 input. Each line has a two-digit label that represents the resulting output $X_{0n} X_{1n}$. For example, if the input sequence is 110100 and the initial state of the system is $S_0 = a$, the state follows the path $acdbcba$ and the encoder output will be 111010000111.

The ladder diagram is the extension of the state diagram in time. The ladder diagram for the encoder of Figure 8.1 is shown in Figure 8.3. Each column of four dots in Figure 8.3 represents the states of the system at $t = j\tau_s$ with $j = 0, 1, 2, \ldots$. In going from $S_j$ to $S'_{j+1}$, a solid line represents a 0 input and a broken line represents a 1 input. The 2-bit sequences on the lines correspond to the output at each transition. The encoder output stream can be found by tracing the appropriate path through the ladder. For example, the input stream 110100 . . . corresponds to the path $a_0 c_1 d_2 b_3 c_4 b_5 a_6$ . . . and the output sequence 111010000111 . . . .

In practice, it is necessary to work with a truncated version of a convolutional code. If the stream of information is truncated after $N$ digits, it is usually preferred to input a sufficient number of zeros so that the last bit can pass through the shift register. For the encoder of Figure 8.1, the required number of zeros is 2, and the last few stages of the ladder diagram for a code truncated after $N$ input letters are shown in Figure 8.4. Notice that in the last two stages all the lines are solid; this is because the last two input letters are zeros. The truncated convolutional code can, in fact, be thought of as a single-block code

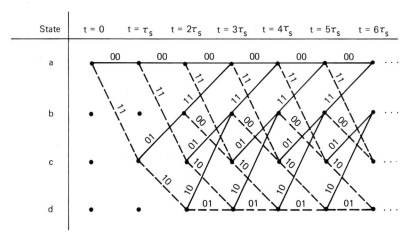

**Figure 8.3**  Ladder diagram. (From R. J. McEliece, *The Theory of Information and Coding*, Addison-Wesley, Reading, Mass., 1977.)

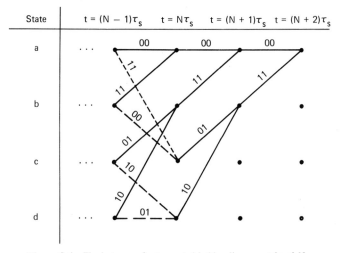

**Figure 8.4**  Final stages of a truncated ladder diagram at level $N$.

of length $2N + 4$ with $N$ information digits. The rate, $R = N/(2N + 4)$, approaches $\frac{1}{2}$ as $N \to \infty$. Moreover, it is not difficult to show that this linear block code is in fact a parity check code (see Problem 8.17).

## 8.13 MAXIMUM LIKELIHOOD DECODING AND THE VITERBI ALGORITHM

The Viterbi algorithm is a maximum likelihood (minimum distance) decision scheme for convolutional codes. If the sequence $V_j = (y_{01} y_{11} \ldots y_{0,N+2} y_{1,N+2})$ is received at the channel output, the decoder must identify a sequence of states $S_0 S_1 \ldots S_{N+2}$ that corresponds to the code word $W_i = x_{01} x_{11} \ldots x_{0,N+2}, x_{1,N+2}$

with minimum distance from $V_j$. The sequence of states $S_0 S_1 \ldots S_{N+2}$ is not arbitrary; it represents a continuous path in the ladder diagram. Moreover, the initial and final states are always known in advance: $S_0 = S_{N+2} = a$.

For a given received sequence $V_j$, we assign a "length" to each branch of the ladder diagram. A branch that connects the state $S$ in level $(j - 1)$ (i.e., $S_{j-1}$) to state $S'$ in level $j$ (i.e., $S_j'$) will have a length equal to the Hamming distance between its corresponding encoder output $(x_{0j} x_{1j})$ and the corresponding 2 bits in the received sequence $(y_{0j} y_{1j})$. Figure 8.5 shows the ladder diagram of the encoder of Figure 8.1, truncated at $N = 6$. A received sequence $V_j = 1011001110111100$ is also shown.

As an example, consider the branch that connects $d_2$ to $b_3$. For this branch, $x_{03} x_{13} = 10$ and $y_{03} y_{13} = 00$; therefore, the length of $d_2 b_3$ is 1. Figure 8.6 shows the lengths of all the branches of Figure 8.5.

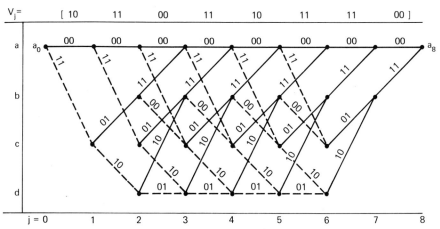

**Figure 8.5**    (From R. J. McEliece, *The Theory of Information and Coding,* Addison-Wesley, Reading, Mass., 1977.)

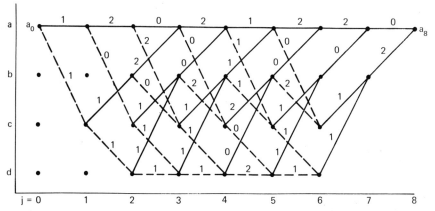

**Figure 8.6**    (From R. J. McEliece, *The Theory of Information and Coding,* Addison-Wesley, Reading, Mass., 1977.)

The minimum-distance decoding scheme can now be stated as follows: For a given received sequence $V_j$, determine the sequence of states $a_0 S_1 S_2 \ldots S_N S_{N+1} a_{N+2}$ that connects $a_0$ to $a_{N+2}$ through a continuous path of minimum total length.

### Example

It is possible to verify in Figure 8.6 that the path $a_0 a_1 c_2 b_3 a_4 c_5 b_6 a_7 a_8$ is the shortest path between $a_0$ and $a_8$. The total length of this path is equal to 4.

The problem of maximum likelihood decoding is now reduced to the problem of identification of the shortest path between $a_0$ and $a_{N+2}$. Viterbi recognized that if $a_0 S_1 S_2 \ldots S_j \ldots S_{N+1} a_{N+2}$ is such a path then the sequence $a_0 S_1 S_2 \ldots S_j$ must also correspond to the shortest path between $a_0$ and $S_j$. Now assume that for all states $S_j$ at level $j$, that is, $a_j$, $b_j$, $c_j$, and $d_j$, the shortest path leading to $S_j$ is known (one path for each state). Then for every state at level $(j + 1)$, say $S_{j+1}$, determination of the shortest path between $a_0$ and $S_{j+1}$ is as simple as comparing two possible paths and choosing the shorter one. This is because every path that leads to $S_{j+1}$ must first visit some state in level $j$, and there are only two states in level $j$ from which $S_{j+1}$ can be reached. Considering the preceding arguments, the Viterbi algorithm can be described as follows:

1. Set $j = 1$.
2. For every state $S_j$ of level $j$, find the shortest path leading to $S_j$ from $a_0$.
3. If $j = N + 2$, stop. Otherwise, set $j = j + 1$ and go to step 2.

Figure 8.7 shows this process for the ladder diagram of Figure 8.6. The numbers appearing on the states represent the length of the shortest path that leads to them. The shortest path to $a_8$ is readily seen to be $a_0 a_1 c_2 b_3 a_4 c_5 b_6 a_7 a_8$. The decoding is now complete.

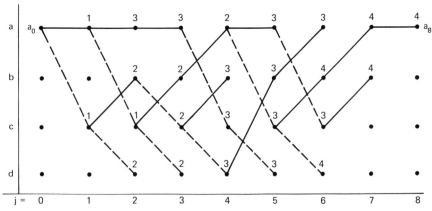

**Figure 8.7** The Viterbi algorithm. (From R. J. McEliece, *The Theory of Information and Coding*, Addison-Wesley, Reading, Mass., 1977.)

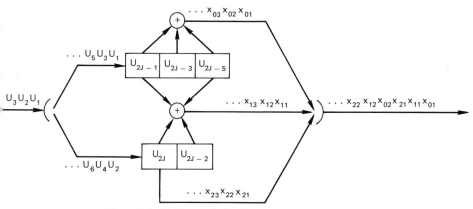

**Figure 8.8**   (3, 2) convolutional encoder with eight states.

So far we have restricted our study of convolutional codes to a simple $(2, 1)$ code with a small number of states. The ideas, however, can be readily generalized to include $(N, K)$ convolutional codes with any number of states. Figure 8.8 shows a $(3, 2)$ convolutional encoder with eight states. The ladder diagram for this encoder has eight dots in each column, representing the eight states. Each state can go to four states in the next level and can be reached from four states in the previous level. The lines must be of four different types (say —————— , — — — — , — · — · — , ∿∿∿∿∿∿) corresponding to four different inputs $U_{2j-1}U_{2j} = 00, 01, 10, 11$. Each line in the ladder diagram will be labeled with a 3-bit output sequence. It is easy to see that the Viterbi algorithm is applicable to the general case of $(N, K)$ codes with an arbitrary number of states. In practice, however, as the number of states grows, the storage and computation requirements become prohibitive. Decoding techniques that are almost as good as Viterbi's can be applied in such situations. We mention sequential decoding and threshold decoding techniques but will not discuss the specifics here.

## PROBLEMS

**8.1.** The Hamming code is a parity check code whose matrix $A$ has the following property: column $n$ of $A$ is the binary number $n$. For example, the matrix of a Hamming code with $m = 3$, $N = 7$ is

$$A = \begin{pmatrix} 0 & 0 & 0 & 1 & 1 & 1 & 1 \\ 0 & 1 & 1 & 0 & 0 & 1 & 1 \\ 1 & 0 & 1 & 0 & 1 & 0 & 1 \end{pmatrix}$$

(a) For a given $m$, what is the maximum code-word length $N$?

(b) Construct the largest Hamming matrix for $m = 4$ and show that it corrects all single errors of transmission.

**(c)** Show that errors of magnitude 2 and larger cannot be corrected by the Hamming code.

**8.2. (a)** Show that a parity check code will correct $\nu$-tuple (and all smaller) errors and detect (but not necessarily correct) $(\nu + 1)$-tuple errors if and only if every set of $2\nu + 1$ columns of the parity check matrix is linearly independent.

**(b)** Given a $\nu$-tuple error correcting parity check code with parity check matrix $A = [I_m | A_1]$, where $I_m$ is an identity matrix of order $m$, show that the code defined by the matrix

$$A_0 = \left[\begin{array}{ccc|c|ccc} & & & 0 & & & \\ & & & 0 & & & \\ & I_m & & \vdots & & A_1 & \\ & & & \vdots & & & \\ & & & 0 & & & \\ \hline 1 & 1 \;\cdots\; 1 & & 1 & 1 & 1 \;\cdots\; 1 \end{array}\right]$$

will correct $\nu$-tuple errors and detect $(\nu + 1)$-tuple errors. (This corresponds to adding one check digit that performs a parity check on all the digits of a code word.)

**(c)** Find a parity check matrix of a single-error-correcting, double-error-detecting code with five check digits and eight information digits.

**(d)** What is the analog of the Varsharmov–Gilbert condition for codes that correct $\nu$-tuple and detect $(\nu + 1)$-tuple errors?

**8.3.** Consider the following parity check matrix:

$$A = \begin{pmatrix} 1 & 0 & 0 & 0 & 1 & 1 \\ 1 & 1 & 0 & 0 & 0 & 1 \\ 1 & 0 & 1 & 0 & 0 & 1 \\ 0 & 1 & 1 & 1 & 0 & 1 \end{pmatrix}$$

**(a)** Find the code words of the code corresponding to $A$.

**(b)** Show that it is possible to replace the rightmost column of $A$ such that the resulting code will correct single errors and detect double errors. Show that not all double errors can be corrected.

**8.4.** The simplest error-control code is obtained by adding a single parity check bit at the end of a binary sequence of length $N - 1$ to make the total number of 1's in the sequence even. For this code:

**(a)** Determine the parity check matrix $A$ and the rate $R$.

**(b)** What is the minimum distance of the code? How many errors can be corrected? How many errors can be detected?

**(c)** Describe the decoding sets (cosets) and the corrector vectors. How many error patterns can be corrected?

**8.5.** It is desired to construct a parity check code to detect $\nu$-tuple and all smaller errors. If an error of magnitude $\le \nu$ is made, the decoder must decide that an error has occurred; it is not required that the decoder provide any information about the nature of the error.

**(a)** Find the necessary and sufficient conditions on the parity check matrix for this type of error detection.

**(b)** Find a convenient condition on the code words that is equivalent to the condition of part (a).

**(c)** Given a parity check code with $2^K$ words of length $N$, find the number of error patterns that can be detected by the code. [Note that this number is the same for all $(N, K)$ codes.]

**8.6.** A generator matrix for an $(N, K)$ binary code $S$ is a matrix $G$ whose rows consist of $K$ linearly independent code words of $S$. Every code word of $S$ may be obtained as a linear combination of the rows of $G$. Assuming that the last $K$ columns of $G$ are linearly independent (if not we can interchange columns), we may reduce $G$ by elementary row transformations to a new generator matrix

$$G^* = [B \mid I_K]$$

where $B$ is $K$ by $m$ ($m$ = rank of the parity check matrix = $N - K$) and $I_K$ is an identity matrix of order $K$.

**(a)** Show the matrix $A = [I_m \mid B^T]$ is a parity check matrix for $S$.

**(b)** Find parity check matrices for the codes whose generator matrices are

(i) $G = \begin{bmatrix} 1 & 1 & 0 & 0 & 1 & 0 \\ 0 & 0 & 1 & 1 & 0 & 1 \\ 0 & 1 & 0 & 1 & 1 & 1 \\ 0 & 1 & 0 & 0 & 0 & 1 \end{bmatrix}$     (ii) $G = \begin{bmatrix} 1 & 1 & 1 & 1 & 1 \end{bmatrix}$

**8.7.** The parity check matrix $A$ represents a single-error-correcting, double-error-detecting code. By eliminating a row and a column from $A$, it is always possible to obtain the matrix of a single-error-correcting code. How do you go about selecting the row and column that must be eliminated for this purpose?

**8.8.** The circuit in Figure P8.8 is used to encode binary digits for transmission over a binary symmetric channel with crossover probability $\varepsilon < \frac{1}{2}$. The shift register is initially filled with 0's; then four information digits are shifted into the shift register and simultaneously transmitted. Next three check digits are transmitted; the four information digits in the shift register shift one place to the right between each check digit calculation.

Find the parity check matrix, the generator matrix, a decoding table, and the probability of decoding error for the code.

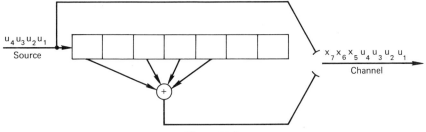

**Figure P8.8**

**8.9.** **(a)** Show that in a parity check code either all the code words contain an even number of ones or half the code words contain an odd number of ones and half an even number.

**(b)** Let $x_{m,n}$ be the $n$th digit in the $m$th code word of a parity check code. Show that, for any given $n$, either exactly half or all the $x_{m,n}$ are zero. If all the $x_{m,n}$ are zero for a given $n$, explain how the code could be improved.

**(c)** Show that the average number of ones per code word, averaged over all code words in a parity check code of block length $N$, must be at most $N/2$.

**8.10.** Consider two parity check codes. Code I is generated by the rule

$$x_1 = u_1 \qquad x_4 = u_1 \oplus u_2$$

$$x_2 = u_2 \qquad x_5 = u_1 \oplus u_3$$

$$x_3 = u_3 \qquad x_6 = u_2 \oplus u_3$$

$$x_7 = u_1 \oplus u_2 \oplus u_3$$

Code II is the same except that $x_6 = u_2$.

**(a)** Write down the generator matrix and parity check matrix for code I.

**(b)** Write out a decoding table for code I, assuming a BSC with crossover probability $\varepsilon < \frac{1}{2}$.

**(c)** Give an exact expression for the probability of decoding error for codes I and II. Which is larger?

**(d)** Find $d_{\min}$ for codes I and II.

**(e)** Give a counterexample to the conjecture that, if one $(N, K)$ parity check code has a larger minimum distance than another $(N, K)$ parity check code, it has a smaller error probability on a BSC.

**8.11.** Consider a parity check code of block length $N$, and let $W_0 = 000 \ldots 0$ be the all-zero code word and $W_1$ be an arbitrary code word of this code. Show that the number of code words that have a given distance, say $n$, from $W_0$ is the same as the number of code words at the same distance $n$ from $W_1$.

**8.12.** A binary code has minimum distance $d_{\min}$. Show that if this code is used on a binary erasure channel (see Problem 6.1), as long as the number of erasures is less than $d_{\min}$, the error can be corrected.

**8.13.** Let $S_1$ and $S_2$ be two binary parity check codes of equal block length. Show that the intersection of $S_1$ and $S_2$, that is, the set of all code words that belong to both codes, is also a parity check code. Describe a method for obtaining the matrix of the new code from the matrices of the original codes.

**8.14.** Consider the $m \times N$ parity check matrix $A$. Define a new matrix $A_1$ by adding a row of all 1's to $A$; that is,

$$A_1 = \left[ \begin{array}{c} A \\ \hline 1 \quad 1 \quad 1 \quad \ldots \quad 1 \end{array} \right]$$

**(a)** Can you obtain the code words of $A_1$ from the code words of $A$? If the answer is positive, describe a procedure.

**(b)** In terms of $N$ and $m$, how many code words belong to $A_1$?

**(c)** If $A$ is a $\nu$-tuple error-correcting code, prove that $A_1$ is at least $\nu$-tuple error correcting, $(\nu + 1)$-tuple error detecting.

**8.15.** Let the $m \times N$ parity check matrix $A$ be expressed as $A = [B \,|\, I_m]$, where $B$ is $m \times (N - m)$ and $I_m$ is the $m \times m$ identity matrix. Construct a new matrix $A_1$ by eliminating the first column of $A$ (i.e., $A_1 = [B_1 \,|\, I_m]$).

    **(a)** Describe a procedure for obtaining the code words of $A_1$ from the code words of $A$.

    **(b)** In terms of $N$ and $m$, how many code words belong to $A_1$?

    **(c)** Show that the minimum distance $(d_{min})$ for the new code is $\geq d_{min}$ for the original code.

**8.16.** Suppose you were approached by a customer who told you that his (binary) channel accepts words of length $n = 7$ and that the only kind of error pattern ever observed is one of the eight patterns 0000000, 1000000, 1100000, 1110000, 1111000, 1111100, 1111110, 1111111. Design a parity check code that will correct all such patterns with as large a rate as possible.

**8.17.** Using the equivalence between parity check codes and group codes, show that a truncated linear convolutional code is a parity check block code.

**8.18.** The convolution of a sequence $\{a_0, a_1, \ldots\}$ with another sequence $\{b_0, b_1, \ldots\}$ is defined as the sequence $\{c_0, c_1, \ldots\}$, where $c_n = \sum_{i=0}^{n} a_i b_{n-i}$. Using modulo 2 addition and multiplication, show that each of the sequences $x_{01} x_{02} x_{03} \ldots$ and $x_{11} x_{12} x_{13} \ldots$ of Figure 8.1 can be expressed as the convolution of the input sequence $U_1 U_2 U_3 \ldots$ with an appropriate (finite) sequence.

# 9

# ADVANCED TOPICS

**Introduction**    In this final chapter we introduce some of the more advanced topics of information theory. This presentation is neither detailed nor exhaustive; its only aim is to convey to the reader the sense that the concepts of information theory that have been developed in this book in connection with simple discrete memoryless sources and channels are far more general and can be extended in a variety of directions. In Section 9.1, for example, we remove the restriction of memorylessness from the discrete source and show that entropy can be defined in a natural way for discrete stationary sources. We then show that this generalized entropy has the same practical significance that was associated with its restricted version for the discrete memoryless source; that is, the entropy of a stationary source is the minimum average code-word length that one has to use in order to represent the source accurately. In Section 9.2, we generalize the concept of likely or typical sequences by proving the Shannon–McMillan theorem for a broad subclass of discrete stationary sources. By imposing the constraint of ergodicity, we will be able to show the generality of the relationship between entropy and typical sequences that was studied in Chapter 2.

Another direction in which the results of information theory can be extended is in relation to continuous messages and channels. Although some information generation, storage, and transmission systems in use today are discrete in nature, the vast majority of such systems remain continuous. Microwave channels, telephone lines, fiber-optic networks, and magnetic disk and tape drives are all examples of continuous systems. A great deal of effort has been expended to extend the results of information theory to such practical situations. The cornerstone of all these efforts is the concept of differential entropy, which will be introduced in Section 9.3. Although we shall not build upon this concept here to investigate the properties of continuous (or waveform) messages and channels, we will point out its major differences with conventional (discrete) entropy. Our analysis of a continuous channel in Section 9.4 is based on intuition rather than rigor, but the derivation of the formula for the capacity of a band-limited Gaussian channel in this section is expected to give the reader a great deal of insight.

Section 9.5 describes a numerical algorithm for the calculation of the capacity of discrete memoryless channels. This is a simple, yet elegant method, which was not discovered until later in the development of information theory [13, 14]. The discussion here takes advantage of the knowledge developed in Chapters 5 and 6 with regard to the information theoretic functions.

## 9.1 DISCRETE STATIONARY SOURCES

In Chapter 2 we studied sources that produced a sequence of letters $u_1 u_2 u_3 \ldots$ from a finite alphabet. There we required the letters to be independent and identically distributed. It was shown that the entropy $H(\mathbf{u})$ of the source was intimately related to the optimum encoding of information sequences produced by the source, and that $H(\mathbf{u})$ represented the minimum number of bits per source letter that was required for perfect reconstruction. In this section we generalize this result by removing the requirement of independence among the letters.

Consider the sequence of letters $u_1 u_2 u_3 \ldots$ produced by the information source $S$. Each letter $u_i$ is a selection from a discrete alphabet. A complete description of this stochastic process requires the assignment of probabilities $p(u_{j+1} u_{j+2} \ldots u_{j+N})$ for all starting points $j \geq 0$, all sequence lengths $N \geq 1$, and all realizations of the sequence $u_{j+1} \ldots u_{j+N}$. The source is defined as stationary if its probabilistic description is independent of a time origin, that is, if $p(u_{j+1} u_{j+2} \ldots u_{j+N})$ is independent of $j$ for all values of $N$ and for all realizations of the sequence. According to this definition, the individual letters are identically distributed but are not necessarily independent. A source with i.i.d. letters is a stationary source, but so is a source whose sequences are formed by mere repetition of the first letter. For example, a binary source that produces the output $11111 \ldots$ with probability $p$ and $00000 \ldots$ with probability $1 - p$ is a stationary source.

Let $S_N$ be a sequence of $N$ letters from a discrete stationary source, and let $\mathbf{u}_1 \mathbf{u}_2 \ldots \mathbf{u}_N$ be the joint ensemble for $S_N$. We define the entropy per letter in a sequence of $N$ letters as

$$H_N(\mathbf{u}) = \frac{1}{N}\left\{-\sum_{S_N} p(S_N) \log p(S_N)\right\} \tag{9.1}$$

Obviously, $H_N(\mathbf{u}) \geq 0$ for all $N$. We now prove that $H_N(\mathbf{u})$ is a nonincreasing function of $N$.

**Lemma 1.**  $H(\mathbf{u}_N | \mathbf{u}_1\mathbf{u}_2 \dots \mathbf{u}_{N-1})$ is nonincreasing with $N$.*

*Proof.* Using first the fact that conditioning cannot increase entropy and then the stationarity of the source, we obtain

$$H(\mathbf{u}_N | \mathbf{u}_1\mathbf{u}_2 \dots \mathbf{u}_{N-1}) \leq H(\mathbf{u}_N | \mathbf{u}_2 \dots \mathbf{u}_{N-1}) = H(\mathbf{u}_{N-1} | \mathbf{u}_1 \dots \mathbf{u}_{N-2}) \tag{9.2}$$

**Lemma 2.**

$$H_N(\mathbf{u}) \geq H(\mathbf{u}_N | \mathbf{u}_1\mathbf{u}_2 \dots \mathbf{u}_{N-1}) \tag{9.3}$$

*Proof*

$$H_N(\mathbf{u}) = \frac{1}{N} H(\mathbf{u}_1\mathbf{u}_2 \dots \mathbf{u}_N)$$

$$= \frac{1}{N}\{H(\mathbf{u}_1) + H(\mathbf{u}_2 | \mathbf{u}_1) + H(\mathbf{u}_3 | \mathbf{u}_1\mathbf{u}_2) + \cdots + H(\mathbf{u}_N | \mathbf{u}_1\mathbf{u}_2 \dots \mathbf{u}_{N-1})\}$$

From Lemma 1, the last term on the right side of the preceding equation is a lower bound to each of the other terms. Inequality (9.3) then follows.

**Theorem 1.**  $H_N(\mathbf{u})$ is nonincreasing with $N$.

*Proof.* Using Lemma 2, we write

$$H_N(\mathbf{u}) = \frac{1}{N} H(\mathbf{u}_1 \dots \mathbf{u}_N)$$

$$= \frac{1}{N} H(\mathbf{u}_1 \dots \mathbf{u}_{N-1}) + \frac{1}{N} H(\mathbf{u}_N | \mathbf{u}_1 \dots \mathbf{u}_{N-1})$$

$$\leq \frac{N-1}{N} H_{N-1}(\mathbf{u}) + \frac{1}{N} H_N(\mathbf{u}) \tag{9.4}$$

Rearranging Eq. (9.4) now yields

$$H_N(\mathbf{u}) \leq H_{N-1}(\mathbf{u}) \tag{9.5}$$

The proof is thus complete.

Using Theorem 1 and the fact that $H_N(\mathbf{u}) \geq 0$ for all $N$, we conclude that the limit of $H_N(\mathbf{u})$ as $N \to \infty$ exists. The entropy per letter for a stationary source can now be defined as follows:

$$H(\mathbf{u}) = \lim_{N\to\infty} H_N(\mathbf{u}) \tag{9.6}$$

---

*From R. G. Gallagher, *Information Theory and Reliable Communications*. New York: Wiley, 1968, p. 57. Reprinted by permission of John Wiley & Sons, Inc.

In the special case of independent identically distributed letters, we have $H(\mathbf{u}_1 \ldots \mathbf{u}_N) = H(\mathbf{u}_1) + \cdots + H(\mathbf{u}_N) = NH(\mathbf{u})$, and thus the preceding definition is equivalent to the earlier definition for memoryless sources.

The entropy for the discrete stationary source can be defined from several other perspectives, but all definitions turn out to be equivalent. One such definition is given in Theorem 2, which follows, and another is the subject of Problem 9.1.

**Lemma 3.**

$$H(\mathbf{u}) \leq H(\mathbf{u}_N \mid \mathbf{u}_1 \ldots \mathbf{u}_{N-1}), \qquad \text{for all } N \geq 1 \tag{9.7}$$

*Proof*

$$H_{N+M}(\mathbf{u}) = \frac{1}{N+M} H(\mathbf{u}_1 \ldots \mathbf{u}_{N+M})$$

$$= \frac{1}{N+M} H(\mathbf{u}_1 \ldots \mathbf{u}_{N-1}) + \frac{1}{N+M}$$

$$\cdot \{ H(\mathbf{u}_N \mid \mathbf{u}_1 \ldots \mathbf{u}_{N-1}) + H(\mathbf{u}_{N+1} \mid \mathbf{u}_1 \ldots \mathbf{u}_N)$$

$$+ \cdots + H(\mathbf{u}_{N+M} \mid \mathbf{u}_1 \ldots \mathbf{u}_{N+M-1}) \}$$

Using Lemma 1, this can be written as

$$H_{N+M}(\mathbf{u}) \leq \frac{1}{N+M} H(\mathbf{u}_1 \ldots \mathbf{u}_{N-1}) + \frac{M+1}{M+N} H(\mathbf{u}_N \mid \mathbf{u}_1 \ldots \mathbf{u}_{N-1})$$

In the limit when $M \to \infty$, we have

$$H(\mathbf{u}) \leq H(\mathbf{u}_N \mid \mathbf{u}_1 \ldots \mathbf{u}_{N-1})$$

The proof is now complete.

**Theorem 2.**  The limit of $H(\mathbf{u}_N \mid \mathbf{u}_1 \ldots \mathbf{u}_{N-1})$ as $N \to \infty$ exists and is equal to $H(\mathbf{u})$.

*Proof.* From Lemma 1 and the fact that $H(\mathbf{u}_N \mid \mathbf{u}_1 \ldots \mathbf{u}_{N-1})$ is larger than or equal to zero for all $N$, we conclude that the limit exists. Lemma 2 asserts that the limit is $\leq H(\mathbf{u})$, while from Lemma 3 the limit must be $\geq H(\mathbf{u})$. Therefore, $H(\mathbf{u}) = \lim_{N \to \infty} H(\mathbf{u}_N \mid \mathbf{u}_1 \ldots \mathbf{u}_{N-1})$. This completes the proof.

The following theorem establishes the relationship between the entropy of a discrete stationary source and the average code-word length required for its perfect reconstruction.

**Theorem 3.**  Let $H(\mathbf{u})$ be the entropy per letter for a discrete stationary source with a finite alphabet, and let $\delta > 0$ be arbitrary. Given a code alphabet of $D$ symbols, it is possible to encode source sequences into a prefix-free code with the average code-word length per source letter $\bar{n}$ satisfying the following relation:

$$\frac{H(\mathbf{u})}{\log D} \le \bar{n} < \frac{H(\mathbf{u})}{\log D} + \delta \tag{9.8}$$

$\bar{n}$ cannot violate the left inequality for any uniquely decodable code.

*Proof.* The proof is similar to the proof of the corresponding theorem for memoryless sources given in Chapter 2. By encoding sequences of length $N$ at a time, we can achieve

$$\frac{H_N(\mathbf{u})}{\log D} \le \bar{n} < \frac{H_N(\mathbf{u})}{\log D} + \frac{1}{N} \tag{9.9}$$

Since $H_N(\mathbf{u}) \ge H(\mathbf{u})$, the left inequality in Eq. (9.9) yields $H(\mathbf{u})/\log D \le \bar{n}$, and any uniquely decodable code must satisfy this inequality. By choosing a large enough value for $N$, the term on the right side of Eq. (9.9) can be made less than $H(\mathbf{u})/\log D + \delta$. The proof is thus complete.

## 9.2 ERGODICITY AND THE SHANNON–MCMILLAN THEOREM

Consider a source with alphabet $\{a_1, a_2, a_3\}$ and two modes of behavior, each occurring with probability $\frac{1}{2}$. In the first mode the source produces an infinite sequence of repetitions of $a_1$. In the second mode the source produces an infinite sequence of statistically independent, equiprobable selections of the letters $a_2$ and $a_3$. This is obviously a stationary source, since the probability of a given sequence does not depend on the starting point. A sequence of length $N$ has either probability $\frac{1}{2}$ (if it is all $a_1$'s) or $(\frac{1}{2})^{N+1}$ (if it is composed of $a_2$'s and $a_3$'s). We then have

$$H_N(\mathbf{u}) = \frac{1}{N}\left(-\sum_{S_N} p(S_N) \log p(S_N)\right)$$

$$= \frac{1}{N}\left\{\frac{1}{2}\log 2 + 2^N\left(\frac{N+1}{2^{N+1}}\log 2\right)\right\} = \frac{N+2}{2N}\log 2$$

The entropy per source letter is thus given by $H(\mathbf{u}) = \lim_{N \to \infty} H_N(\mathbf{u}) = \frac{1}{2}$ bit.

If we encode sequences of length $N$ into binary code (using either Shannon–Fano coding or Huffman coding), it is not hard to see that the sequence of $a_1$'s is encoded into a single binary digit, and each of the $2^N$ sequences composed of $a_2$'s and $a_3$'s is encoded into a binary sequence of length $N + 1$. The average code-word length is $\frac{1}{2} + (N + 1)/2 = (N + 2)/2$, and the average number of bits per source letter is $(N + 2)/2N$, which is close to $H(\mathbf{u})$ for large $N$. However, it is clear that neither $\bar{n}$ nor $H(\mathbf{u})$ are quantities of great significance in this case.

Sources that cannot be separated into different persisting modes of behavior are known as ergodic sources. A stationary ergodic source has the property that statistical averages of functions defined on its output sequences are arbitrarily close to the time averages with probability close to 1; that is, the probability that the time average differs significantly from the statistical average is almost zero. For the stationary ergodic source, the following theorem, which is a generalization of the results of Section 2.4, can be proved.

**The Shannon–McMillan Theorem.**   Let a discrete stationary ergodic source have entropy $H(\mathbf{u})$. For arbitrary $\varepsilon > 0$, $\delta > 0$, there exists $N_0$ such that, for $N \geq N_0$,

$$P\left\{\left|-\frac{1}{N}\log p(u_1 u_2 \ldots u_N) - H(\mathbf{u})\right| > \delta\right\} < \varepsilon \qquad (9.10)$$

*Proof.*   The proof will be given in two steps. First we prove the theorem for sources with finite memory; then we show that a stationary source can be arbitrarily closely approximated by a finite-memory source.

*Part 1:*   Let

$$p(u_1 \ldots u_N) = p(u_1 \ldots u_m) \prod_{n=m+1}^{N} p(u_n \mid u_{n-m} \ldots u_{n-1})$$

This represents a source with a memory of length $m$. Now

$$-\frac{1}{N}\log p(u_1 \ldots u_N) = -\frac{1}{N}\log p(u_1 \ldots u_m)$$
$$-\frac{N-m}{N}\left[\frac{1}{N-m}\sum_{n=m+1}^{N}\log p(u_n \mid u_{n-m} \ldots u_{n-1})\right] \qquad (9.11)$$

Since $m$ is fixed, in the limit $N \to \infty$ the first term on the right side of Eq. (9.11) approaches zero and the coefficient of the second term approaches unity. The second term is now the time average of $-\log p(u_n \mid u_{n-m} \ldots u_{n-1})$ and, because of ergodicity, it approaches the statistical average with probability 1. The statistical average of this quantity is

$$E(-\log p(u_n \mid u_{n-m} \ldots u_{n-1})) = -\sum_{\substack{\text{all sequences} \\ u_{n-m} \ldots u_n}} p(u_{n-m} \ldots u_n) \log p(u_n \mid u_{n-m} \ldots u_{n-1})$$
$$= H(\mathbf{u}_n \mid \mathbf{u}_{n-m} \ldots \mathbf{u}_{n-1}) \qquad (9.12)$$

Since the memory is finite and equal to $m$, the conditional entropy in Eq. (9.12) is equal to $H(\mathbf{u})$. Therefore, in the limit of large $N$, Eq. (9.10) will be satisfied.

*Part 2:*   We now show that, for sufficiently large $m$, the quantity

$$\hat{p}(u_1 \ldots u_N) = p(u_1 \ldots u_m) \prod_{n=m+1}^{N} p(u_n \mid u_{n-m} \ldots u_{n-1})$$

closely approximates $p(u_1 \ldots u_N)$ with probability close to 1.

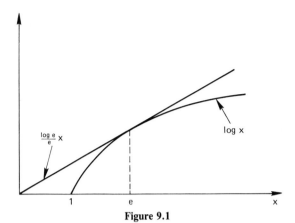

**Figure 9.1**

$$P\left\{\frac{1}{N}\left|\log \hat{p}(u_1 \ldots u_N) - \log p(u_1 \ldots u_N)\right| > \varepsilon\right\}$$

$$= P\left\{\left|\log \frac{\hat{p}(u_1 \ldots u_N)}{p(u_1 \ldots u_N)}\right| > N\varepsilon\right\}$$

$$\leq \frac{1}{N\varepsilon}E\left(\left|\log \frac{\hat{p}(u_1 \ldots u_N)}{p(u_1 \ldots u_N)}\right|\right) \tag{9.13}$$

The last inequality follows from a version of Chebyshev inequality for positive random variables (see Problem 1.4).

Let us digress momentarily to prove the following inequality concerning the absolute value of the function $\log x$:

$$|\log x| \leq \frac{2 \log e}{e}x - \log x \tag{9.14}$$

The function $\frac{1}{2}(\log x + |\log x|)$ is shown in Figure 9.1. It is equal to $\log x$ for $x \geq 1$ and is zero otherwise. The tangent to this function passing through the origin is $(\log e/e)x$, which is also shown in the figure. Thus $\frac{1}{2}(\log x + |\log x|) \leq (\log e/e)x$, which is equivalent to Eq. (9.14).

Using Eq. (9.14) in Eq. (9.13), we obtain

$$P\left\{\frac{1}{N}\left|\log \hat{p}(u_1 \ldots u_N) - \log p(u_1 \ldots u_N)\right| > \varepsilon\right\}$$

$$\leq \frac{1}{N\varepsilon}\left\{\frac{2 \log e}{e}E\left[\frac{\hat{p}(u_1 \ldots u_N)}{p(u_1 \ldots u_N)}\right] - E\left[\log \frac{\hat{p}(u_1 \ldots u_N)}{p(u_1 \ldots u_N)}\right]\right\} \tag{9.15}$$

However,

$$E\left[\frac{\hat{p}(u_1 \ldots u_N)}{p(u_1 \ldots u_N)}\right] = \sum_{\substack{\text{all sequences} \\ u_1 \ldots u_N}} p(u_1 \ldots u_N)\frac{\hat{p}(u_1 \ldots u_N)}{p(u_1 \ldots u_N)} = \sum \hat{p}(u_1 \ldots u_N)$$

$$= \sum_{u_1 \ldots u_m}\left[p(u_1 \ldots u_m)\sum_{u_{m+1}} p(u_{m+1}|u_1 \ldots u_m) \ldots \sum_{u_N} p(u_N|u_{N-m} \ldots u_{N-1})\right] = 1 \tag{9.16}$$

And

$$E\left(\log \frac{p(u_1 \ldots u_m) \, \Pi_{n=m+1}^{N} p(u_n \mid u_{n-m} \ldots u_{n-1})}{p(u_1 \ldots u_N)}\right)$$

$$= NH_N(\mathbf{u}) - mH_m(\mathbf{u}) - (N-m)H(\mathbf{u}_{m+1} \mid \mathbf{u}_1 \ldots \mathbf{u}_m) \qquad (9.17)$$

Therefore,

$$P\left\{\frac{1}{N} \left|\log \hat{p}(u_1 \ldots u_N) - \log p(u_1 \ldots u_N)\right| > \varepsilon\right\}$$

$$\leq \frac{1}{\varepsilon}\left\{\frac{2 \log e}{Ne} - [H_N(\mathbf{u}) - H(\mathbf{u}_{m+1} \mid \mathbf{u}_1 \ldots \mathbf{u}_m)]\right.$$

$$+ \frac{m}{N}[H_m(\mathbf{u}) - H(\mathbf{u}_{m+1} \mid \mathbf{u}_1 \ldots \mathbf{u}_m)]\right\} \qquad (9.18)$$

For sufficiently large $m$, the terms in the brackets on the right side of Eq. (9.18) will be as close to zero as desired; and since $N$ is always larger than $m$, the first term can be made arbitrarily small as well. Therefore, for sufficiently large $m$,

$$P\left\{\frac{1}{N} \left|\log \hat{p}(u_1 \ldots u_N) - \log p(u_1 \ldots u_N)\right| > \varepsilon\right\} < \delta \qquad (9.19)$$

for any $\varepsilon > 0$, $\delta > 0$ chosen arbitrarily. This result, combined with the result of part 1, completes the proof of the Shannon–McMillan theorem.

## 9.3 DIFFERENTIAL ENTROPY

Consider the continuous random variable $\mathbf{x}$ with density function $p(x)$. The differential entropy of $\mathbf{x}$ is defined as follows:

$$H(\mathbf{x}) = -\int_{-\infty}^{\infty} p(x) \log p(\mathbf{x}) \, dx \qquad (9.20)$$

Unlike the entropy for a discrete r.v., the preceding function is not necessarily positive, not necessarily finite, and not necessarily invariant under transformations of $\mathbf{x}$. Therefore, its interpretation as the amount of uncertainty associated with $\mathbf{x}$ is no longer valid. The following examples demonstrate these facts clearly.

**Example 1**

Let $\mathbf{x}$ be uniformly distributed between $a$ and $b$. Then

$$H(\mathbf{x}) = -\int_a^b \frac{1}{b-a} \log \frac{1}{b-a} \, dx = \log(b-a) \qquad (9.21)$$

As $b - a$ assumes values in the interval $(0, \infty)$, the function $H(\mathbf{x})$ in Eq. (9.21) takes on negative, zero, and positive values.

**Example 2**

Let **x** have the following density function:

$$p(x) = \begin{cases} 0, & x < e \\ \dfrac{1}{x \ln^2 x}, & x \geq e \end{cases} \tag{9.22}$$

Then

$$H(\mathbf{x}) = \int_e^\infty \frac{\ln x + 2 \ln \ln x}{x \ln^2 x} \, dx \geq \int_e^\infty \frac{dx}{x \ln x} = \int_e^\infty \frac{d(\ln x)}{\ln x} = \int_1^\infty \frac{dy}{y} = \infty \tag{9.23}$$

Differential entropy can thus be infinite.

**Example 3**

Let **x** be a Gaussian random variable with average $\mu$ and variance $\sigma^2$. Then

$$H(\mathbf{x}) = -\int_{-\infty}^\infty \frac{1}{\sqrt{2\pi}\,\sigma} \exp\left[ -\frac{(x-\mu)^2}{2\sigma^2} \right] \left[ -\log(\sqrt{2\pi}\,\sigma) - \frac{(x-\mu)^2}{2\sigma^2} \log e \right] dx$$

$$= \log(\sqrt{2\pi}\,\sigma) + \frac{\sigma^2}{2\sigma^2} \log e = \frac{1}{2} \log(2\pi e \sigma^2) \tag{9.24}$$

The entropy in Eq. (9.24) is independent of $\mu$ and, depending on the value of $\sigma$, could be positive, zero, or negative.

Now consider the reversible (one-to-one) transformation $\mathbf{y} = \alpha \mathbf{x}$. Since $E(\mathbf{y}) = \alpha\mu$ and $\text{Var}(\mathbf{y}) = \alpha^2\sigma^2$, we have $H(\mathbf{y}) = \frac{1}{2} \log(2\pi e \alpha^2 \sigma^2)$. Clearly, the differential entropy is not invariant under this reversible transformation.

The differences between entropy for a discrete r.v. and differential entropy for a continuous r.v. can be traced to the fact that differential entropy is not a limiting case obtained by approximating a continuous distribution with a discrete one. If the real axis is divided into intervals of length $\Delta$ and each interval is assigned the probability $p(n\Delta)\Delta$, then the discrete approximation to the entropy will be

$$\hat{H}(\mathbf{x}) = -\sum_{n=-\infty}^\infty p(n\Delta)\Delta \, \log[\, p(n\Delta)\Delta\,]$$

$$= -\log \Delta \sum_{n=-\infty}^\infty p(n\Delta)\Delta - \sum_{n=-\infty}^\infty [\, p(n\Delta) \log p(n\Delta)\,]\Delta$$

In the limit of small $\Delta$, the approximation becomes

$$\hat{H}(x) = -\log \Delta - \int_{-\infty}^\infty p(x) \log p(x) \, dx \tag{9.25}$$

where $-\log \Delta$ approaches infinity. It is the absence of this infinitely large term from the differential entropy that is responsible for its odd behavior.

Among the continuous random variables with fixed standard deviation $\sigma$, the Gaussian r.v. has the largest differential entropy. To prove this, we need the following lemma.

**Lemma.**   Let $p(x)$ and $q(x)$ be two continuous density functions. Then, assuming the integrals exist, we will have

$$-\int_{-\infty}^{\infty} p(x) \log p(x)\, dx \ \leq\ -\int_{-\infty}^{\infty} p(x) \log q(x)\, dx \qquad (9.26)$$

with equality iff $p(x)$ and $q(x)$ are equal.

*Proof*

$$-\int_{-\infty}^{\infty} p(x) \log p(x)\, dx \ +\ \int_{-\infty}^{\infty} p(x) \log q(x)\, dx$$

$$= \int_{-\infty}^{\infty} p(x) \log\left[\frac{q(x)}{p(x)}\right] dx \ \leq\ \int_{-\infty}^{\infty} p(x) \left[\frac{q(x)}{p(x)} - 1\right] dx$$

$$= \int_{-\infty}^{\infty} q(x)\, dx \ -\ \int_{-\infty}^{\infty} p(x)\, dx \ =\ 0$$

Equality holds iff $p(x) = q(x)$. The proof is now complete.

Now let the r.v. $\mathbf{x}$ have average $\mu$, variance $\sigma^2$, and probability density function $p(x)$. Define

$$q(x) = \frac{1}{\sqrt{2\pi}\,\sigma} \exp\left[-\frac{(x-\mu)^2}{2\sigma^2}\right]$$

Application of Eq. (9.26) yields

$$H(\mathbf{x}) = -\int_{-\infty}^{\infty} p(x) \log p(x)\, dx$$

$$\leq -\int_{-\infty}^{\infty} p(x) \left[-\log(\sqrt{2\pi}\,\sigma) - \frac{(x-\mu)^2}{2\sigma^2} \log e\right] dx$$

$$= \log(\sqrt{2\pi}\,\sigma) + \frac{\sigma^2}{2\sigma^2} \log e = \frac{1}{2} \log(2\pi e \sigma^2) \qquad (9.27)$$

The right side of Eq. (9.27) is the entropy for a Gaussian r.v. with variance $\sigma^2$ (see Example 3). Thus the Gaussian distribution has the largest differential entropy, as stated before. Moreover, in Eq. (9.27) equality holds iff $p(x) = q(x)$ everywhere.

Joint and conditional entropies as well as average mutual information for continuous random variables can be defined in a similar way. For instance, if $\mathbf{x}$ and $\mathbf{y}$ are continuous random variables with joint density $p(x, y)$, conditional densities $p(x\,|\,y)$ and $p(y\,|\,x)$, and marginal densities $p(x)$ and $p(y)$, we define

$$H(\mathbf{x}, \mathbf{y}) = -\iint_{-\infty}^{\infty} p(x, y) \log p(x, y)\, dx\, dy \qquad (9.28)$$

$$H(\mathbf{x}\,|\,\mathbf{y}) = -\iint_{-\infty}^{\infty} p(x, y) \log p(x\,|\,y)\, dx\, dy \qquad (9.29)$$

$$I(\mathbf{x}, \mathbf{y}) = \iint\limits_{-\infty}^{\infty} p(x, y) \log \frac{p(x, y)}{p(x)p(y)} \, dx \, dy \qquad (9.30)$$

It is not difficult to verify that most of the relationships between information theoretic functions that were derived in the previous chapters for discrete random variables also hold among their continuous counterparts defined here. We do not intend to pursue this subject any further in this book since the problems of information theory in the continuous domain are beyond the scope of our treatment. Let us just mention that much of the theory of continuous waveforms and channels parallels the discrete theory with the central role played by the differential entropy.

## 9.4 A SIMPLE CONTINUOUS CHANNEL

In this section we derive the expression for the capacity of a band-limited channel with average power constraint and signal-independent, additive, Gaussian noise. The arguments used here are not mathematically rigorous but are intuitively acceptable, and in fact the final result, which is the expression for the channel capacity, is an exact result. The channel is diagramatically shown in Figure 9.2. The Fourier spectrum of the input waveform $x(t)$ is limited to frequencies between $-W$ and $+W$ cycles/second, and its average power, defined as

$$P = \lim_{T \to \infty} \frac{1}{2T} \int_{-T}^{+T} x^2(t) \, dt \qquad (9.31)$$

is confined to values below $P_0$. The noise $z(t)$ is white, Gaussian, and independent of $x(t)$. Its spectral density is $\frac{1}{2}N_0$, independent of frequency.

To analyze the system, we first sample the waveforms at the Nyquist rate of $2W$ samples per second. This preserves the information content of the waveforms and allows us to confine attention to the samples alone. Let us denote the total number of samples in the time interval $[-T, T]$ by $K$; then $K = 4WT$. For sufficiently large $K$, the input power constraint can be expressed as

$$\frac{1}{K} \sum_{i=1}^{K} x_i^2 \leq P_0 \qquad (9.32)$$

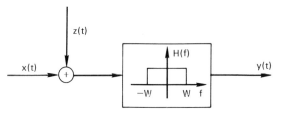

**Figure 9.2**    Schematic diagram of an ideal band-limited channel with additive noise.

where $x_i$ are the samples of $x(t)$ in the interval $[-T, T]$. The noise samples $\mathbf{z}_i$ are zero-mean, Gaussian random variables with variance $\sigma_z^2 = N_0 W$. These samples are independent of the samples of $x(t)$ and of each other. From the law of large numbers, one can deduce that

$$\frac{1}{K} \sum_{i=1}^{K} \mathbf{z}_i^2 \approx \sigma_z^2 \tag{9.33}$$

for sufficiently large $K$. Finally, the output samples $y_i$ must satisfy the following inequality:

$$\frac{1}{K} \sum_{i=1}^{K} y_i^2 \leq P_0 + \sigma_z^2 \tag{9.34}$$

Now consider a $K$-dimensional Euclidean space and assign the $K$ coordinates of the space to the $K$ samples of the wave forms. In this way, each waveform is uniquely identified with a point in the $K$-dimensional space. Inequality (9.32) then states that the input signal $x(t)$ must be within a sphere of radius $\sqrt{P_0}$. Similarly, the output signal $y(t)$ is within a sphere of radius $\sqrt{P_0 + \sigma_z^2}$, and each realization of the noise waveform $z(t)$ is, with a probability close to 1, inside a sphere of radius $\sigma_z$. As the diagram in Figure 9.3 shows, when an input signal such as $x_0(t)$ is transmitted, the output signal $y_0(t)$ must be somewhere within a sphere of radius $\sigma_z$ around $x_0(t)$. If the input signals that are used for communication over the channel are far enough from each other, their

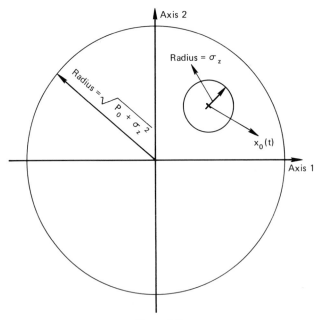

**Figure 9.3**

corresponding noise spheres will not overlap and, consequently, the receiver can correctly identify the transmitted signals.

The problem of calculating the channel capacity is now reduced to that of calculating the maximum number of spheres of radius $\sigma_z$ that can be packed inside a sphere of radius $\sqrt{P_0 + \sigma_z^2}$ without overlap. Since the dimensionality $K$ of the space is large, this is approximately the ratio of the volumes of the two spheres. Thus, if $M$ denotes the maximum number of input signals that can be correctly identified at the receiver, we can write

$$M = \frac{(\sqrt{P_0 + \sigma_z^2})^K}{\sigma_z^K} \tag{9.35}$$

The maximum rate of transfer of data over the channel is then given by

$$C = \frac{1}{2T} \log_2 M = \frac{K}{4T} \log_2 \left( 1 + \frac{P_0}{\sigma_z^2} \right) \quad \text{bits/second}$$

But $K = 4WT$ and $\sigma_z^2 = N_0 W$; therefore,

$$C = W \log_2 \left( 1 + \frac{P_0}{N_0 W} \right) \quad \text{bits/second} \tag{9.36}$$

As a numerical example, consider a telephone channel with a bandwidth of 3 kHz, maximum useful power of 1 W, and noise spectral density of 1 mV/$\sqrt{\text{Hz}}$. From Eq. (9.36), the capacity is found to be $C \approx 25$ Kbit/second.

## 9.5 THE ARIMOTO–BLAHUT ALGORITHM

In this section we describe an iterative method of calculating the channel capacity for a discrete memoryless channel and prove its convergence. The algorithm was discovered by S. Arimoto [13] and, independently, by R. Blahut [14]; our proof of convergence here follows that of Arimoto. This algorithm can be applied without any restrictions to a DMC with transition matrix $[p(y_j|x_k)]$ and can easily be programmed on a personal computer. To begin with, let us rewrite the mutual information between the input and output of the channel in the following form:

$$I(\mathbf{x}, \mathbf{y}) = H(\mathbf{x}) - H(\mathbf{x}|\mathbf{y}) = -\sum_{k=1}^{K} p(x_k) \log p(x_k) + \sum_{k=1}^{K} p(x_k) a_k \tag{9.37}$$

where

$$a_k = \sum_{j=1}^{J} p(y_j|x_k) \log p(x_k|y_j) \tag{9.38}$$

is a function of both the channel matrix and the input distribution $P = \{p(x_1),$ $\ldots, p(x_K)\}$. It will be assumed throughout the section that the input distribution $P$ is strictly positive; that is, $p(x_k) > 0$ for $1 \leq k \leq K$. Under this condition the conditional probabilities $p(x_k | y_j)$ can always be defined, and consequently the coefficients $a_k$ exist for all $k$. We define $A = \{a_1, a_2, \ldots, a_K\}$ for simplicity of future reference.

To calculate the capacity $C$, one must find an input distribution $P^*$ for which $I(\mathbf{x}, \mathbf{y})$ is maximum. The Arimoto–Blahut algorithm achieves this goal by starting with an arbitrary distribution $P^{(1)}$ and calculating a sequence of distributions $P^{(1)}, P^{(2)}, \ldots, P^{(n)}, \ldots$ for which the corresponding sequence of $I(\mathbf{x}, \mathbf{y})$'s, that is, $I^{(1)}(\mathbf{x}, \mathbf{y}), I^{(2)}(\mathbf{x}, \mathbf{y}), \ldots, I^{(n)}(\mathbf{x}, \mathbf{y}), \ldots$ converges to the capacity. The algorithm is iterative and $P^{(n+1)}$ can be directly calculated from $P^{(n)}$. The initial distribution $P^{(1)}$ must be strictly positive, but is otherwise arbitrary. In general, a good choice for $P^{(1)}$ is the uniform distribution $p(x_1) = \cdots = p(x_K) = 1/K$.

To obtain $P^{(n+1)}$ from $P^{(n)}$, one calculates $A = \{a_1, \ldots, a_K\}$ from Eq. (9.38). Since $A$ thus obtained depends on $P^{(n)}$, it will be referred to as $A^{(n)}$. With $A$ fixed at $A^{(n)}$, the right side of Eq. (9.37) is maximized over $P$, and the distribution that achieves maximum is chosen as $P^{(n+1)}$. The maximum value of the expression on the right side of Eq. (9.37), which is obtained by setting $P = P^{(n+1)}$, is denoted $\Gamma^{(n)}$, while the value of $I(\mathbf{x}, \mathbf{y})$ at the $n$th iteration, which is obtained by setting $P = P^{(n)}$, is denoted $I^{(n)}(\mathbf{x}, \mathbf{y})$. Therefore,

$$I^{(n)}(\mathbf{x}, \mathbf{y}) = -\sum_{k=1}^{K} p^{(n)}(x_k) \log p^{(n)}(x_k) + \sum_{k=1}^{K} p^{(n)}(x_k) a_k^{(n)} \tag{9.39}$$

$$\Gamma^{(n)} = -\sum_{k=1}^{K} p^{(n+1)}(x_k) \log p^{(n+1)}(x_k) + \sum_{k=1}^{K} p^{(n+1)}(x_k) a_k^{(n)} \tag{9.40}$$

$$I^{(n+1)}(\mathbf{x}, \mathbf{y}) = -\sum_{k=1}^{K} p^{(n+1)}(x_k) \log p^{(n+1)}(x_k) + \sum_{k=1}^{K} p^{(n+1)}(x_k) a_k^{(n+1)} \tag{9.41}$$

We now show how $P^{(n+1)}$ can be derived in terms of $P^{(n)}$. Let $Q = \{q_1, \ldots, q_K\}$ be defined in terms of $A = \{a_1, \ldots, a_K\}$ in the following way:

$$q_k = \frac{e^{a_k}}{\sum_{k=1}^{K} e^{a_k}} \tag{9.42}$$

Obviously, $q_k > 0$ and $\sum_k q_k = 1$. The right side of Eq. (9.37) can then be written as

$$-\sum_{k=1}^{K} p(x_k) \log p(x_k) + \sum_{k=1}^{K} p(x_k) a_k = \sum_{k=1}^{K} p(x_k) \log \frac{q_k}{p(x_k)} + \log\left(\sum_{k=1}^{K} e^{a_k}\right)$$

$$\leq \log\left(\sum_{k=1}^{K} e^{a_k}\right) \tag{9.43}$$

In Eq. (9.43), equality holds iff $p(x_k) = q_k$ for all $k$ (that is, the maximizing distribution is $Q$). Therefore, $P^{(n+1)} = Q$ and $\Gamma^{(n)} = \log(\sum_k e^{a_k})$; the values of $a_k$ are obtained from Eq. (9.38) with $P = P^{(n)}$.

If at some stage in the computation $P^{(n+1)}$ becomes equal to $P^{(n)}$, the algorithm has come to successful completion because now $P^{(n)}$ is the distribution that maximizes the mutual information. In this case, $C = I^{(n)}(\mathbf{x}, \mathbf{y})$. We are thus interested in situations where $P^{(n+1)} \neq P^{(n)}$ for all $n$. In such cases the inequality in Eq. (9.43) is strict and we have

$$I^{(n)}(\mathbf{x}, \mathbf{y}) < \Gamma^{(n)} \tag{9.44}$$

We now prove that the sequence $\{I^{(n)}(\mathbf{x}, \mathbf{y})\}$ is strictly increasing. This is done by proving the following inequality:

$$I^{(n+1)}(\mathbf{x}, \mathbf{y}) \geq \Gamma^{(n)} \tag{9.45}$$

Using Eqs. (9.40) and (9.41) and replacing for $a_k$ from Eq. (9.38), we have

$$
\begin{aligned}
\Gamma^{(n)} - I^{(n+1)}(\mathbf{x}, \mathbf{y}) &= \sum_{k=1}^{K} p^{(n+1)}(x_k)\left[a_k^{(n)} - a_k^{(n+1)}\right] \\
&= \sum_{k=1}^{K}\sum_{j=1}^{J} p^{(n+1)}(x_k)p(y_j|x_k) \log \frac{p^{(n)}(x_k|y_j)}{p^{(n+1)}(x_k|y_j)} \\
&\leq \sum_{k=1}^{K}\sum_{j=1}^{J} p^{(n+1)}(x_k, y_j)\left[\frac{p^{(n)}(x_k|y_j)}{p^{(n+1)}(x_k|y_j)} - 1\right] \\
&= \sum_{j=1}^{J} p^{(n+1)}(y_j)\sum_{k=1}^{K} p^{(n)}(x_k|y_j) - 1 = 0
\end{aligned}
$$

This proves the validity of Eq. (9.45) and consequently the claim that the sequence $\{I^{(n)}(\mathbf{x}, \mathbf{y})\}$ is strictly increasing. Since the sequence is bounded from above by the channel capacity $C$, it must have a limit $\hat{C}$ that is less than or equal to $C$. Our task is now reduced to proving that $\hat{C}$ is in fact equal to $C$.

**Lemma.**    Define $\delta^{(n)} = C - \Gamma^{(n)}$, where $C$ is the capacity, and denote the input distribution that achieves capacity by $P^* = \{p^*(x_1), \ldots, p^*(x_K)\}$. Then

$$\delta^{(n)} \leq \sum_{k=1}^{K} p^*(x_k) \ln \frac{p^{(n+1)}(x_k)}{p^{(n)}(x_k)} \tag{9.46}$$

*Proof.*    From Eq. (9.42) and the discussion following Eq. (9.43), we can write

$$\Gamma^{(n)} = \ln\left(\sum_{k=1}^{K} e^{a_k^{(n)}}\right) = \ln \frac{e^{a_k^{(n)}}}{p^{(n+1)}(x_k)} = a_k^{(n)} - \ln p^{(n+1)}(x_k) \tag{9.47}$$

Replacing for $a_k^{(n)}$ from Eq. (9.38) yields

$$
\begin{aligned}
\Gamma^{(n)} &= \sum_{j=1}^{J} p(y_j|x_k) \ln \frac{p^{(n)}(x_k)p(y_j|x_k)}{p^{(n)}(y_j)} - \sum_{j=1}^{J} p(y_j|x_k) \ln p^{(n+1)}(x_k) \\
&= \sum_{j=1}^{J} p(y_j|x_k) \ln \frac{p^{(n)}(x_k)p(y_j|x_k)}{p^{(n+1)}(x_k)p^{(n)}(y_j)}
\end{aligned}
\tag{9.48}
$$

Equation (9.48) is valid for all $k$. Thus we can write

$$\delta^{(n)} = C - \Gamma^{(n)} = \sum_{k=1}^{K} \sum_{j=1}^{J} p^*(x_k) p(y_j \mid x_k) \ln \frac{p(y_j \mid x_k)}{p^*(y_j)}$$

$$- \sum_{k=1}^{K} \sum_{j=1}^{J} p^*(x_k) p(y_j \mid x_k) \ln \frac{p^{(n)}(x_k) p(y_j \mid x_k)}{p^{(n+1)}(x_k) p^{(n)}(y_j)}$$

$$= \sum_{k} \sum_{j} p^*(x_k) p(y_j \mid x_k) \ln \frac{p^{(n+1)}(x_k) p^{(n)}(y_j)}{p^{(n)}(x_k) p^*(y_j)}$$

$$= \sum_{k=1}^{K} p^*(x_k) \ln \frac{p^{(n+1)}(x_k)}{p^{(n)}(x_k)} + \sum_{j=1}^{J} p^*(y_j) \ln \frac{p^{(n)}(y_j)}{p^*(y_j)} \qquad (9.49)$$

The last term in Eq. (9.49) is always less than or equal to zero and thus the inequality in Eq. (9.46) is valid.

**Theorem.**    The limit of $I^{(n)}(\mathbf{x}, \mathbf{y})$ as $n \to \infty$ is $C$.

*Proof.* We prove that $\delta^{(n)} \to 0$ as $n \to \infty$ (i.e., the limit of $\Gamma^{(n)}$ is $C$). In light of inequalities (9.44) and (9.45), this is equivalent to the statement of the theorem.

$\{\delta^{(n)}\}$ is a positive, monotonically decreasing sequence. If it does not converge to zero it will converge to some positive value, and consequently $\sum_{n=1}^{\infty} \delta^{(n)}$ will be infinite. But this is impossible because

$$\sum_{n=1}^{N} \delta^{(n)} \leq \sum_{k=1}^{K} p^*(x_k) \ln \frac{p^{(N+1)}(x_k)}{p^{(1)}(x_k)} \leq \sum_{k=1}^{K} p^*(x_k) \ln \frac{p^*(x_k)}{p^{(1)}(x_k)} \qquad (9.50)$$

and the right side is independent of $N$. This completes the proof of the theorem.

Finally, we remark on the speed of convergence. Assuming the initial distribution $P^{(1)}$ to be uniform, Eq. (9.50) can be written as

$$\sum_{n=1}^{N} \delta^{(n)} \leq \ln K - H^*(\mathbf{x}) \leq \ln K \qquad (9.51)$$

But $\{\delta^{(n)}\}$ is a positive, monotonically decreasing sequence; therefore,

$$\sum_{n=1}^{N} \delta^{(n)} \geq N \delta^{(N)} \qquad (9.52)$$

Combining Eqs. (9.51) and (9.52), we obtain

$$\delta^{(N)} \leq \frac{\ln K}{N} \qquad (9.53)$$

The inequality in Eq. (9.53) provides a simple criterion for terminating the algorithm. A more sophisticated criterion is discussed in Problem 9.6.

## PROBLEMS

**9.1.** One method of obtaining the entropy for a discrete stationary source $\mathbf{u}_1 \mathbf{u}_2 \ldots$ $\mathbf{u}_N \ldots$ is to consider

$$H_{N|N}(\mathbf{u}) = \frac{1}{N}H(\mathbf{u}_{2N} \ldots \mathbf{u}_{N+1} | \mathbf{u}_1 \ldots \mathbf{u}_N)$$

(a) Show that $H_{N|N}(\mathbf{u})$ is nonincreasing with $N$.

(b) Prove that, in the limit $N \to \infty$, $H_{N|N}(\mathbf{u})$ approaches $H(\mathbf{u})$.

**9.2.** Let $\mathbf{x}$ and $\mathbf{y}$ be continuous random variables with joint density $p(x,y)$ and individual (marginal) densities $p(x)$ and $p(y)$. The average mutual information between $\mathbf{x}$ and $\mathbf{y}$ is defined as follows:

$$I(\mathbf{x}, \mathbf{y}) = \iint\limits_{-\infty}^{\infty} p(x,y) \log \frac{p(x,y)}{p(x)p(y)} \, dx \, dy$$

(a) Prove that, in general, $I(\mathbf{x}, \mathbf{y}) \geq 0$ with equality iff $\mathbf{x}$ and $\mathbf{y}$ are independent.

(b) Assuming that $H(\mathbf{x})$, the differential entropy of $\mathbf{x}$, exists, is it always true that $I(\mathbf{x}, \mathbf{y}) \leq H(\mathbf{x})$?

**9.3.** Let $\mathbf{x}$ and $\mathbf{z}$ be independent, Gaussian random variables with $E(\mathbf{x}) = E(\mathbf{z}) = 0$ and $\text{var}(\mathbf{x}) = \sigma_x^2$, $\text{var}(\mathbf{z}) = \sigma_z^2$, and let $\mathbf{y} = \mathbf{x} + \mathbf{z}$. What is the average mutual information between $\mathbf{x}$ and $\mathbf{y}$?

**9.4.** The input $\mathbf{x}$ to a channel has uniform distribution on the interval $(0, 2\pi)$. The noise $\mathbf{z}$ is independent of $\mathbf{x}$ with an arbitrary distribution $p(z)$. The output $\mathbf{y}$ is the sum modulo $2\pi$ of $\mathbf{x}$ and $\mathbf{z}$ (i.e., the addition takes place on the unit circle). Determine $I(\mathbf{x}, \mathbf{y})$ in terms of $p(z)$ and evaluate it in the special case where $\mathbf{z}$ is uniformly distributed on the interval $(\alpha, \beta)$, with $\beta - \alpha \leq 2\pi$.

**9.5.** A channel has an input ensemble $X$ consisting of the numbers $+1$ and $-1$ used with the probabilities $p(+1) = p(-1) = \frac{1}{2}$. The output $\mathbf{y}$ is the sum of the input $\mathbf{x}$ and an independent noise random variable $\mathbf{z}$ with the probability density $p(z) = \frac{1}{4}$ for $-2 < z \leq 2$ and $p(z) = 0$ elsewhere.

(a) Find and sketch the output probability density for the channel.

(b) Find $I(\mathbf{x}, \mathbf{y})$.

(c) Suppose the output is transformed into a discrete processed ouput $\mathbf{u}$ defined by $u = 1$ for $y > 1$, $u = 0$ for $-1 < y \leq 1$, and $u = -1$ for $y \leq -1$. Find $I(\mathbf{x}, \mathbf{u})$ and interpret your result.

**9.6.** Let $I(x_k, \mathbf{y})$ be the conditional mutual information between the input and output of a DMC for an arbitrary input distribution $P = \{p(x_1), \ldots, p(x_K)\}$. Prove that

$$\text{Max}_k \, I(x_k, \mathbf{y}) \geq C$$

This provides a way to terminate the Arimoto–Blahut algorithm by calculating the quantity

$$\text{Max}_k \, I(x_k, \mathbf{y}) - I(\mathbf{x}, \mathbf{y})$$

at each iteration and stopping the search when this value is sufficiently small. [*Hint:* Let $P_1$ and $P_2$ be two arbitrary input distributions and show that

$$I_2(\mathbf{x}, \mathbf{y}) \leq \sum_{k=1}^{K} p_2(x_k)I_1(x_k, \mathbf{y})$$

by considering the partial derivative of $I(\mathbf{x}, \mathbf{y})$ with respect to $P_1$.]

# APPENDIX

We prove that, for $N$ sufficiently large and $\alpha < \frac{1}{2}$, the following inequality is always valid:

$$\sum_{k=0}^{N\alpha} \binom{N}{k} < 2^{NH(\alpha)}$$

where $N\alpha = K$, an integer, and $H(\alpha) = -\alpha \log_2 \alpha - (1 - \alpha) \log_2(1 - \alpha)$.

*Proof.* The following inequalities are easily verified:

$$\binom{N}{K-1} = \frac{N!}{(K-1)!\,(N-K+1)!} = \binom{N}{K} \cdot \frac{K}{N-K+1} < \binom{N}{K}\frac{\alpha}{1-\alpha}$$

$$\binom{N}{K-2} = \frac{N!}{(K-2)!\,(N-K+2)!}$$

$$= \binom{N}{K-1} \cdot \frac{K-1}{N-K+2} < \binom{N}{K}\left(\frac{\alpha}{1-\alpha}\right)^2$$

$$\vdots$$

$$\binom{N}{1} < \binom{N}{K}\left(\frac{\alpha}{1-\alpha}\right)^{K-1}$$

$$\binom{N}{0} = \binom{N}{1}\frac{1/N}{1} < \binom{N}{1}\left(\frac{K/N}{1-K/N}\right) < \binom{N}{K}\left(\frac{\alpha}{1-\alpha}\right)^K$$

Therefore, using the fact that $\alpha < \frac{1}{2}$, we write

$$\sum_{k=0}^{K} \binom{N}{k} < \binom{N}{K}\sum_{k=0}^{K}\left(\frac{\alpha}{1-\alpha}\right)^k < \binom{N}{K}\sum_{k=0}^{\infty}\left(\frac{\alpha}{1-\alpha}\right)^k = \binom{N}{K}\frac{1-\alpha}{1-2\alpha}$$

Using Stirling's formula, we derive a bound on $\binom{N}{K}$ as follows:

$$\binom{N}{K} = \frac{N!}{K!\,(N-K)!} \leq \frac{N^N e^{-N}\sqrt{N}e}{K^K e^{-K}\sqrt{K} \cdot (N-K)^{N-K} e^{-(N-K)}\sqrt{N-K}\,e^{7/4}}$$

$$< \sqrt{\frac{N}{K(N-K)}}\left(\frac{N}{K}\right)^K\left(\frac{N}{N-K}\right)^{N-K}$$

$$= \frac{1}{\sqrt{N\alpha(1 - \alpha)}} \cdot \alpha^{-N\alpha} \cdot (1 - \alpha)^{-N(1-\alpha)}$$

$$= \frac{1}{\sqrt{N\alpha(1 - \alpha)}} 2^{N[-\alpha \log_2 \alpha - (1-\alpha) \log_2(1-\alpha)]}$$

Therefore,

$$\sum_{k=0}^{N\alpha} \binom{N}{k} < \sqrt{\frac{1 - \alpha}{N\alpha(1 - 2\alpha)^2}} \cdot 2^{NH(\alpha)}$$

Since $\alpha$ is a constant, for sufficiently large $N$ the coefficient of $2^{NH(\alpha)}$ on the right side will be less than unity. Consequently,

$$\sum_{k=0}^{N\alpha} \binom{N}{k} < 2^{NH(\alpha)}$$

The proof is now complete.

# BIBLIOGRAPHY

1. C. E. Shannon and W. Weaver, *The Mathematical Theory of Communication*, University of Illinois Press, Urbana (1964).
2. N. Abramson, *Information Theory and Coding*, McGraw-Hill, New York (1963).
3. R. G. Gallager, *Information Theory and Reliable Communication*, Wiley, New York (1968).
4. R. Ash, *Information Theory*, Wiley-Interscience, New York (1965).
5. R. J. McEliece, *The Theory of Information and Coding*, Addison-Wesley, Reading, Mass. (1977).
6. R. W. Hamming, *Coding and Information Theory*, Prentice-Hall, Englewood Cliffs, N.J. (1980).
7. T. Berger, *Rate Distortion Theory*, Prentice-Hall, Englewood Cliffs, N.J. (1971).
8. D. Slepian, ed., *Key Papers in the Development of Information Theory*, IEEE Press, New York (1974).
9. B. M. Fitingof, "Optimal Coding in the Case of Unknown and Changing Message Statistics," *Problemy Peredachi Informatsii*, 2, 3–11 (1966).
10. B. M. Fitingof, "The Compression of Discrete Information," *Problemy Peredachi Informatsii*, 3, 28–36 (1967).
11. A. N. Kolmogorov, "Three Approaches to the Quantitative Definition of Information," *Problemy Peredachi Informatsii*, 1, 3–11 (1965).
12. L. D. Davisson, "Universal Noiseless Coding," *IEEE Trans. Info.*, 19, 783–795, (1973).
13. S. Arimoto, "An Algorithm for Computing the Capacity of Arbitrary Discrete Memoryless Channels," *IEEE Trans. Info.*, 18, 14–20 (1972).
14. R. Blahut, "Computation of Channel Capacity and Rate Distortion Functions," *IEEE Trans. Info.*, 18, 460–473 (1972).

# INDEX